Education Madness

A SAPIENT Being's Guide to Fixing America's Dysfunctional & Illiberal Educational Systems

By

Corey Lee Wilson

Education Madness

Fratire Publishing books can be purchased in bulk with exclusive discounts for educational purposes, association gifts, sales promotions, and special editions can be created to specifications. All inquiries for such can be made below.

FRATIRE PUBLISHING LLC
4533 Temescal Canyon Rd. # 308
Corona, CA 92883 USA
www.FratirePublishing.com
FratirePublishing@att.net
1+ (951) 638-5502

FratirePublishing
Relevant Books for **SAPIENT** Beings

Fratire Publishing is all about common sense and relevant books for sapient beings. If this sounds like you and you can never have enough common sense, wisdom, and relevancy, then visit us and learn more about the 40 *MADNESS* series of book titles at www.fratirepublishing.com/madnessbooks.

Printed paperback and eBook ePUB by Ingram Spark in La Vergne, Tennessee, USA
Copyright © 2022: First Edition December 2022
ISBN 978-0-9994603-2-0 (Paperback)
ISBN 978-1-953319-36-4 (eBook)
Education Madness-01-PDF (pdf)
LCCN 2022922627

Special thanks for the cover design by Jenny Barroso, J20Graphics, j20graphics@gmail.com and ebook conversion by Redeemer SoftTech, redeemer.softtech@gmail.com.

Contents

Acknowledgements

I owe a debt of gratitude to the following for "heavily" borrowing at times pieces of their and/or outright sections. I do this unashamedly to use the sapient phrase, "if it ain't broke—don't try to fix it." Most of the borrowed works and research cannot be improved upon—so why try? It's better to assemble these meaningful parts, profound messages, and eloquent arguments into a cohesive whole, told with high school and college students in mind, and that's what I've done and where my talent lies.

Below in alphabetical order are the major contributors to The SAPIENT Being that I borrowed verbatim, quoted, and conceptualized much of their content from a little to a lot. Wherever this happened, I did my best to acknowledge my source. If I didn't at times within the 15 chapters, I did so intentionally because doing so would have distracted from their message. Nonetheless, they are more than acknowledged in the References and Index sections of this textbook.

ACTA: Founded in 1995, the American Council of Trustees and Alumni (ACTA) is an independent, nonprofit organization committed to academic freedom, excellence, and accountability at America's colleges and universities.

City Journal: Is a public policy magazine and website, published by the Manhattan Institute for Policy Research, that covers a range of topics on urban affairs, such as policing, education, housing, and other issues. The *City Journal* and its authors were the most widely used resource for *Education Madness.*

Epoch Times, The: Is America's fastest-growing independent news media, founded in 2000, and their mission is to bring readers a truthful view of the world free from the influence of any government, corporation, or political party. Contrary to fake news organizations, their aim is to tell readers what they see, not how to think; and they strive to deliver a factual picture of reality that lets readers form their own opinions.

Greene, Ph.D., Jay P.: Is a Senior Research Fellow at the Heritage Foundation and his research was cited four times in the U.S. Supreme Court's opinions in the landmark *Zelman v. Simmons-Harris* case on school vouchers.

Hirsch Jr., E. D.: Is an American educator, literary critic, and theorist of education and is the founder and chairman of the non-profit Core Knowledge Foundation. He is best known for his 1987 book *Cultural Literacy: What Every American Needs to Know*, which was a national best-seller and a catalyst for the standards movement in American education. A prolific writer, his other education policy books include, *The Dictionary of Cultural Literacy* (1988), *The Schools We Need and Why We Don't Have Them* (1996), *The Schools Our Children Deserve: Moving Beyond Traditional Classrooms and Tougher Standards* (1999), *The Knowledge Deficit* (2006), *The Making of Americans: Democracy and Our Schools* (2009), *The Making of Americans* (2010), *Why*

Knowledge Matters: Rescuing our Children from Failed Educational Theories (2016), and *How to Educate a Citizen: The Power of Shared Knowledge to Unify a Nation* (2020).

Mac Donald, Heather: Is an American political commentator, essayist, attorney, author, a Thomas W. Smith Fellow of the Manhattan Institute, and a contributing editor of the institute's *City Journal*. She has written numerous editorials and is the author of several books like the bestseller *The Diversity Delusion: How Race and Gender Pandering Corrupt the University and Undermine Our Culture*.

McManus, Bob: Is a contributing editor at *City Journal* covering Richard Carranza and his stories have appeared in the *New York Post*, Fox News, RealClear Politics, HotAir, Commentary Magazine, RealClear Markets, RealClear Policy, and more publications and media.

National Association of Scholars: Is an American non-profit politically conservative advocacy organization, with a particular interest in education, utilizing a network of scholars and citizens united by a commitment to academic freedom, disinterested scholarship, and excellence in American higher education.

***National Review*:** Is an American semi-monthly editorial magazine, focusing on news and commentary pieces on political, social, and cultural affairs and its authors contributed a considerable number of articles to this textbook. The magazine was founded by the author William F. Buckley Jr. in 1955 and has played a significant role in the development of conservatism in the United States, and is a leading voice on the American right.

Randall, David: Is the Director of Research at the National Association of Scholars and a Policy Advisor to The Heartland Institute and leads research studies on education and trends in the curriculum.

Rufo, Christopher F.: Is a senior fellow at the Manhattan Institute, contributing editor of *City Journal,* and the foremost leader exposing progressive indoctrination taking place throughout our education systems.

The Heritage Foundation: Is an American conservative think tank that is primarily geared toward public policy and the foundation took a leading role in the conservative movement during the presidency of Ronald Reagan, whose policies were taken from Heritage's policy study Mandate for Leadership. The Heritage Foundation has had a major influence in U.S. public policy making and is among the most influential conservative public policy organizations in America.

The James G. Martin Center for Academic Renewal: Is a private nonprofit institute dedicated to improving higher education policy and their mission is to renew and fulfill the promise of higher education in North Carolina and across the USA.

A SAPIENT Being's Preface

According to many government statistics, America's education system is failing due to lower expectations and the shift in focus from academic excellence in mathematics, science, reading, and history toward the implementation of social constructs like critical race theory equals fewer literate graduates.

"Public records and other evidence show that state-level and some local education officials are no longer focused on maintaining high academic standards and providing the best public education possible to students," according to Liv Finne.

"Instead, a concern for learning has been replaced by an aggressive political agenda designed to instill doubt, mental pain and low expectations in students. This race-centered agenda also seeks to divide children from teachers, their own communities and from each other.

This harmful trend can only be resolved through policies that return high-quality academic standards to public education and well-funded and supportive education-choice programs that allow families to access alternatives services to meet the learning needs of all children."

Finne, a former adjunct scholar now serving as Director of the Center for Education at Washington Policy Center, has been analyzing education policy for the past 13 years. Her research suggests the unmistakable decline in the literacy of America's students from fourth to twelfth grade is a direct result of the shift from academic excellence toward social constructs such as CRT.

"Internationally, we do pretty well at the fourth grade," Finne told *The Epoch Times*, "but we decline from there." Recent statistics support her claim.

Government data for 2019 shows the average fourth grader has a 41 percent proficiency level in mathematics. By the eighth grade, the proficiency level drops to 34 percent. By the twelfth grade, America's students have an average math proficiency level of only 24 percent. In reading, fourth graders have an average proficiency rate of 35 percent. By eighth grade, the proficiency level drops to 34 percent, and by the twelfth grade, America's average student shows only a slight proficiency improvement to 37 percent. In writing, the proficiency levels are 28 percent in fourth grade with eighth and twelfth graders sharing a score of 27 percent.

America's students fare worse in science, with fourth-graders having only a 36 percent proficiency rate and eighth-graders dropping to 35 percent. Twelfth-graders have only a 22 rate of proficiency in science. The worst scores come in history, with fourth-graders starting out with only 20 percent proficiency and dropping to 15 percent by the eighth grade. By grade 12, America's students have a paltry 12 percent proficiency level in history.

Are you interested in how bad is America's union and leftist dominated public education system is and how to reverse their 'D-' grade to an 'A+' grade? If yes, read on but be forewarned: For some of you this *MADNESS* textbook will be a revelation, an epiphany, a sapient being moment. For others, it will be a triggering event, denial of truth, and a painful intervention.

For our civic leaders, elected officials, policy advisors, school board members, college trustees, public and private school officials, state legislatures and departments of education, house and senate members—*Education Madness* provides an essential resource to fight the illiberal, woke, Marxist, racist, ethnic studies, and progressive programs designed to fundamentally change America and destroy our republic.

If these essential resources interested you, please read on and if you also believe in the message of this textbook and willing to fight for it—please considering supporting, joining and/or participating in one of the three SAPIENT Being programs below.

Sapient Conservative Textbooks (SCT) Program is a relevant and current events textbooks program (published by Fratire Publishing LLC) to help return conservative values, viewpoint diversity, and sapience to high school and college campuses—and enlighten them on the many blessings to humankind that are the direct result of Western European culture, American exceptionalism, and Judeo-Christian values.

Free Speech Alumni Ambassador (FSAA) Program helps create faculty and administrative positions, throughout America's predominantly liberally staffed college campuses, that can serve as much needed conservative club advisors—because conservative students are facing many obstacles when they attempt to start and charter a right-leaning student organization on campus due to faculty members fearful of losing their jobs or tenure for becoming these organization's advisors.

Make Free Speech Again On Campus (MFSAOC) Program is an interactive opportunity and nexus for high school and college students to start SAPIENT Being campus clubs, chapters, and alliances where independent, liberal, and conservative minded students can meet, discuss, and debate important issues by utilizing the sapient principles of viewpoint diversity, freedom of speech, and intellectual humility—and develop sapience in the process.

Are You a Sapient Being or Want to Be One?

Sapience, also known as wisdom, is the ability to think and act using knowledge, experience, understanding, common sense and insight. Sapience is associated with attributes such as intelligence, enlightenment, unbiased judgment, compassion, experiential self-knowledge, self-actualization, and virtues such as ethics and benevolence.

Being a sapient being is not about identity politics, it's about doing what is right and borrows many of the essential qualities of Centrism that supports strength, tradition, open mindedness, and policy based on evidence not ideology.

Sapient beings are independent minded thinkers that achieve common sense solutions that appropriately address America's and the world's most pressing issues. They gauge situations based on context and reason, consideration, and probability. They are open minded and exercise conviction and willing to fight for it on the intellectual battlefield. Sapient beings don't blindly and recklessly follow their feelings or emotions.

Their unifying ideology is based on the truth, reason, logic, scientific method, and pragmatism—and not necessarily defined by compromise, moderation, or any particular faith—but is considerate of them.

Most importantly, per a letter written by Princeton professor Robert George in 2017 and endorsed by 28 professors from three Ivy League universities for incoming freshmen, "Think for yourself!"

George's letter continues:

Thinking for yourself means questioning dominant ideas even when others insist on their being treated as unquestionable. It means deciding what one believes not by conforming to fashionable opinions, but by taking the trouble to learn and honestly consider the strongest arguments to be advanced on both or all sides of questions—including arguments for positions that others revile and want to stigmatize and against positions others seek to immunize from critical scrutiny.

The love of truth and the desire to attain it should motivate you to think for yourself. The crucial point of a college education is to seek truth and to learn the skills and acquire the virtues necessary to be a lifelong truth-seeker. Open-mindedness, critical thinking, and debate are essential to discovering the truth. Moreover, they are our best antidotes to bigotry.

Merriam-Webster's first definition of the word "bigot" is a person "who is obstinately or intolerantly devoted to his or her own opinions and prejudices." The only people who need fear open-minded inquiry and robust debate are the actual bigots, including those on campuses or in the broader society who seek to protect the hegemony of their opinions by claiming that to question those opinions is itself bigotry.

So, don't be tyrannized by public opinion. Don't get trapped in an echo chamber. Whether you in the end reject or embrace a view, make sure you decide where you stand by critically assessing the arguments for the competing positions. Think for yourself. Good luck to you in college!

Now, that might sound easy. But you will find—as you may have discovered already in high school—that thinking for yourself can be a challenge. It always demands self-discipline, and these days can require courage.

In today's climate, it's all-too-easy to allow your views and outlook to be shaped by dominant opinion on your campus or in the broader academic culture. The danger any student—or faculty member—faces today is falling into the vice of conformism, yielding to groupthink, the orthodoxy.

At many colleges and universities what John Stuart Mill called "the tyranny of public opinion" does more than merely discourage students from dissenting from prevailing views on moral, political, and other types of questions. It leads them to suppose that dominant views are so obviously correct that only a bigot or a crank could question them.

Since no one wants to be, or be thought of as, a bigot or a crank, the easy, lazy way to proceed is simply by falling into line with campus orthodoxies. Don't do it!

To be sure, our overly-politicized culture has a tough time viewing any "verbal cacophony" as a sign of strength and vibrancy. And perhaps nowhere is this truer than on many college campuses where political correctness is rampant, groupthink is common, and social media "mobs" arise in a flash to intimidate anyone who openly strays from the prevailing orthodoxy.

At the SAPIENT Being we're not intimidated—and our primary purpose is to seek the truth by enhancing viewpoint diversity, promoting intellectual humility, protecting freedom of speech and expression while developing sapience in the process—no matter what the cost on the intellectual battlefield, campus classroom, and marketplace of ideas. This is our ethos! Is it yours?

Best regards and sapiently yours,

Corey Lee Wilson

Corey Lee Wilson

S.A.P.I.E.N.T. Being

1 – How Bad Are America's High School, Community College & University Systems?

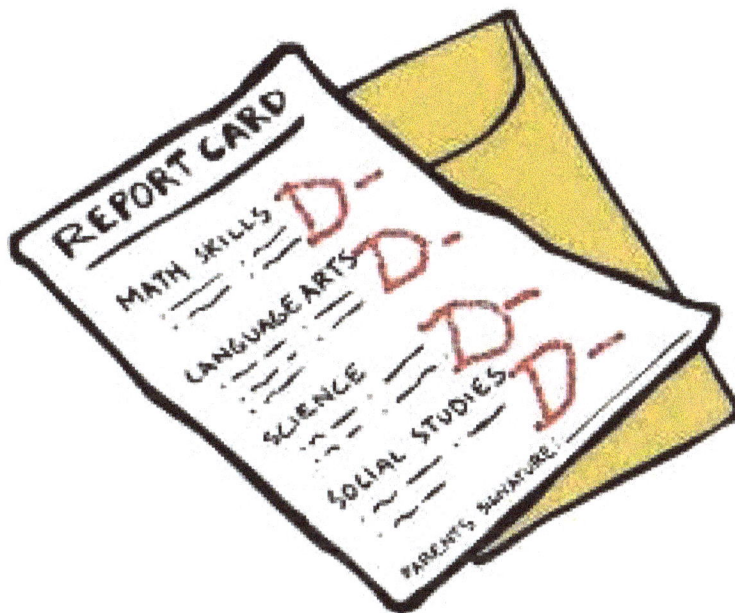

Credit: EAG.

Learning has been replaced by an aggressive political agenda designed to instill doubt, mental pain, and low expectations in students. According to government statistics, America's education system is failing. According to one expert, lower expectations and the shift in focus from academic excellence in mathematics, science, reading, and history toward the implementation of social constructs like critical race theory equals fewer literate graduates.

As noted by Thomas Sowell, a senior fellow at the Hoover Institution, Stanford University, decades of dumbed-down education no doubt have something to do with this, but there is more to it than that. Education is not merely neglected in many of our schools today, but is replaced to a great extent by ideological indoctrination. Moreover, it is largely indoctrination based on the same set of underlying and unexamined assumptions among teachers and institutions.

If our educational institutions—from the schools to the universities—were as interested in a "diversity of ideas" as they are obsessed with racial diversity, students would at least gain experience in seeing the assumptions behind different visions and the role of logic and evidence in debating those differences.

The failure of our educational system goes beyond what they fail to teach. It includes what they do teach, or rather indoctrinate, and the graduates they send out into the world, incapable of seriously weighing alternatives for themselves or for American society.

"Public records and other evidence show that state-level and some local education officials are no longer focused on maintaining high academic standards and providing the best public education possible to students," Liv Finne wrote in her September 2021 report regarding the lowering of academic standards by school officials in Washington state as they implement CRT.

"Instead, a concern for learning has been replaced by an aggressive political agenda designed to instill doubt, mental pain and low expectations in students. This race-centered agenda also seeks to divide children from teachers, their own communities and from each other. This harmful trend can only be resolved through policies that return high-quality academic standards to public education and well-funded and supportive education-choice programs that allow families to access alternatives services to meet the learning needs of all children."

Statistics Show America's Education System is Failing

Per the Patricia Tolson "Statistics Show America's Education System is Failing: CRT and Lower Expectation Equals Fewer Literate Graduates, Expert Says" *Epoch Times* article in January 2022:

Liv Finne, a former adjunct scholar now serving as Director of the Center for Education at Washington Policy Center, has been analyzing education policy for the past 13 years. Her research suggests the unmistakable decline in the literacy of America's students from fourth to twelfth grade is a direct result of the shift from academic excellence toward social constructs such as CRT.

"Internationally, we do pretty well at the fourth grade," Finne told *The Epoch Times*, "but we decline from there." Recent statistics support her claim.

Government data for 2019 shows the average fourth grader has a 41 percent proficiency level in mathematics. By the eighth grade, the proficiency level drops to 34 percent. By the twelfth grade, America's students have an average math proficiency level of only 24 percent. In reading, fourth graders have an average proficiency rate of 35 percent. By eighth grade, the proficiency level drops to 34 percent, and by the twelfth grade, America's average student shows only a slight proficiency improvement to 37 percent. In writing, the proficiency levels are 28 percent in fourth grade with eighth and twelfth graders sharing a score of 27 percent.

America's students fare worse in science, with fourth-graders having only a 36 percent proficiency rate and eighth-graders dropping to 35 percent. Twelfth-graders have only a 22 rate of proficiency in science. The worst scores come in history, with fourth-graders starting out with only 20 percent proficiency and dropping to 15 percent by the eighth grade. By grade 12, America's students have a paltry 12 percent proficiency level in history.

Recent numbers from USA Facts show similar results. According to Finne, there are a number of reasons for the steady decline in literacy among America's students the longer they remain in school. Number one is "the low expectations we have of our teachers."

Lowering the Academic Achievement Bar

Rather than develop curriculum that provides students with the qualifications needed to graduate high school, Finne says the education system has opted to lower the bar of academic standards.

"They're lowering the bar in a couple of ways," Finne explained. "Like the Ethnic Studies framework passed by the State of Washington in 2019, critical race theory concepts are now woven into the learning standards of all of the different subjects."

As Finne explains, traditional educational standards have been reorganized into systems of oppression and the whole CRT construct—a "false philosophy from radical professors in higher education" is now being "imposed as the truth" in the standards of learning in K-12 schools.

"When you take attention away from the basics, and focus on teaching this ideology, you're going to get a lowered level of knowledge and skill acquisition of the basics in reading, math, history, and science; not to mention learning falsehoods in history like the 1619 Project," Finne insisted. "It's astonishing."

The Status Quo System

According to Finne, the new push by the school system to abandon efforts of academic achievement and shift toward social constructs like CRT is an effort to hide the fact that they have failed in their jobs to educate our children.

"The whole idea is that if the community knew that their schools are not educating their children to basic levels they would rise up," Finne said. "Just look what's happening now with the uprising of parents against CRT in places like Loudoun County [Virginia] and they're still going forward with it. It's a huge uphill battle for parents."

"The whole system has promoted children whether they learn the content or not," Finne said. "So why should they care if a whole generation of children lost the content of a year (from the pandemic)? It's consistent with their practice. They do not individualize education. They don't make sure each, individual child is ready to go on to the next grade. They move them along, especially minority children. The only people blocking real reform are the defenders of the status quo, the ones who like it just the way it is."

Teachers Unions are indeed the ones who fight against charter schools, school choice, and parental involvement and fought to keep kids out of classrooms during the COVID-19 outbreak. According to Finne, "if they really cared about black lives, they would be expanding their options for charter schools. But they're not. If these critical race theorists are truly intent on helping the children, they would be going after the unions. But they're not."

The Silver COVID-19 Lining

Ironically, Finne believes the greatest hope for the education of America's children will rise from the ashes of the COVID-19 school lockdowns.

"The silver lining is we will eventually figure out how terrible it has been," Finne said. "Through the COVID shutdowns it has become clear how far behind so many kids are and the movements to expand school choice is not going away, because parents have woken up. That's what's so exciting about the COVID school shutdowns. Together with the takeover of the schools by this crazy critical race theory idea that children are bad and if they're white they're racist and if they're not white they're victims, that is going to lead to lawsuits.

"Maybe out of the ashes of this, school choice will arise," Finne opined of the educational chaos that ensued during the lockdowns. "This is still a democracy. The exchange of ideas is still happening in education because we do care about our children. That's what I'm hoping; that people will see the wisdom of giving parents real control, not just window dressing like involving parents and having parent involvement coordinators, but real control."

What Are Public Schools For?

From the Oren Cass "What Are Public Schools For?" *City Journal* article in December 2021:

Recent battles over racially divisive curricula prompted Virginia gubernatorial candidate Terry McAuliffe to remark, "I don't think parents should be telling schools what they should teach." But those battles, and the peculiar response that parents are best kept away from the process of educating their children, are signs of a much larger crisis. The gap in perspective between professional educators and the communities they serve about what public education is for has grown unsustainably large.

The gap is most evident, and costly, on the question of what outcome a good education should lead toward. For the current generation of reformers, the answer is simple: a college degree.

Embracing this college-for-all mentality, secondary schools have become college-prep academies held accountable to rigorous testing regimes and college-going rates, while policymakers have plowed hundreds of billions of dollars into subsidizing higher education. Leading proposals for "free college" and student-loan forgiveness reinforce those commitments.

American parents disagree. In partnership with YouGov, the organization, American Compass, surveyed 1,000 American parents with a child between the ages of 12 and 30 about their priorities for the public education system. We asked: Which is more important, helping students "maximize their academic potential and gain admission to colleges and universities with the best possible reputations," or helping them "develop the skills and values to build decent lives in the communities where they live?" By more than two to one, parents chose life preparation over academic excellence.

Uncommon for contentious issues in American life, this opinion holds across all the usual divisions. "Build decent lives" earns 68 percent among Democrats, 69 percent among Republicans, and 77 percent among Independents. It earns 68 percent among lower-class parents (defined by education level and income), 69 percent in the working class, 75 percent in the middle class, and 71 percent in the upper class; 68 percent with women and 74 percent with men, 76 percent with whites, and 63 percent with nonwhites.

Parents also express this view across various experiences for their own children. While having a child drop out of college is correlated most strongly with a preference for life preparation (79 percent), parents whose children have completed college still choose it over academic excellence 69 percent of the time. The preference also holds by similar margins regardless of whether parents report their children are "living the American dream," "getting by," or "struggling."

An optimistic educator might argue that developing the skills and values to build decent lives is what public schools already do, but parents would again disagree. Most rate their school system's performance as good or excellent at teaching students academic skills and engaging students in extracurriculars, but not on life preparation. In a parallel survey, young people aged 18–30 were even more frustrated with their schools' academic focus. They gave priority to life preparation by a four-to-one margin; fewer than one-third rated their school's performance on that task positively.

College isn't always the answer

Parents and young people with recent experience in America's education system seem to understand something that the experts designing it do not: college isn't always the answer. Nationwide, only one in five young people moves smoothly from high school to college to career. Twice as many never enroll in college at all; twice as many enroll in college but drop out, or graduate into a job that doesn't require a degree.

The main constituency for the college fixation is Democrats with postgraduate degrees, who prefer the idea of full-tuition scholarships by more than two-to-one. Yet that perspective seems to dominate public debates. For all the political energy expended on college costs and college debt, meaningful non-college programs that would help students develop the skills to build decent lives in the communities where they live are scarce.

Most parents want options that meet the needs of their children; this means not only that high schools should cater to the majority of students who will not succeed in college, but also that public education should offer as much after high school to this non-college majority as it offers those fortunate enough to pursue a college degree.

In *The Making of Americans*, education scholar E. D. Hirsch observes that our tradition of public education began with an emphasis on "common knowledge, virtue, skill, and an allegiance to the larger community shared by all children no matter what their origin." Our schools were "the central and main hope for the preservation of democratic ideals and the endurance of the nation as a republic."

Today, they resemble strip-mining operations—serving the needs of the academically talented by extracting them from their hometowns to ivory towers in faraway lands from which they will never return. Some go on to run the education system and see nothing wrong with this state of affairs. For reformers to succeed in improving public education, they will need to remember what public education is for.

Learning for Self-Government

From the David Randall "Learning for Self-Government" National Association of Scholars article in February 2022:

In 2021, the American people awoke to the longstanding crisis in K–12 civics education. Not the old crisis of plummeting test scores and abysmal knowledge of our republic's structure and our nation's history, but the new crisis—that radical advocates have seized control of our K–12 public education system and have imposed a curriculum that forwards their dogmas in the guise of civics and history—and, indeed, not only in these subjects but also in classes ranging from literature to science to mathematics.

Critical Race Theory (CRT) has emerged as the flashpoint of political conflict regarding the Woke Educators' curriculum, but subjects of dispute include action civics (vocational training in community organizing) and a host of other radical distortions of our school curricula, imposed piecemeal over several generations.

Radical advocates have seized control of our K–12 public education system and have imposed a curriculum that forwards their dogmas in the guise of civics and history. American schools traditionally have upheld the principle that classroom instruction, above all in the public K–12 schools, should be nonpartisan—that students should not be taught to support a particular party, political position, or ideology.

Teachers knew that they had great power to influence young minds, so they chose pedagogies that restricted their ability to impose their personal predilections on the students entrusted to their care. Civics and history, in particular, sought to convey a broadly consensual account of American history and government, which would teach students an intelligent love of their country founded on knowledge of how it came to be, how its system of government worked, and what their fellow Americans had done since their country's founding. Students would be prepared by this education to act as they saw fit as self-reliant citizens of the United States of America.

The new radical pedagogy destroys virtually every aspect of the old curriculum

Above all, it replaces the old commitment to nonpartisan education with a commitment to partisan education.

The partisan positions they support are, in substance, revolutionary and illiberal departures from the American tradition, including the primacy of group "identity" over individual membership in the republic, the replacement of equality of individual opportunity with equity (equal outcomes for each identity group in every component of the polity, society, and culture), quasi-Marxist economics, a commitment to revolutionary "liberation" from an "oppressive" status quo, and a redefinition of intellectual inquiry from the collective pursuit of truth to the imposition of power. These positions in themselves appall most Americans—but even more appalling is the basic fact that the advocates of this new radical pedagogy believe that school instruction should forward any partisan position.

Radical activists are defined by their basic commitment to remolding America's education system to facilitate ever more avowedly partisan teaching by means of a host of obscurely denominated pedagogies—and by their equally basic redefinition of "civics education" to mean "exercises in political activism" instead of "classroom instruction in American history and government."

The national coalition Educating for American Democracy (EAD) has published a Pedagogy Companion to the EAD Roadmap that usefully catalogues a substantial number of the new curriculum's pedagogies and their unsapient program aspects as follows, and more details about them can be found in the Appendix:

Action Civics, Applied Civic Learning in Community, Carpet-Time Democracy, Chrono-Thematic, Civic Agency, Civic-Focused Schools, Collaborative Teaching, Community-Based, Constructivist Teaching, Cooperative Approach, Culturally Responsive Teaching, Democratic Competency-Based, Democratic School Climate, Experiential Learning, Inquiry-Centered Learning, Open Climate, Problem-Based Learning, Positive School Climate, Project-Based Learning, Service Learning, Simulation of Democratic Processes and Roles, Social Emotional Learning.

These pedagogies are articulated in impenetrable, jargon-heavy terms that are hardly clarified by the Appendix's paragraph-length definitions. "Action civics," for example, was defined above as "vocational training in community organizing." What this means is that in "action civics" history and government classes, students spend class time and receive class credit for work with "nongovernmental community organizations."

This substitution degrades teachers' and students' esteem for classroom instruction, which is deemed not to have sufficient civic purpose in itself. It reduces the scarce time available for students actually to learn about the history of their country and the nature of their republic. Most importantly, it introduces a pedagogy that facilitates teachers' ability to impose their personal predilections on their students, by influencing the process by which students choose "community partners" with which to work.

It also facilitates the ability of peer pressure to impose group predilections on individual, dissenting students. We may note that the advocates of "action civics" explicitly distinguish this activity from volunteering: action civics is meant to change the political system, not to support civil society.

Action civics is meant to change the political system, not to support civil society

Practically speaking, it is extraordinary how many "action civics" projects support groups affiliated with progressive political goals, such as environmental justice or immigration amnesty, and how few—to my knowledge, none—support conservative goals such as Second Amendment rights or immigration enforcement. "Action civics" exemplifies a putatively nonpartisan pedagogy that is, in fact, a means to commit students' to work, during school time and for class credit, for progressive nonpartisan organizations. It is essentially a form of Saul Alinskyite organizational tactics, with students serving a double role as the subjects and the means of community organizing.

In substance, this radical curriculum reduces to disaffecting Americans' children from their country, providing tactical tips on how to undermine it, and providing a moral education to fit our children to be the subjects of a managerial-therapeutic regime, divided into identity groups, rather than the self-governing citizens of a republic, united by their common membership in the American nation.

The radical activists seek to introduce this curriculum by an extraordinarily wide variety of means, which includes federal grants, national "frameworks," state laws and curriculum standards, school district policies, and teacher initiatives in the classroom. The careful combination of putatively bipartisan compromise, impenetrable jargon, and euphemized but extensive ideological commitments together radicalize America's sprawling K–12 civics education.

These means, cumulatively, have been extraordinarily effective. Scarcely a school in America has not marbled some portion of the radical catechism into its curriculum, camouflaged by education-school jargon.

Patriotism Starts in the Classroom

The effort to indoctrinate students in progressive, anti-American ideologies that pervades our universities is also ravaging K–12 education as noted in the Kennin M. Spivak "Patriotism Starts in the Classroom" *National Review* article in July 2022:

State education departments issue standards that public and charter K–12 schools, and their teachers, must follow. Particularly in larger states, these standards determine the content of textbooks and standardized tests, influence private and homeschool curricula, and impact public-college admission requirements.

Traditional standards are aggressively being usurped by the principles of critical race theory, social justice, and "action civics," which promotes student involvement in protests for progressive causes. The National Association of Scholars (NAS) has identified at least 45 state education standards in 25 states that incorporate radical doctrine, including CRT, the 1619 Project, and other expressions of anti-American animus.

More than twelve federal and 200 state bills have been introduced that would incorporate progressive civics education in K–12 schooling. By July 2020, more than 4,500 schools taught the 1619 Project as truth, despite its author's admission that it is a parable. That number is likely considerably greater today.

Concurrently, states are eliminating or dumbing down tests and otherwise lowering standards, imposing, for example, "equitable grading," which excludes factors such as class participation and returning homework on time. The motivations for doing so vary but consistently include an effort to reduce or obscure performance differences to promote "equity."

This debasement is occurring against a backdrop of declining test scores, with proficiency ranging from just 12 percent to 46 percent in the eleven subjects included in the Department of Education's national assessment of fourth-, eighth-, and twelfth-graders. As in our universities and colleges, if a radical canon supplants traditional content standards in K–12 schools, we can expect a steep drop in patriotism among our youth, and in their understanding and support for American institutions and principles.

The hostility to Western civilization in our universities

Douglas Murray well describes the hostility to Western civilization in our universities. If strong remedies are not swiftly applied, our K–12 schools are about to catch up. Eliminating the foundations and premises of Western civilization, American exceptionalism, and liberty leaves students uninformed about America's history and unique story.

Even after tests have been watered down, national scores in history and geography have declined, and scores for civics are flat. In 2018, only 15 percent of eighth-graders scored "proficient" or above in U.S. history, along with about a quarter in civics and geography. Many students do not even know why the American Revolution was fought, how a city differs from a state, or how to locate the United States on a map of the world. Replacing history, geography, and civics with ethnic studies and protest politics will not fix this.

It is particularly disturbing this Fourth of July weekend that so many Americans are graduating ignorant of, and estranged from, America's history and ideals. A 2020 Echelon Insights poll of high-school and college students underscores how progressive indoctrination in college changes beliefs.

For example, 66 percent of high-schoolers view the U.S. as exceptional and unique, compared with 47 percent of college students; 63 percent of high-schoolers are proud of the U.S., compared with 40 percent of college students; 70 percent of high-schoolers have a favorable view of U.S. history, compared with 44 percent of college students; and 58 percent of high-schoolers are patriotic, compared with just 35 percent of college students. In other results, high-school students were consistently more supportive than college students of American institutions.

This conclusion is bolstered by a poll that the Institute of Politics at the Harvard Kennedy School conducted among Americans 18 to 29 in October and November 2021. Those with a college education were 82 percent more likely to identify as liberal. Sixty percent of respondents with a college degree, and 52 percent of those who did not attend college, believed that America's democracy was "in trouble" or "failing."

Nearly two-thirds of respondents with a college degree believed that there were "other nations as great or greater than America," compared with 44 percent of those who did not attend college. Just one-quarter of respondents with a degree said that America was the greatest country, compared with a third of those who did not attend college. In other poll results, those with a degree were consistently less supportive of American institutions than were those who had not attended college.

If progressives achieve the same success degrading K–12 standards that they have achieved in our universities, there is no reason to expect a different result.

Universities Breed Anger, Ignorance, and Ingratitude

As per the Victor Davis Hanson "Universities Breed Anger, Ignorance, and Ingratitude" *National Review* article in October 2019:

In turning out woke and broke graduates, our higher education system has a lot to answer for like the question of: What do widely diverse crises such as declining demography, increasing indebtedness, Generation Z's indifference to religion and patriotism, static rates of home ownership, and a national epidemic of ignorance about American history and traditions all have in common?

Answer: 21st-century higher education.

A pernicious cycle begins even before a student enrolls

A typical college-admission application is loaded with questions to the high-school applicant about gender, equality, and bias rather than about math, language, or science achievements.

How have you suffered rather than what you know and wish to learn seems more important for admission. The therapeutic mindset preps the student to consider himself a victim of cosmic forces, past and present, despite belonging to the richest, most leisured, and most technologically advanced generation in history.

Without a shred of gratitude, the young student learns to blame his ancestors for what he is told is wrong in his life, without noticing how the dead made sure that almost everything around him would be an improvement over 2,500 years of Western history.

Once admitted, students take classes from faculty who, polls reveal, are roughly 90 percent liberal. According to one recent survey, Democrat professors on average outnumber Republican faculty by a 12-to-1 ratio on the nation's supposedly diverse campuses.

But such political asymmetries are magnified by a certain progressive messianic self-righteousness that turns the lectern into the pulpit, the captive class into a congregation. The rare conservative professor is more resigned to the tragedy of the universe and, in live-and-let-live fashion, vacates the campus arena to the left-wing gladiators who wish to slay any perceived heterodoxy.

Campus activism has replaced the old university creed of disinterested inquiry

Students are starting to resemble military recruits in boot camp, prepping to become hardened social-justice warriors on the frontlines of America's new wars over climate change, gun control, abortion, and identity politics. In Camp Yale or Duke Social Warrior Base, they learn just enough about purported historical oppression to make them dangerous, as they topple statues, demand the renaming of streets and buildings, and swarm professors deemed politically incorrect.

No wonder that certain issues—abortion, global warming, illegal immigration—are mostly off-limits to campus disagreement. Safe spaces, racial theme houses, and censorship have replaced the 1960s ideals of unfettered free speech and racial and ethnic integration and assimilation.

Today's students often combine the worst traits of bullying and cowardice

They are quite ready as a mob to dish it out against unorthodox individuals, and yet they're suddenly quite vulnerable and childlike when warned to lighten up about Halloween costumes or a passage in *Huckleberry Finn*. The 19-year-old student is suddenly sexually mature, a Bohemian, a cosmopolitês when appetites call—only to revert to Victorian prudery and furor upon discovering that callousness, hurt, and rejection are tragically integral to crude promiscuity and sexual congress without love.

The curricula in the social sciences and humanities are largely politicized

Culture, history, and literature are often taught through the binary lenses of victims and victimizers, as a deductive zero-sum melodrama. There is little allowance for tragedy, irony, and paradox or simply the complexities of the human experience. That preexisting slavery, imperialism, and atrocity were as common in the New World, Asia, and Africa as in Europe is rarely mentioned in the boilerplate campus indictment of the West.

Regarding the cost of a university education, the federal government guarantees student loans to pay skyrocketing tuition, room, and board. That guarantee has empowered crony-capitalist universities to hike their annual costs far above the rate of inflation—without much worry over what happens to their customers when and if they graduate.

Eighteen-year-olds entering college are seldom warned by campus financial officers exactly how long their debt obligations will last—or which majors are likely to lead to better salaries after graduation. None are given itemized bills that are broken down to show where their money is going. Many who will remain in debt for years might have wished to know how much they paid for the vast swamp of non-teaching facilitators and high-paid administrators.

Colleges today can never assure students that after graduation they will at least test higher on the standardized tests than when they entered

If colleges could do that, they'd long ago have required exit examinations to boast of their success. Instead, the higher-education industry insists that almost any baccalaureate degree is a good deal, without worrying about how much it costs or whether their brand certifies any real knowledge. Again, the logic is that of consumer branding—as we see with Coca-Cola, Nike, and Google—in which status rather than cost-benefit efficacy is purchased. Does anyone believe that a graduating senior of tony Harvard, Yale, or Stanford knows more than a counterpart at Hillsdale or St. John's?

The net result is a current generation that owes $1.6 trillion in college loans to the federal government. And that debt is now affecting the entire country, including those who never went to college, who as taxpayers eventually may be asked to forgive some if not all the debt. An entire generation of Americans has costly degrees; many cannot use them to find well-paying jobs, and they increasingly forgo or delay marriage, child-rearing, and buying a car or home until their mid-twenties or thirties. All that pretty much sums up the profile of Antifa, Black Lives Matter, and Occupy Wall Street adherents—or the environmental-studies major who is shocked that a skilled electrician makes three times more than he does.

Colleges are turning out woke and broke graduates

They are not up to ensuring the country that they will pass on to the next generation an America that's as prosperous, secure, and ethical as what they inherited and have so often faulted.

Ignorance, arrogance, and ingratitude are now the brands of the undergraduate experience. No wonder a once duly honored institution, higher education, is now either the butt of jokes or cynically seen as a credentialing factory.

National Suicide by Education

Per the Philip Carl Salzman "National Suicide by Education" Minding the Campus story in September 2022:

It's true that children are our future, for good or ill, depending on their education. Ill-educate children, as we are doing in the United States and Canada, and the result will be cultural decay, social breakdown, and political decline.

We now teach our children that our country is illegitimate, based on genocide and racism, and is systemically evil. Will this lead the next generation to love or despise their country? Who will volunteer for the military, to risk their lives to protect their evil country? When generals assert that the military is racist and sexist, homophobic and transphobic, and harbors white supremacists and domestic terrorists, who will volunteer for the military, to risk their lives to protect their country? Recruitment for the military in both the United States and Canada is severely down, and no one can figure out how to increase it.

We teach our children that our society is divided between helpless victims and cruel oppressors. BIPOC (black, indigenous, people of color) and females are all and everywhere oppressed, and whites and males, Christians and Jews, and (astonishingly) Asians are privileged, evil villains. Children learn to fear and hate their fellow citizens of other races, sexes, religions, and ethnicities. What kind of society will we have when we teach children that race hatred, sexism, and ethno-supremacy are justified and virtuous?

Children are taught that speaking and writing correct English is racist, and so they must not learn correct English

Math too is racist, when really, there are no correct answers, and to deny that two plus two can equal anything is oppressive. The demand for correct answers, logic, and scientific proof are sins of "whiteness" that must be eradicated from the socially just society. Thus, it isn't a weakness that American children perform poorly on international tests of reading, math, and science, but a demonstration of virtue, of social justice.

When schools teach the counterfactual lie that police every day murder innocent black and brown people, a lie refuted by every serious study, is it a surprise that police are viewed by black and brown children with fear and hatred? The constant insults and attacks on police by BIPOC children as well as adults are a predictable result of such inculcation. So too is the low morale of police in almost all urban jurisdictions, their unwillingness to engage in proactive policing, the flood of resignations, early retirements, transfers to rural jurisdictions, and suicides, and the lack of recruits to fill the large gaps in almost every urban police force. It's no surprise that the crime rate has shot up in every urban jurisdiction.

Race and gender disparities in academic participation and performance are explained by one and only one possible factor: racist and sexist discrimination. The other likely causes—family weakness in single-parent homes, community pathologies, and individual choices—may not be mentioned or investigated. In this way, disparities in participation or performance are deemed illegitimate, and therefore must be wiped out in order to achieve "equity," that is, equal results among census categories of the population, and "social justice."

Thus, poor performers are "victims," and measures must be taken to ensure that outcomes are the same

This is done by giving preferences to underperforming BIPOC pupils and students, canceling accelerated programs for which they do not qualify, canceling examinations in which they do poorly, and setting aside performance standards. Programs in which females are underrepresented must prioritize recruiting females through special preferences and benefits.

BIPOC pupils and students are taught that their academic participation and performance is not their responsibility, but the responsibility of others who victimize them, and who owe them preference, benefits, and reparations. This is the perfect pedagogical plan for destroying individual motivation and a sense of responsibility. There's always someone else to blame.

In order to advance "equity," based on demographic "representation" of race, sex, ethnicity, etc., alternative criteria for judgment, such as individual achievement, merit, and potential, are denounced as, you know, "racist," and rejected. So recruitment to academia, science, media, professions, and government will be of the demographically underrepresented, not of the most capable candidates.

The foundation of this plan is the racism of low expectations, assuming that people from BIPOC categories could never make it on merit. This guarantees mediocrity or complete incompetence throughout our institutions: in medical care, scholarship and teaching, engineering, the press, law, and governance. The consequent trajectory is a societal decline and decay.

Female pupils and students are taught that they are being excluded due to sexist discrimination

This counterfactual claim ignores the reality that females are the majority in universities and in most schools and programs. Those few programs where they are not, in spite of all of the heavy recruiting—physical sciences, mathematics, computer science—is a result of the choices of females who prefer to enter other fields. Yet females are continually told that they are victims of sexist discrimination. And male pupils and students are told that non-existent female victimhood is their fault.

Given the understanding that reason, logic, the search for evidence and correct answers, and science are taught as features of oppressive "whiteness," it should come as no surprise that schools discourage students from basing their understandings on scientific facts. A particular focus of teaching from kindergarten through graduate studies is the rejection of biology and its knowledge of biological factors in human life. Biological sex is now taught to be irrelevant to human life; the only thing that counts is one's feelings about gender.

Children are taught that they can be any of a hundred genders that they choose. Some teachers groom children to be supporters and "allies" of LGBTQ+, and to join in wherever they choose. Some children who are uncomfortable with their sex or confused about it are in some schools recruited into the trans community. Schools funnel pupils to sex transition clinics run by people, who still call themselves doctors, where children are subjected to life-changing chemical treatments and surgical mutilation in the futile effort to transform children from their biological sex to a replica of the other.

What devious force brought all of this cultural destruction into being?

Who injected this destructive poison into our educational system? The source, of course, is our universities. They were taken over by grievance studies advanced by various particular interest groups. First and most decisive were the feminists who established women's and gender studies to advance what they defined as the narrow interests of women.

They adopted the Marxist model of society divided into two warring classes; in place of the proletariat versus the bourgeoisie, they defined the conflicting classes as females versus the patriarchy, all men. The feminists inspired queer studies and LGBTQ+ activism. Black studies, Latinx studies, and Asian studies all championed their races in alleged conflict with the other races. Universities no longer were about what can we learn about the world and its people, but about what you could do through propaganda and activism to advance the narrow interests of your category.

All of these activisms were absorbed in social science and humanities programs, often by joint appointed professors with one or another grievance study. Administrators were either activists themselves or were won over and instituted "social justice" measures of "diversity, equity, and inclusion," hiring "diversity officers" to police the staff and students to ensure that no "wrong think" was allowed to flourish.

Faculties of education, being weak in academic content and lax in pursuing that, adopted grievance theory with a vengeance, and trained their students, the future school administrators and teachers, in the most radical forms of grievance activism. The faculties of education have contaminated our K-12 schools and made them what they are now.

2 – NEA & AFT Teacher Unions: The Worst of the Worst Are Failing Our Students

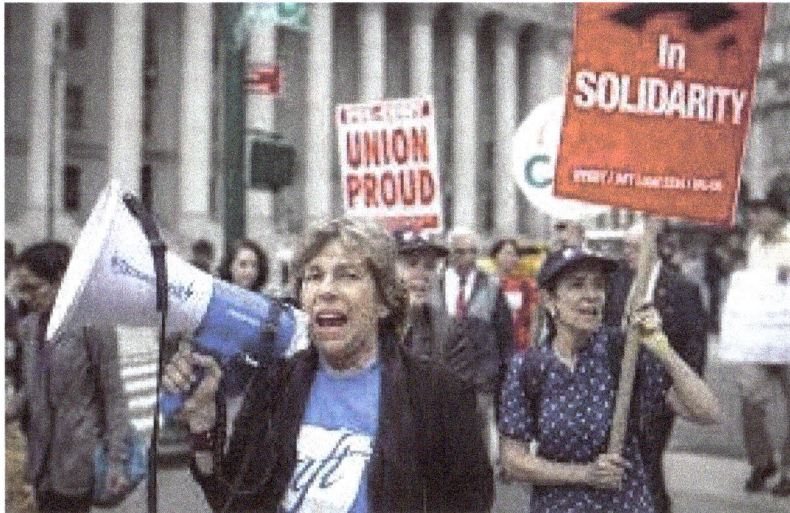

Credit: American Federation of Teachers president Randi Weingarten - The Times of Israel.

Parents are outraged after the National Education Association (NEA), a national teachers union, tweeted teachers "know better than anyone" what students need in the classroom. President of Parents Defending Education Nicole Neily joined "Fox & Friends First" to discuss the "astonishing" claim after the top teachers union appeared to play clean-up after the polarizing post.

"They know better than anybody how to spend money on Democratic candidates and undermine American education, but certainly not how to let children learn and thrive," Neily told co-host Todd Piro. "So really an astonishing claim by them. Four Pinocchios."

The NEA posted the controversial tweet over the weekend saying, "Educators love their students and know better than anyone what they need to learn and to thrive." The union turned off replies to the tweet after thousands of responses poured in, appearing to begin clean-up efforts, as parents nationwide push for more influence in the classroom.

One of those responses was former Education Secretary Betsy DeVos, who said, "You misspelled parents." The NEA fired back to DeVos' response saying, "Together, families and educators are an essential team for the resources and opportunities all students need. Out-of-touch billionaires, however, are not."

"They are trying to gaslight the American people about their role in lockdowns, about the role in learning loss," Neily said. "We have seen from those NAEP scores that came out recently, how American children fell off a cliff during COVID. And let's be honest, achievement, proficiency in America was not good before that, despite the fact that the amount of money we have spent on American education has gone through the roof."

"Families know best," she continued. "Families should decide where their children go and how that money is spent, and the teachers unions need to be cut out of this process entirely." Most recently, teachers union have sparred with parents nationwide over COVID lockdowns after a national report card indicated massive decline in math and reading scores.

The NEA, along with the American Federation of Teachers (AFT), was caught up in controversial emails with the Centers for Disease Control and Prevention. The correspondence, obtained by Americans for Public Trust, found that the nation's two largest teachers' unions appeared to influence last-minute changes to school reopening guidance and a slow walking of getting kids back to school.

"They don't care what we think because they have their own agenda, and I think the sooner the American people realize this union is not in it for us or our children, they're in it for their money and their power, the better off we will be," Neily said.

Why These Teachers Unions Are the Worst of the Worst

From the Alex Newman "How Socialists Used Teachers Unions Such as the NEA to Destroy Education" *Epoch Times* article in May 2020:

Along with other leading unions, the NEA and its affiliates at the state and local level played a leading role in transforming American education into the dangerous disaster that it has become. The extremism has been getting progressively more extreme for more than a century now. But it's not new by any means.

The destructive role played by the NEA is so serious, and so widely understood, that in 2004, even then-U.S. Secretary of Education Rod Paige described the union as a "terrorist organization." But in reality, the NEA has done far more damage to the United States than a simple terrorist organization ever could.

Consider that terrorists merely kill individuals, even if sometimes in large numbers. But the NEA and its allied unions have helped to practically kill a nation—the greatest, freest nation that ever existed. While terrorists destroy human bodies, the NEA has worked to destroy human minds and human freedoms.

For at least a century, the NEA, founded in 1857 as a professional association, has barely bothered to conceal its leadership's affinity for communism, collectivism, socialism, humanism, globalism, and other dangerous "isms" that threaten individual liberty. Nor has the union shied away from vitriolic attacks on the United States, the free-market system, Christianity, the family, or educational freedom.

Perhaps the most important exposé ever written on the NEA was the 1984 book "NEA: Trojan Horse in American Education" by Dr. Samuel Blumenfeld. Packed with examples and references, Blumenfeld's book proved that, contrary to popular mythology, which holds that the NEA's extremism is a more recent phenomenon, the union's leaders have been radicalizing teachers against America for a century or more.

More Federal Power, War on Competition

More than a century ago, the NEA began lobbying Congress for federal funding of education. NEA bosses knew that with federal aid comes federal control. They finally succeeded in 1965 with the passage of the Elementary and Secondary Education Act. From there, the next stop was the creation of a cabinet-level Department of Education, an NEA wish that President Jimmy Carter granted the union in exchange for its critical support.

NEA bosses often get their way in government, even if it takes a while. That is because the NEA has been a well-oiled lobbying machine for decades. For one, by collecting dues from millions of members, the NEA and its state affiliates are able to pour endless resources into the campaign coffers of politicians. And by prodding its members to vote a certain way, write letters, and even protest, it can keep the politicians it gets elected in line indefinitely.

With almost 3 million members today, the NEA is the largest labor union in the United States. It has pumped well over $100 million into federal political campaigns since the early 1990s alone. And data from the Center for Responsive Politics show that more than 97 percent of that money went to Democrats. The tiny donations to Republicans virtually all went to the most liberal among them. Similar trends exist at the state and local level among NEA affiliates.

Today, the NEA is still trying to quash competition, seeking onerous restrictions on private schools and even waging a war on homeschooling families. In 1988 and the years following (amended in 2006 to the current version), the NEA adopted a resolution that formalized its hatred of families operating outside the government system.

"The National Education Association believes that home schooling programs based on parental choice cannot provide the student with a comprehensive education experience," the union declared.

Of course, not all of the millions of NEA members agree with the totalitarian ideologies and ideas peddled by the union's leadership. But until recently, at least, in many states, they were required to be members, forced to fund political campaigns and extremist views that they may have vehemently disagreed with. Thankfully, Illinois child support specialist Mark Janus sued and won, ending compulsory union dues. But many teachers still don't realize they don't have to fund the extremism of the NEA and its affiliates.

Examples of Just How Much Harm the Teachers Union Has Done

From the August 2018 S.A.P.I.E.N.T. Being article "Why Teachers Unions are the Worst of the Worst California" by the California Policy Center's Edward Ring:

One of the most compelling examples of just how much harm the teachers union has done to California's schools was the 2014 case *Vergara v. the State of California.*

In this case, attorneys representing public school students argued that union negotiated work rules harmed their ability to receive a quality education. In particular, they questioned rules governing tenure (too soon), dismissals (too hard), and layoffs (based on seniority instead of merit). In the closing arguments, the plaintiff's lead attorney referenced testimony from the defendant's expert witnesses to show that these and other rules had a negative disproportionate impact on students in disadvantaged communities.

Despite winning in the lower courts, the Vergara case was eventually dismissed by the California Supreme Court. Teachers still get tenure after less than two years of classroom observation. Incompetent teachers are still nearly impossible to fire. And whenever it is necessary to reduce teacher headcount in a district, the senior teachers stay and the new teachers go, regardless of how well or poorly these teachers were doing their jobs. The consequences of these self-serving work rules are more than academic.

The evidence that California's public schools are failing is everywhere. Los Angeles, a city whose residents are–perhaps more than anywhere else–representative of America's future, is home to the Los Angeles Unified School District (LAUSD), with 640,000 K-12 students. And as reported in a 2018 LA School Report, according to the new "California School Dashboard," a ratings system that replaced the Academic Performance Index,

LAUSD is failing to educate hundreds of thousands of students. In the most recent year of results, 52 percent of LAUSD's schools earned a D or F in English language arts, and 50 percent earned a D or F in math. Fifty percent of LAUSD's schools are failing or nearly failing to teach their students English or math.

They Attack Innovative Charter Schools

In the face of failure, you would think LAUSD, and other failing school districts would embrace bipartisan, obvious reforms such as those highlighted in the Vergara case. But instead, these unions are relentlessly trying to unionize charter schools, which would force those schools to adhere to the same union work rules. In Los Angeles, the Alliance Network of charter schools has delivered demonstrably better educational outcomes for less money, while serving nearly identical student populations.

How does it help to impose union work rules on charter schools that are succeeding academically? How does that help the children who are America's future?

They Promote a Left-Wing Political Agenda

The other way the teachers union is unique among public sector unions is their hyper-partisanship. Despite and often in defiance of their memberships, nearly all unions are left-wing partisan organizations. Nearly all of them support left-wing causes and Democratic political candidates. But the teachers unions do so with a zeal that dwarfs their counterparts. Larry Sand, a former LAUSD teacher and prolific observer of teachers union antics, has spent years documenting their left wing agenda.

For example, reporting on the annual conventions of the two largest national teachers unions, Sand writes: "The National Education Association (NEA) convention...gave us a clue which theory would become reality when the union passed quite a few über liberal New Business Items, maintained its lopsided leftward political spending, and gave rogue quarterback Colin Kaepernick a human rights award. And here in the Golden State, the California Teachers Association (CTA) continues its one-way spending on progressive initiatives and endorsed 35 state legislators in the 2018 June primary–all Democrats."

They Support Left-Wing Student Indoctrination

This left-wing political agenda finds its way into the classroom, of course. At the same time as California's K-12 public school students are not being effectively taught English or math skills, they are being exposed to agenda-driven political and cultural indoctrination.

Again, as documented by Larry Sand: "Nor are textbooks safe. Communist and notorious America-hater Howard Zinn's "A People's History of the United States" is assigned in many high school history classes. Zinn felt that the teaching of history "should serve society in some way" and that "objectivity is impossible, and it is also undesirable." As a Marxist, he'd prefer a society that resembles Stalin's Russia.

Additionally, Pacific Research Institute's Lance Izumi notes that pages and pages of the latest California History, Social Science Framework are devoted to identity politics, and the environmentalist, sexual, and anti-Vietnam War movements, with detailed and extensive bibliographical references. In contrast, the contemporaneous conservative movement, which succeeded in electing Californian Ronald Reagan as president, with its complex mixture of social, economic, and national security sub-movements, is given cursory and passing mention, with no references provided.'"

Public sector unions are going to be with us for a long time. But in the wake of the Janus ruling, members who don't agree with the political agenda of these unions can quit, depriving them of the dues that–to the tune of nearly a billion per year just in California–make them so powerful.

Teachers, in particular, should carefully consider this option. America's future depends on it.

The Politics of Closing Schools

As American schools reopen for the fall—or attempt to, amid a new surge of coronavirus cases related to the Delta variant—what, if anything, can be learned from the experience of Europe asks Susanne Wiborg from her "The Politics of Closing Schools" Education Next August 2021 article:

Governments in Europe have wrangled over when to close and reopen schools, weighing the risk of children spreading the virus at school against the economic and education-related disruptions of keeping them at home. During the first months of the pandemic, when most schools were shut, research supported reopening schools for younger age groups, given the evidence of low infection in and from young children. Governments attempted to follow this science and have, from almost the beginning of the pandemic, tried to keep schools open as much as possible to avoid children losing out on education. Teachers unions, on the other hand, have tried to keep the schools closed.

Teachers unions have persistently argued that schools were too unsafe for teachers, who could risk contracting the virus and spreading it to their communities and vulnerable people. The unions put enormous pressure on governments to close down schools, even when governments deemed it safe enough to open or partially open them. When the unions were unsatisfied with government action, they sought to block their members from returning to work, filed lawsuits, issued strike threats, and held strikes and mass protests to compel governments to delay school reopenings.

When scientific advice indicated it would be safe for more children to return to school in England at the beginning of June 2020, Mary Bousted, the leader of the National Education Union, told members not to engage with any government planning based on a wider reopening of schools and hit schools with 22 pages of demands, including a ban on grading.

The union also launched the Escalation App, a smartphone app devised to help teachers challenge attempting to keep classrooms open during lockdown and initiate local strike actions. Across the channel, the French teachers unions— the most strike-prone unions in Europe— launched three major strikes during the pandemic, criticizing the government's handling of the crisis and calling for more teachers, higher salary, and an increase to the 2021 education budget.

Teachers-union activism has routinely goaded governments into accepting union demands and allowing politics rather than science and medical advice, to drive decisions. Parents, who are in favor of some in-person learning for children, have been largely marginalized in the political battles of school closures and reopenings.

They have found it frustrating when governments negotiate with unions rather than parents, who prefer to trust public-health professionals. Consequently, more resourceful parents have sought to find alternative ways of schooling, while low-income families, who often do not have access to such opportunities, have had no other choice but to live with union-enforced decisions.

Teachers Unions Continue to Exploit COVID to Serve Themselves

From the Steven Greenhut "Teachers Unions Continue to Exploit COVID to Serve Themselves" *American Spectator* article in September 2022:

Those who believe there's hope for reforming the current union-controlled public school system ought to pay close attention to the response by United Teachers Los Angeles (UTLA) to a seemingly unobjectionable recent teaching proposal. The district is offering "Accelerated Days" in October to help students who have lagged far behind in their studies because of the COVID-19 shutdowns.

The Los Angeles Unified School District wants to offer several additional teaching days for "students identified as in need of intensive intervention … to accelerate students' progress toward grade-level proficiency, social emotional learning and high school graduation, while providing teachers and other employees an opportunity to earn extra pay."

The extra schooling is optional for students and employees. The district will pay the teachers. The accelerated days would focus on tutoring and hands-on assistance, especially for English learners and those with disabilities. A few additional school days are unlikely to accomplish much given the depth of the pandemic-related educational setbacks, but it's hard to imagine anyone objecting to that modest effort.

Yet in a recent union tally, 93 percent voted not only to boycott any participation in the program, but also to file an unfair labor practice grievance with the state's union-controlled Public Employment Relations Board. As the *Los Angeles Times* reported, "The union wants the labor board to advise—and, if necessary, compel—L.A. Unified to 'immediately' withdraw the four school days" and bargain with it over additional remediation efforts.

Using the overwrought language we've come to expect, United Teachers Los Angeles said the days "distract from the district's refusal to support an equitable education for all students by denying our children support and services proven to ensure student success." Instead, union officials want higher salaries, additional staff, more school nurses, and smaller classes. Hey, why let a good crisis go to waste?

This is the same union, by the way, that resisted Los Angeles Unified School District's reopening plans and bungled at-home learning—not that it was the only culprit. California teachers unions placed absurd hurdles in the way of school officials who were trying to get the kids back to class. California unions tried—and largely succeeded—in limiting online charters, which were among the few schools that handled distance learning with any competence.

Post-Pandemic Educational Report Card

Now only days after the union's latest action, the National Center for Education Statistics released its special post-pandemic educational report card, which found, "Average scores for age 9 students in 2022 declined 5 points in reading and 7 points in mathematics compared to 2020. This is the largest average score decline in reading since 1990, and the first ever score decline in mathematics."

That's an appalling but predictable statistic. It's a nationwide travesty that's not the result of the pandemic per se, but "the result of choices made by COVID-panicked teachers unions and progressive politicians who failed to carefully consider the educational damage at stake," as the libertarian *Reason* magazine aptly put it. Students in California's cities, which are most dominated by unions and progressive pols, bore the worst of it.

Los Angeles Unified School District and other large California districts struggle to provide a quality education in the best of times. In the 2012 Vergara decision in Los Angeles Superior Court, Judge Rolf Treu invalidated the state's vast system of teacher protections (such as tenure) because they left "grossly ineffective teachers" in the classroom, with a result that "shocks the conscience." Higher courts overturned that ruling, but we know that Treu's words were on point.

After Gov. Gavin Newsom replaced charter-friendly Gov. Jerry Brown, lawmakers have been targeting the state's remarkably successful charter school system and especially online charters.

"Democratic lawmakers demonized parent choice and routinely pushed harmful legislation creating obstacles for students to attend a non-classroom based school," said Mike MeCey, who represents a coalition of virtual charter schools.

"Students enrolled in public online charter schools during the pandemic didn't suffer the tremendous learning loss their counterparts in traditional neighborhood schools did," he added. "Once school closures happened, our kids continued to learn and our teachers continued to teach—with remarkable and measurable progress."

Such schools, by the way, were particularly adept at serving the disadvantaged students United Teachers Los Angeles says it wants to help. Obviously, poor students had less access to computer technology, quiet at-home learning spaces, and tutors. Who couldn't see this—and growing educational gaps among minority students—coming when the state shut down its schools?

"In mathematics, the 13-point score decrease among Black students compared to the 5-point decrease among White students resulted in a widening of the White–Black score gap from 25 points in 2020 to 33 points in 2022," according to the federal report card.

Instead of figuring out ways to boost the education of their students, United Teachers Los Angeles and other California teachers unions used the crisis to lobby for higher salaries and more spending—even though state public school spending has soared even as student enrollment dropped.

For instance, when the governor was trying to prod districts into ending their COVID-19 shutdowns, the California Teachers' Association released a statement saying, "CTA believes all schools will need additional funding and supports to open for in-person instruction safely whenever the local parents, educators and communities make those decisions."

Now that schools are back in session and local districts are trying, however inadequately, to provide left-behind kids with some modest additional help, the local teachers union doesn't like that, either. If something as modest as a few extra paid school days merits a complaint, then there's little hope the public schools can make any substantive changes.

Hypocrisy, Inc.

Per the Larry Sand "Hypocrisy, Inc." *City Journal* report in February 2018:

Back in 2018, the American Federation of Teachers (AFT) president Randi Weingarten pilloried President Trump's health plan in the Huffington Post: "GOP Rewards The Rich, Rips Off The Rest Of Us," she declared. Is Weingarten among "the rest of us?" The union leader hauled in $472,197 in 2017.

Weingarten is hardly the only fat-cat teachers' union leader. According to the Department of Labor, National Education Association executive director John Stocks bagged $355,721 in 2017, while NEA president Lily Eskelsen García scraped by on $317,826. At the 2017 California Democratic Party Convention, California Teachers Association (CTA) president Eric Heins ranted about billionaires without acknowledging his own $317,000 total compensation package. CTA executive director Joe Nunez's compensation is $460,000; associate ED Emma Leheny makes $480,000, and deputy ED Karen Kyhn gets by on $427,000 yearly. New York City's United Federation of Teachers (UFT) boss Michael Mulgrew is practically working class by comparison, making $288,000.

Funny how Alex Caputo-Pearl and other union leaders neglect to point out that teachers' unions are themselves de facto corporations, though with a difference: all their income—money they get from teachers, voluntarily or otherwise—is tax-free. No teachers' union—or any union—pays a penny in taxes.

Teachers' union leaders grandstand about evil corporations while drawing fat salaries and howl about the rich and how corporations don't pay their "fair share in taxes," but they support the biggest corporations with their own untaxed income—income that puts many union leaders themselves into the 1 Percent Club.

Chicago's Big Education, Inc.

On Super Bowl Sunday in 2021, the Chicago Teachers Union (CTU) announced its intention to return to the classroom, per the Adam Andrzejewski "Chicago's Big Education, Inc." *City Journal* report in February 2021:

Finally, Chicago's 347,476 public school students can receive the same in-person instruction that many private and parochial students have already been receiving throughout the pandemic. Why does this seem like such a big achievement?

Other "essential" workers such as grocery clerks, doctors and nurses, and package-delivery workers haven't enjoyed the same luxury of working remotely—and they've kept doing their jobs without the generous pay and benefits earned by Chicago's public-school teachers.

In 2020, Chicago had 20,927 full-time teachers at a total payroll cost of $2.3 billion, according to a response to a Freedom of Information Act request by our organization, OpenTheBooks.com. Our auditors found that the average Chicago teacher earned $108,730 in 2017—$81,422 in salary and another $27,307 in benefits. Further, teachers are allowed to accumulate up to 244 sick days for use or pension credit. (A full school year runs only 175 days.)

It's not just unionized teachers who enjoy excellent pay, perks, and pension benefits. The most highly compensated Chicago Public Schools (CPS) employee was the CEO, Janice K. Jackson, who made $322,839—a $260,000 salary and an additional $62,839 in benefits. Jackson's salary alone was $61,000 higher than that of the U.S. Secretary of Education, a cabinet-level position. And Chicago's 522 school principals averaged $194,000 in pay and benefits in 2017, with the most highly compensated earning up to $219,000. Another 304 acting, interim, assistant, and resident principals averaged $171,315 in pay and perks.

In fact, pay is lucrative across all 908 job titles in Chicago's public school system. Custodians, for example, earned compensation packages as high as $101,177. Twenty-two custodians, with base pay up to $75,066, out-earned the $70,000 salary of the governor of Maine.

The 1,823 employees in six departments with names containing some usage of the word "diverse"—Business Diversity, Diverse Learner Superintendent and Services, Diverse Learner Related Services, Diverse Learner Quality Instruction, Diverse Learner Pupil Personnel Service, and Diverse Learner Service Delivery—cost Chicago taxpayers $221.8 million in 2017, with the top 1,193 employees taking home six-figure salaries. The district would probably contend that these departments are fundamental to the social safety net, but its spokespersons ignored our requests for comment.

Employed within the six departments are social workers making pay and benefits of $163,431; speech pathologists making $163,406; managers collecting $155,617; psychologists earning $141,912; school nurses earning $141,982; and many others. Maurice Swinney, Chicago Public Schools' Chief Equity Officer, made $214,605 in salary and benefits while managing a group of six employees. We were unable to locate any public comments that Swinney made denouncing the educational losses experienced by minority students during the past year. Stephanie N. Jones, chief of the Office of Diverse Learner Supports and Services, made $211,868 in pay and benefits. Latonya S. Seanior-Smith, executive director of Business Diversity, made $164,394.

The Chicago Teachers Union understands the power of the strike in the battle to secure high pay. In November 2019, the CTU walked off the job for the third time in the last eight years. After a ten-day strike, its members were awarded a five-year contract that included a 16-percent pay hike. During the pandemic, the union threatened another strike.

CTU critics say that its strike threats amount to hostage-taking. Illinois is one of the few states where teachers can strike, leaving the students as pawns in high-stakes "negotiations" between the union and the school board.

Several options exist for restoring balance between the interests of teachers and taxpayers. The Illinois General Assembly could eliminate the union's ability to strike for pay and benefits. Or lawmakers could follow the lead of State Representative Blaine Wilhour, who supports giving parents and students more choice in education. Wilhour has introduced H.B. 273 in the Illinois legislature, which would give students a state-aid scholarship, letting state dollars follow the student, not the bureaucracy. "The teachers union has become the biggest obstacle to upward mobility and to breaking the cycle of poverty for poor and minority students," Wilhour says.

Reining in the CTU's power would provide significant benefits to taxpayers, students, and parents—all of whom could use some help right now.

Teachers Unions Are More Powerful Than You Realize—But That May Be Changing

Per the Kerry McDonald "Teachers Unions Are More Powerful Than You Realize—but That May Be Changing." Cato Institute article in August 2020:

School reopenings are closely linked to the power and influence of teachers unions in a given location—not to virus-related safety concerns. Teachers unions throughout the US claim to be looking out for the best interests of teachers and students, but they are deeply political organizations with significant influence over what, how, where, and with whom most children learn.

While the nation's largest teachers' unions have long been deeply connected to the Democratic Party and left-wing ideology, this political affiliation has become increasingly apparent in recent months. From hinging their support for reopening schools on outrageous policy demands to launching court battles, threatening strikes, and openly supporting disturbing actions during recent protests, today's teachers unions are more powerful and dangerous than many parents may realize.

Public sector unions by their nature are problematic because they are funded by taxpayers under a threat of force and often have monopoly power. Unlike private sector unions where consumers have more choice, no taxpayer can opt out of paying their portion of public sector union dues (which come from government employee salaries), including what those dues fund.

School reopenings are closely linked to the power and influence of teachers unions in a given location—not to virus-related safety concerns.

In July 2020, the Los Angeles teachers union released a report detailing the conditions they identified for a safe reopening of schools. This document went far beyond requesting social distancing plans and personal protective equipment to an agenda that eclipsed both COVID-19 and educational matters. Specifically, it laid out policy requirements for school reopening, including passing Medicare for All at the federal level, raising state taxes, defunding the police, and imposing a moratorium on charter schools.

In Florida, the teachers union waged a court battle against the state's school reopening plans this fall. In New York City, the teachers union is threatening to strike this week over in-person school reopening plans. And in Massachusetts, teachers unions recently succeeded in delaying the school start date to later in September, ensuring no funding cuts, and pushing for remote-only learning in many districts.

As Corey DeAngelis of the Reason Foundation observed, school reopenings are closely linked to the power and influence of teachers unions in a given location—not to virus-related safety concerns. Citing mounting data on school reopening plans across the country, DeAngelis reports that the "relationship between unionization and reopening decisions remains substantively and statistically significant even after controlling for school district size and coronavirus deaths and cases per capita in the county during the month of July."

Shining an Illuminating Spotlight on Teachers Unions and Their Established Political Affiliations

According to EducationNext, the nation's two top teachers unions have been among the leading financial contributors to national elections since 1990: "They have forged an alliance with the Democratic Party, which receives the vast majority of their hard-money campaign contributions as well as in-kind contributions for get-out-the-vote operations." Teachers union members comprise 10 percent of the delegates at the Democratic National Convention, where they represent "the single largest organizational bloc of Democratic Party activists."

At their July convention, the American Federation of Teachers (AFT), the nation's second-largest teachers union, voted almost unanimously to endorse Joe Biden's presidential bid. In her convention speech, AFT president Randi Weingarten made no secret of the far-left policies and politics her union and its members endorse. She said:

Imagine a world with: universal pre-K; debt forgiveness for educators; triple Title I funding; expanded community schools; supports for kids with special needs; high-stakes testing thrown out the window; charter school accountability; public colleges and universities tuition-free for families who earn less than $125,000

That's not from an AFT resolution. That's straight from the Democratic Party platform, born out of the Biden-Sanders Unity Task Force recommendations we helped draft.

Additionally, the AFT endorsed other progressive policies at their convention that are unrelated to education, such as the Green New Deal, affordable housing, and universal healthcare. For many of the parents of the nearly 50 million K-12 public school students in the US, these policies likely go against their personal and political beliefs, and they should be concerned that this leftist ideology is creeping into their child's classroom.

Going All In

From the Christopher F. Rufo "Going All In" *City Journal* article in July 2021:

On June 30, members of the National Education Association, the nation's largest teachers' union, voted to approve a plan to promote critical race theory in all 50 states. Union delegates representing 3 million public school employees approved funding for three separate items related to "increasing the implementation" of "critical race theory" in K-12 curricula; promoting critical race theory in 14,000 local school districts; and attacking opponents of critical race theory, including parent organizations and conservative research centers.

The public vote represents a significant strategic pivot. For the past month, many liberal pundits and activists have insisted that critical race theory is not taught in K-12 schools. This was always a bad-faith claim; the ideology has made inroads in public schools for more than a decade. But the NEA's official endorsement puts the final nail in the coffin of this rhetorical dodge.

In the resolution, the union agreed publicly to "convey its support" for critical race theory, oppose restrictions in state legislatures, and use schools to promote political activism. The delegates pledged to "join with Black Lives Matter at School and the Zinn Education Project" to hold a "national day of action" on George Floyd's birthday, recruiting teachers to hold political demonstrations and "teach lessons about structural racism and oppression."

The resolution also promised to develop a study to critique "empire, white supremacy, anti-Blackness, anti-Indigeneity, racism, patriarchy, cisheteropatriarchy, capitalism, ableism, [and] anthropocentrism"—that is, adapting the most fashionable and intellectually bankrupt ideas from the universities for use in grade school classrooms.

Finally, the NEA passed a resolution to "research the organizations" that oppose critical race theory—including grassroots parent organizations—and provide resources to groups and individuals targeting them. The national teachers' union will use union dues, collected from public employees paid by taxpayers, to attack parents who oppose the racial indoctrination of their children.

Yet we might thank the NEA for one thing. Its new militant stance on critical race theory provides much-needed clarity to the debate on this issue. Progressives such as MSNBC host Joy Reid can no longer disingenuously claim that critical race theory is only taught in law schools or is only a "lens" for examining American history. The teachers' union has nationalized critical race theory and committed to the full range of left-wing radicalism, including opposition to "capitalism" and "anthropocentrism."

Moving forward, the question is now clear: Who should decide what happens in public schools—parents, voters, and state legislatures, or the national teachers' union and its allies in the public school bureaucracy?

Fortunately, the American people aren't ready to cede their authority to left-wing ideologues masquerading as educators. According to a recent YouGov survey, 58 percent of Americans who have heard of critical race theory and "have a good idea of what it is" have an unfavorable view of it—and 55 percent of this group, including 72 percent of independents, believe that teaching it in schools is "bad for America." The parents who are standing up and speaking out in local school boards across the country understand that critical race theory is ideological poison, and more are joining their ranks every day.

Charters for All

Per the Wai Wah Chin "Charters for All" *City Journal* article in February 2022:

In the turmoil of the last two years, teachers' unions and their allies have followed the maxim of progressive city engineering: never let a crisis go to waste. Taking advantage of the Covid-19 pandemic and its effects on education, they've sidelined objective standards to implement new admissions criteria, classes, and curricula. It's almost as if, at long last, they've ditched education as the raison d'être of schools, deeming themselves free to pursue radical educator Paulo Freire's vision of schools as instruments for transformative change to serve the "oppressed."

Meantime, charter schools, in contrast to their public-sector counterparts, continue to hold classes, maintain high expectations, and produce capable graduates. Given these conditions, it's no wonder New York City public school enrollment has fallen 9 percent over the past two years, while charter school enrollment has risen by the same measure. Primarily serving black and Hispanic families, these schools increasingly attract Asian-American families, too, who feel ill-served by recent educational reforms.

There's only one problem. Even as demand for charters surges in Gotham, the state stands in the way. Governor Kathy Hochul and the state legislature continue to enforce a charter school cap, preventing new schools from being started. The powerful statewide teachers' union has made its animosity against charter schools clear.

Many public officials up for election in November, including Hochul herself, were listening. In his book *Charter Schools and Their Enemies*, Thomas Sowell wrote that the house of public schools is on fire—yet politicians are keeping the exit doors bolted from outside. Inside the burning house are families of all colors and creeds.

That includes Asian families often left out of the conversation. For a time, many Asian parents weren't aware of the New York State Assessment results that show just how much the high-performing charter schools exceed the results of the zoned schools their children attend. Now, this secret is beginning to circulate, especially by word of mouth.

Neither New York nor the country at large has enough charter school seats. But it's not just blacks and Hispanics who are desperate for them—Asians need charter schools, too. As teachers' unions leverage power to dictate how and when students learn, and as curricula more and more begin to resemble activism playbooks, all neighborhoods, of every race and ethnicity, need more charter schools, in order to provide families with viable alternative options. If Governor Hochul and the state legislature don't want to admit that the house is burning, they can at least open the doors and let the children go.

3 – The Pandemic Mistakes of Masking, Remote Learning & School Shutdowns

Distribution of total COVID-19 deaths in the United States as of October 25, 2022, by age group

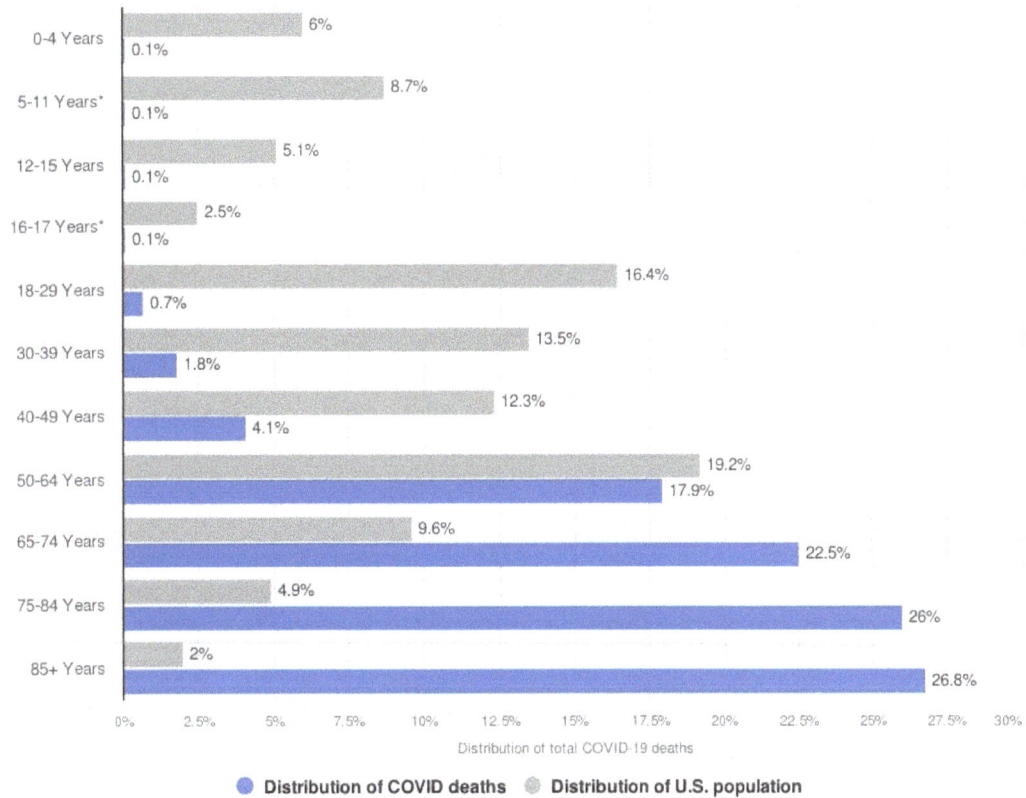

Age group	Distribution of COVID deaths	Distribution of U.S. population
0-4 Years	0.1%	6%
5-11 Years*	0.1%	8.7%
12-15 Years	0.1%	5.1%
16-17 Years*	0.1%	2.5%
18-29 Years	0.7%	16.4%
30-39 Years	1.8%	13.5%
40-49 Years	4.1%	12.3%
50-64 Years	17.9%	19.2%
65-74 Years	22.5%	9.6%
75-84 Years	26%	4.9%
85+ Years	26.8%	2%

Distribution of total COVID-19 deaths

● Distribution of COVID deaths ◉ Distribution of U.S. population

Source
CDC
© Statista 2022

Additional Information:
United States; As of October 25, 2022

Credit: CDC.

As per the "Lockdowns Reduce COVID-19 Mortality?" article by Emel Akan published in the *Epoch Times* in January 2022:

Compared to other age groups, the Covid infection rate and number of deaths of children remain extremely rare as the chart above shows. Since the pandemic began, using an example of America's largest state in population, California, 32 children in California have died from COVID-

19—out of some 65,000 deaths. That's just 0.05% of all COVID deaths in the state, while kids make up 22.5% of the population. Nationwide, experts say there have been 300 to 600 child deaths since the pandemic began—a fraction of 1% of the total, even at the highest estimate.

However, early epidemiological studies predicted large positive effects of these lockdown measures. Researchers at the Imperial College London, for example, estimated that such compulsory interventions could reduce death rates by up to 98 percent.

But the new study by researchers Steve Hanke, Jonas Herby, and Lars Jonung challenges these early predictions. "Overall, we conclude that lockdowns are not an effective way of reducing mortality rates during a pandemic, at least not during the first wave of the COVID-19 pandemic," the researchers wrote in a paper that presented the findings of their study.

Hanke, a co-author of the paper, is a professor of applied economics at Johns Hopkins University and the founder and co-director of the Johns Hopkins Institute for Applied Economics, Global Health, and the Study of Business Enterprise. Herby is special adviser at Center for Political Studies in Copenhagen, Denmark. And Jonung is professor emeritus in economics at Lund University, Sweden.

Meta-Analysis is a Quantitative Study Method Combining the Results of Previous Research Studies

"Based on review of 18,590 studies related to lockdowns and COVID-19 mortality, we determined that 34 of those studies qualified to address the belief that lockdowns reduce COVID-19 mortality, where lockdowns are defined as the imposition of at least one compulsory, non-pharmaceutical intervention (NPI)," Hanke told *The Epoch Times* in an email.

NPIs are any government mandate that seeks to "limit internal movement, close schools and businesses, and ban international travel," he explained. "An analysis of these qualified studies supports the conclusion that lockdowns have had little to no effect on COVID-19 mortality. Lockdown policies are ill-founded and should be rejected as a pandemic policy instrument," Hanke said.

Governments have taken a wide range of measures in response to the outbreak since the first wave in 2020. A stringency index was created by Oxford University researchers to track and compare these government responses. The index tracked responses in 186 countries.

According to the paper, studies that examine the lockdown strictness based on the stringency index found that "lockdowns in Europe and the United States reduced only COVID-19 mortality by 0.2% on average."

Johns Hopkins Analysis: 'Lockdowns Should be Rejected Out of Hand'

From the Wesley J. Smith "Johns Hopkins Analysis: 'Lockdowns Should be Rejected Out of Hand'" *National Review* report in February 2022: As we can now see, with lessons learned, the aura of "expert" has lost its luster during Covid, as our supposedly bigger brains have been proved wrong repeatedly.

Two of these have been Ezekiel Emanuel and Anthony Fauci. Both were enthusiastic proponents of societal lockdowns as a means of preventing deaths and the spread of Covid. We now know from a Johns Hopkins blockbuster meta-analysis that "shutting it down," in Donald Trump's awkward phrase, did very little to prevent deaths.

Per Smith, "It's a long, arcane, and detailed analysis, and I can't present every nuance or statistic here. But I think these are the primary takeaways." From the study:

Lockdowns are not an effective way of reducing mortality rates during a pandemic

Overall, we conclude that lockdowns are not an effective way of reducing mortality rates during a pandemic, at least not during the first wave of the COVID-19 pandemic. Our results are in line with the World Health Organization Writing Group (2006), who state, "Reports from the 1918 influenza pandemic indicate that social-distancing measures did not stop or appear to dramatically reduce transmission […]

In Edmonton, Canada, isolation and quarantine were instituted; public meetings were banned; schools, churches, colleges, theaters, and other public gathering places were closed; and business hours were restricted without obvious impact on the epidemic." Our findings are also in line with Allen's (2021) conclusion: "The most recent research has shown that lockdowns have had, at best, a marginal effect on the number of Covid 19 deaths."

Why might that be?

Mandates only regulate a fraction of our potential contagious contacts and can hardly regulate nor enforce handwashing, coughing etiquette, distancing in supermarkets, etc. Countries like Denmark, Finland, and Norway that realized success in keeping COVID-19 mortality rates relatively low allowed people to go to work, use public transport, and meet privately at home during the first lockdown. In these countries, there were ample opportunities to legally meet with others.

Worse, the lockdowns caused tremendous harm

Unintended consequences may play a larger role than recognized. We already pointed to the possible unintended consequence of SIPOs, which may isolate an infected person at home with his/her family where he/she risks infecting family members with a higher viral load, causing more severe illness.

But often, lockdowns have limited peoples' access to safe (outdoor) places such as beaches, parks, and zoos, or included outdoor mask mandates or strict outdoor gathering restrictions, pushing people to meet at less safe (indoor) places. Indeed, we do find some evidence that limiting gatherings was counterproductive and increased COVID-19 mortality

What lessons should be learned (my emphasis)?

The use of lockdowns is a unique feature of the COVID-19 pandemic. Lockdowns have not been used to such a large extent during any of the pandemics of the past century. However, lockdowns during the initial phase of the COVID-19 pandemic have had devastating effects. They have contributed to reducing economic activity, raising unemployment, reducing schooling, causing political unrest, contributing to domestic violence, and undermining liberal democracy.

These costs to society must be compared to the benefits of lockdowns, which our meta-analysis has shown are marginal at best. Such a standard benefit-cost calculation leads to a strong conclusion: lockdowns should be rejected out of hand as a pandemic policy instrument.

We can never squelch free discourse and debate on public-health issues again

People who argued against the "scientific consensus" about the lockdowns were stifled, censored by Big Tech, denigrated by the media, and mocked by establishment scientists. That was essentially "anti-science." The scientific method needs heterodox voices to speak freely if it is to function properly.

This subsequent look-back shows why. To a large degree, those with the officially disfavored views–such as the signers of the Great Barrington Declaration—were correct on this matter. Will we learn the lesson? Yes, if our goal is to ably discern and apply the best policy options, which can be a messy process. No, if the point is to allow those in charge of institutional science to exert societal control.

What School Shutdowns Have Wrought

From the Larry Sand "What School Shutdowns Have Wrought" *City Journal* article in March 2021: Comparing the state of pandemic lockdown statistics, a look at the national map shows that the most populous state, California, is also the most locked down, while the third-most populous, Florida, is almost completely back to normal.

In October 2020, Brown University reported that politics and teachers' union strength best explain how school boards approached reopening. In a September 2020 study, researchers Corey DeAngelis and Christos Makridis found that school districts in places with strong teachers' unions were much less likely to offer full-time, in-person instruction in the fall.

In the early days of the lockdowns, medical experts were mixed on reopening schools, but a solid consensus now exists in favor of doing so. In February 2021, the CDC urged the nation's elementary and secondary schools to admit students for in-person instruction as soon as possible.

Around the same time, the *New York Times* "asked 175 pediatric disease experts if it was safe enough to open school." The experts, mostly pediatricians focusing on public health, "largely agreed that it was safe enough for schools to be open to elementary students for full-time and in-person instruction now. Some said that this was true even in communities where Covid-19 infections were widespread, as long as basic safety measures were taken." Reopening doesn't lead to increased cases in a community, and closing classrooms "should be a last resort," according to a March 11, 2021, analysis of more than 130 studies by AEI's John Bailey.

The science is also clear that remote learning has been a disaster for children

A study by FAIR Health, a company that "possesses the nation's largest collection of private healthcare claims data," reveals that young people are suffering profoundly. Comparing August

2019 with August 2020 reveals an almost 334 percent increase in intentional self-harm claims in the Northeast for 13- to 18-year-olds. Drug overdoses more than doubled from April 2019 to April 2020 for the same age cohort. From spring 2020 to November 2020, obsessive-compulsive disorder and tic disorders increased for six- to 12-year-olds.

Additionally, mental-health problems account for a growing proportion of children's visits to hospital emergency rooms. In November, the CDC noted that from March 2020 to October 2020 such visits increased 31 percent for 12- to 17-year-olds and 24 percent for children ages five to 11, compared with the same period in 2019.

Moreover, not all health problems are temporary. Keeping kids away from school will shorten their lifespans, according to the Journal of the American Medical Association.

Beyond the health consequences, school closures also have serious economic ramifications

In September 2020, economists Eric Hanushek and Ludger Woessmann found that accrued lockdown-related learning losses will amount to $14.2 trillion in economic terms.

At last, many liberals in government and the mainstream media are now joining the conservative chorus calling for an end to school closures. Veteran *New York Times* columnist Nicholas Kristof, a self-described progressive, is demanding that schools reopen now. In an opinion piece in late February 2021, he blamed "Democratic governors and mayors who too often let schools stay closed even as bars opened." He also stressed that these leaders have "presided over one of the worst blows to the education of disadvantaged Americans in history. The result: more dropouts, less literacy and numeracy, widening race gaps, and long-term harm to some of our most marginalized youth."

Teachers' unions insist that more cash is needed to reopen schools—for masks, updated ventilation systems, and other Covid-related adjustments. But most private schools have been operating safely already without the benefit of budget windfalls.

As policy analyst Inez Stepman writes, only 5 percent of private schools across the country started all-virtual this fall, and they've done it with fewer resources: "Not only is average private school tuition substantially lower than average public school per-pupil funding (about $11,000 vs. public schools' $14,000), they've received only a tiny fraction of the federal and state aid that has been available to public schools."

Money is not the issue; California spends far more per student than Florida, yet Florida is wide open, and California is not.

Parents of all political stripes have reached the end of their rope. Open Schools California and Reopen California Schools have thousands of members statewide. They have called for campuses to reopen, more transparency from school districts, and a seat at the table to discuss reopening plans. Philadelphia-area parents are so frustrated with remote learning that they're running for office, suing, relocating, or retreating to private schools.

Public schools in 33 states have lost 500,000 students in a one-year period, according to an *Associated Press*-Chalkbeat analysis in December 2020. Data released in February 2021 show that California K-12 public school enrollments have dropped by a record 155,000 students. Nationally, millions have withdrawn from public schools.

It's no surprise that private schools are picking up the slack

A survey of 160 independent schools found that "121 are currently open full time, for face-to-face learning. The remaining 39 are on some sort of hybrid schedule." Education Week disclosed in November 2020 that the number of homeschooled children nationwide has more than tripled, from 3 percent to 10 percent, and it may be even higher now.

Some parents with financial means have enrolled their children in private schools or formed pandemic pods, but most can't take advantage of these options. The good news: legislatures across the country have begun taking steps to empower parents.

The Educational Freedom Institute reports that 29 states have active legislation devoted to funding students instead of school systems. While red states with weaker teachers' unions are over-represented on the list, blue states are present, too. Massachusetts, Oregon, Minnesota, Maryland, and Washington all have Educational Savings Account legislation in the hopper, and Connecticut lawmakers are considering a tax-credit scholarship proposal.

The teachers' union faithful are attempting to stem the rising tide in favor of school choice. When the pandemic hit in March 2020, the Oregon Education Association successfully lobbied to make it illegal for families to switch to virtual charter schools. Here in California, the heavily union-funded state legislature passed Senate Bill 98 in June 2020. The trailer bill effectively put a moratorium on new charter school enrollments by capping per-student state funding to 2020 funding levels. Had the legislators not done that, charter school enrollments would undoubtedly be surging now.

In a recent survey, Beck Research reported across-the-board support for school-choice policies. Released in January 2021, the Democratic polling outfit found that 65 percent of K-12 parents back school choice. African-Americans (74 percent) and Latinos (71 percent), groups that stand to gain the most from choice, are staunch supporters.

School choice is on the rise today because the teachers' unions, along with their allies in legislatures and educational bureaucracies, have made a mess of things. Finally, however, some states are taking steps in the right direction. It's about time.

Schools Are Back and Confronting Severe Learning Losses

Per the Scott Calvert "Schools Are Back and Confronting Severe Learning Losses" *Wall Street Journal* story in September 2022:

For two years, schools and researchers have wrestled with pandemic-era learning setbacks resulting mostly from a lack of in-person classes. They are struggling to combat the learning loss, as well as to measure just how deep it is. Some answers to the second question are becoming clear. National data show that children who were learning to read earlier in the pandemic have the lowest reading proficiency rates in about 20 years.

The U.S. Department of Education in September 2022 released data showing that from 2020 to 2022, average reading scores for 9-year-olds slid 5 points—to 215 out of a possible 500—in the sharpest decline since 1990. Average math scores fell 7 points to 234, the first statistically significant decline in math scores since the long-term trend assessments began in the 1970s.

Learning loss generally is worse in districts that kept classes remote longer, with the effects most pronounced in high-poverty districts, researchers say. Yet reading scores are below 2019 levels for certain grades even in some states that quickly returned to in-person instruction, such as Florida.

Among possible reasons, educators say, are that some students stayed remote after in-person classes resumed, Covid-19 outbreaks led to additional quarantining and class routines were disturbed by practices such as social distancing.

While some students have begun to make up ground, researchers say that, on average, it could take five years or more for today's fourth-graders to read proficiently unless the pace accelerates. By then, billions of dollars in federal pandemic-related aid for education will have run out.

These students are at a pivotal stage

Educators pay particular attention to 9-year-olds' literacy rates because research shows that reading ability by the end of third grade can be predictive of educational success, career earnings and the risk of incarceration. A study released in 2011 by the Annie E. Casey Foundation found that 16% of students who don't read proficiently in third grade fail to graduate from high school on time, a rate four times that of proficient readers.

"If students are not reading at grade level, then what does it mean for the content they're taking in in their other subjects? Are they not as prepared to be able to participate in their math classes and their social studies classes?" said Karyn Lewis, director of the Center for School and Student Progress at NWEA, a nonprofit research firm that has studied how long it may take for proficiency rates on its tests to rebound.

State education leaders were acutely aware of the stakes well before the data from the National Assessment of Educational Progress, and are pumping billions of dollars into hoped-for solutions, from small-group tutoring to expanded summer school, and aiming to offer students more individual attention.

In some cases, the efforts coincide with incremental improvements for struggling students, but educators say they won't know for years whether their efforts are a match for a problem this big.

"Without any prior experience as a guide, practitioners are sort of winging it—providing tutors to some students, double-dose math and summer school to others—and then just hoping that it all adds up to enough," said Thomas Kane, an economist and professor of education at the Harvard Graduate School of Education.

A concern, he said, is that districts might apply solutions and discover their inadequacy only after the federal aid is spent. The biggest pandemic relief program, the American Rescue Plan, earmarked $122 billion for K-12 public schools and required that at least 20% go toward addressing learning loss. In many districts it should be close to 100%, in Prof. Kane's view.

Texas is a rare example of a state where young students' reading scores have more than bounced back to prepandemic levels. In 2022, half of Texas third-graders met or exceeded expectations, up from 37% in 2021 and 43% in 2019, according to state data.

A key part of the learning-loss recovery effort in Texas is a measure passed by the legislature in 2021 that provides 30 hours of tutoring for students on the subject matter of each test where they failed to meet grade level.

Lockdown Addicts

Back in 2020, data from Sweden show it's safe to keep schools open, but Joe Biden's Covid-19 advisors seem more interested in shutting down as noted in the John Tierney "Lockdown Addicts" *City Journal* article in November 2020:

Biden and other leaders claim to be following "the science," but that obviously doesn't include the research showing the high costs and low benefits of lockdowns and school closures. Closing schools was a dubious move in the spring, when the Centers for Disease Control and Prevention warned that it would likely do little to stem the pandemic (and noted that school closings in other countries had failed to make a discernible impact). Today it makes even less sense in light of the accumulated evidence.

For young students, the risk of dying from Covid is lower than the risk of dying from the flu, and researchers have repeatedly found that children do not easily transmit the virus to adults. The clearest evidence comes from Sweden, which did not close elementary schools or junior high schools during the spring Covid wave, and which did not reduce class sizes or encourage students and teachers to wear face masks.

Not a single child died, and there was little effect beyond the schools, as a team of Swedish economists reports after analyzing records of Covid infections and medical treatment for the entire Swedish population. The researchers, from the universities of Stockholm and Uppsala, took advantage of a natural experiment in Sweden by comparing hundreds of thousands of parents at the junior high schools (for students aged 14 to 16), which remained open, against those at the senior high schools, which switched to online instruction for two months in the spring.

There was scant danger from the schools that remained open

The parents at those schools were 15 percent more likely to test positive for the virus than the parents whose children stayed home, but they were no more likely to be treated or hospitalized for Covid. The classroom teachers were twice as likely as the online teachers to test positive, but their infection rate was nonetheless lower than the rate among parents at either type of school. Just 0.2 percent of the classroom teachers were hospitalized for Covid, lower than the rate among parents.

The Swedish researchers suggest additional protections for classroom teachers, like encouraging them to start wearing masks or allowing the older, more vulnerable ones to teach online. But after calculating that a closure of all the junior high schools would have reduced the Swedish national rate of Covid infection by a mere 1 percent, the economists conclude that closing schools is "not a particularly effective way" to stop the spread of the virus.

The chief effect of school closures is to hurt students

Economists at the World Bank estimate that the spring closures will ultimately reduce the affected students' lifetime earnings by 5 percent—a loss totaling $10 trillion worldwide. Extrapolating from the well-established effects of education and income on life expectancy, another team of researchers calculates that the springtime school closures in the United States will shorten students' lives by a cumulative total of more than five million years—more years of life than were lost to the pandemic in the spring.

But those considerations don't carry much weight with teachers' unions—and the politicians who depend on them for reelection. Governors and mayors kept many schools closed or only partially open at the start of the fall, and in November 2020 they've been ordering further shutdowns. Since New York City reopened its schools in September 2020, there has been a minuscule rate of infection among students and staff members—just two cases per thousand. But Mayor Bill de Blasio is so in thrall to the teachers' union that he closed schools anyway even though the city's positivity test rate is well below the threshold used for closing schools in the rest of the state.

The school closures are disproportionately harming African-American and Hispanic students, and other lockdown measures fall hardest on low-income workers who can't do their jobs from home, as was repeatedly pointed out by Trump and the researchers he consulted, like Scott Atlas of the Hoover Institution.

Atlas, whose calculations show that the social costs of lockdowns exceed the benefits, calls them "a luxury of the rich." But despite Biden's professed concern for reducing inequality, he has not urged schools and businesses to remain open. While he says that he will not impose a national lockdown, his advisory board is dominated by public-health professionals eager to impose still more costly restrictions.

Don't Cancel School

Per the Allison Schrager "Don't Cancel School" *City Journal* update in August 2020:

The American Academy of Pediatrics has stressed that reopening is critical for children's emotional and educational development. There is also an overwhelming economic case to be made in favor of reopening. In fact, the cost of not reopening schools will last a generation.

The benefits of universal education are so deep and well-documented that it's unthinkable to consider discounting it for another semester. Education is the most effective means of economic mobility and is critical for long-term success. It explains much of America's income growth and development in the nineteenth and twentieth centuries. Today, moreover, schools provide important child-care services. As Goldman Sachs found, if schools don't open, an estimated 15 percent of America's labor force can't return to work.

Prolonged school closures will also strain communities and undermine cities. Public schools, which remain the foundation of a healthy economy and society, bring children of different socioeconomic backgrounds together. Time away from these schools is associated with more crime and drug use.

The longer the pandemic continues, the harder it will be to open schools, especially as students become unaccustomed to classroom discipline. It could take years to reacclimate children to school attendance.

In recent decades, decent schools and safety were reasons why many upper- and middle-class families stayed in cities. Their presence served as a significant part of the modern urban renaissance. In their absence, cities revert to retaining the very rich, the very poor, and a handful of childless twentysomethings—in other words, communities with limited interaction.

If cities like New York fail to offer decent in-person schooling options for the next year, many middle- and upper-middle-class families will go elsewhere (which they did contributing to a substantial NYC population loss)—and once they enroll their children in suburban schools, it's unlikely they'll return. Considering what's at stake, it's inexcusable that cities like New York wasted time instead of deploying every possible resource to open schools in a meaningful way. It could prove the biggest policy failure of Mayor Bill de Blasio's administration—one that will take years for the city to overcome.

Teachers' Unions Deserve Much of the Blame for Pandemic-Era Learning Loss

Per the Walter Blanks Jr. "Teachers' Unions Deserve Much of the Blame for Pandemic-Era Learning Loss" *National Review* article in September 2022:

Back-to-school season is usually an exciting time for students. But this school year starts under a dark cloud—thanks to political games from adults. In September 2022, for the first time since the start of the pandemic, the National Center for Education Statistics released national test scores.

The news was dismal. The National Assessment of Educational Progress (NAEP) scores for nine-year-olds exposed the erasure of two decades of advancements in math and reading, with performance tumbling to a 20-year low. Who did the erasing? Some of the biggest culprits want you to believe this educational tragedy happened as unexpectedly as the pandemic. That couldn't be further from the truth.

Teacher's union head Randi Weingarten displayed staggering audacity by tweeting, "Thankfully after two years of disruption from a pandemic that killed more than 1 mil Americans, schools are already working on helping kids recover and thrive." It is true that countless teachers in schools across the country are hard at work trying to help struggling students recover. Weingarten failed to mention that teachers and parents are cleaning up the mess she and her union left behind.

Despite gaslighting from unions and their allies, it's no secret that the American Federation of Teachers and its affiliates fought tooth and nail to ensure public schools remained closed. When information about Covid-19 was scarce, closing schools was a reasonable response, but keeping schools closed when the evidence showed it did more harm than help to children was an extreme blunder. While most schools in Europe were open as early as April or May 2020, the unions were hard at work fighting to keep U.S. schools closed long after any point of reasonable concern.

By October 2020, 90 percent of private schools across America were open, providing instruction without the devastating Covid outbreaks unions predicted. Meanwhile, Weingarten and the unions lobbied the CDC to keep kids out of public-school classrooms. This effort continued even after teachers in many states were given priority for vaccines and an overwhelming majority were vaccinated.

Don't forget the intense rhetoric. People who wanted to keep kids learning in classrooms were called sexist, racist, and murderers. Some unions even demanded wealth taxes, charter-school bans, and Medicare for All before schools could reopen.

Ultimately, school closings had far more to do with politics than public health

At a time of national crisis, special interests held hostage the education and future of millions of American children in order to extort billions in tax dollars for "safety"—funds that have, largely, not gone toward safety at all. And when parents demanded school choice to attend schools that actually opened their doors to children, the unions fought that, too.

Now that the truly devastating impact of such fecklessness has been laid bare for all to see, the culprits, unsurprisingly, want to pretend it never happened. We shouldn't let them. Parents and families have the receipts of what really happened. We must demand accountability.

If there is a silver lining, it is just that: Outraged parents are stepping up to create the most meaningful accountability in a generation. Throughout the last several years, a record-breaking number of states passed new or expanded school-choice programs, with 31 states plus Washington, D.C., now offering an escape route for some children the next time they are held hostage by a system that fails to prioritize learning. Most recently, Arizona surpassed Florida as the strongest school-choice state in the nation with its universal education-savings-account program.

The unions' special interests won't go away quietly, but neither will parents. The momentum is with families, many of whom are sending their children to schools of choice for the first time in 2022. As the American Federation for Children's Corey DeAngelis puts it, the unions have overplayed their hand. With this latest tragic proof of how badly unions' games impacted students, parents should be even more determined to demand real choices and break the unions' power once and for all.

The Union Map of School Closings

From the Steven Malanga "The Union Map of School Closings" *City Journal* article in February 2022:

After two years of fighting Covid, public officials are still debating how schools should respond to the virus. Despite ample data showing that virus transmission in schools has been generally weak and that cases among kids are often mild, governors in some states have been slow to ease restrictions on schools even as they lift them on society in general. This makes the U.S. an outlier.

We've imposed tougher restrictions on schools, including closures, than have our peer countries. Meantime, state policy has varied widely, with some states offering much less in-person instruction to children than others. States where teachers' unions are strongest have been slowest to get back to in-person teaching and to lift Covid restrictions on students.

The data can be framed in various ways, but one significant factor is that in places where teachers' unions are the strongest, schools have been closed the longest. No wonder, then, that for the second straight year, public schools appear to be losing students and, according to a new survey, parents are increasingly embracing school choice.

Many of the world's richest industrialized countries boast scientific and medical expertise that approaches that of the United States and have grappled with serious Covid outbreaks for as long as America has. Yet according to UNESCO's latest data, virtually all have closed schools for far less time than the U.S.

In France, where the first wave of the Omicron variant crested in December, schools have been closed for an average of 12 weeks throughout the two years of Covid. Spain has shuttered them for 15 weeks. Italy and Germany have been tougher, having closed schools for 38 weeks apiece. The United Kingdom sits in between those four countries, at 27 weeks. Our woke neighbor to the north, Canada—increasingly seen amid the truckers' protests as endorsing among the most restrictive measures—tallied 41 weeks. American schools have lost a staggering 71 weeks of in-person instruction since Covid began.

Country-wide averages can be misleading, as state reactions to Covid have varied widely

A year ago, as vaccines were becoming widely available, an audit of school districts throughout the country discovered wide variations of in-person instruction. The audit gave states a score between one and 100, with one being the least amount of in-person instruction and 100 the most.

The lowest states were Maryland (with a score of just 9.8), California (11.1), Oregon, and Washington. Illinois scored marginally higher, at 37.6, in the same range as states like New Jersey and Massachusetts. By contrast, Texas was almost completely back to in-person instruction, with a ranking of 90.8 on the in-person index. Florida came in at 99.9. In all, 15 states, mostly in the South and Central Plains, had returned to in-person instruction 80 percent or more of the time.

Asked about the vast differences, California governor Gavin Newsom said at the time that California's school system was like no other and shouldn't be judged against other states. Some parents demurred. As one distraught parent told the *San Jose Mercury News*, "It is unbelievable that despite all the evidence showing that school is safe for students and teachers with a few safety protocols, and hundreds of public health officials and physicians weighing in on the need to return children to classrooms for their mental and physical health, California finds itself almost last in the nation."

Even in February 2022, as Omicron recedes, governors in New York, New Jersey, Delaware, and California have kept mask mandates for kids in place for the time being while already eliminating them in most other settings. The opposite approach can be seen in states such as Florida, Texas, and Utah, where kids have spent the most time in schools and governors have prohibited school districts from imposing mask mandates.

Once again, the distinctions by state are striking

Any map ranking the states by how much school their kids have attended during Covid, or by the severity of mandates for children, corresponds closely to the levels of public-sector unionization and bargaining power of teachers in a state. For instance, all ten states with the highest level of public-sector unionization (from Connecticut to Massachusetts) ranked in the bottom half of the country in terms of days with in-person instruction during the first year of the pandemic, while virtually every state with the lowest levels of public-sector unionization recorded among the most days of in-person school learning.

This isn't hard to understand. Some states grant enormous leverage to unions by imposing onerous collective bargaining requirements on school districts. These states include California, Washington, Oregon, New York, New Jersey, and Illinois—all places where schools have been closed the most. States that impose the fewest requirements on school districts to negotiate— including Utah, Texas, Georgia and South Carolina—have been among those whose students have spent the most time attending school in person, and they are among the places dropping the final Covid restrictions fastest.

The long-term effect of the pandemic on public schools may turn out to be one of the most consequential byproducts of the last two years. In the 2020–21 school year, the number of students attending public schools dropped by 3 percent. The declines were even steeper in earlier grades, suggesting many parents of younger children are exploring other options.

Something similar may be afoot in 2022. Compiling data from 600 districts that represent a cross-section of public schools, NPR recently found that a majority of districts are reporting a second straight year of declines, and that few districts regained the kids they had lost the previous year. Private-school enrollment, however, grew by as much as 6 percent over the last two years.

A recent survey of parents shows that families are looking for options

More than half of those surveyed said they had searched for a new school for their child during the past year. Some 18 percent moved their kids, and another 14 percent were considering a move. According to an earlier survey, that rate of changing schools is some 75 percent greater than pre-Covid. Parents' first concern, the survey found, was simply finding a better school for their child. Covid disruptions were second.

School officials are starting to notice, and the superintendent of schools for Washington State called for an end to mask mandates that have been in place since August 2020. Perhaps not coincidentally, a report became public two days later showing that public school enrollment continues to wane in the state, even faster than projections. A December 2021 poll showed that 71 percent of state residents support school choice, and only 26 percent oppose it.

Is lasting change really on the horizon, though? In 14 states, officials have responded to these kinds of concerns by expanding school choice. But a map of those states would look similar to a map of places where teachers' unions have little power already—highlighting Iowa, Indiana, and Georgia. In November 2022, 36 governorships and more than 6,000 legislative seats will be up for grabs. Virginia governor Glenn Youngkin has pledged to add more charter schools. Given how volatile an issue Covid and schools has become, governors up for election in Democratic-controlled states may have to choose between the wishes of parents and the power of teachers' unions.

4 – Marxist, Progressive, Racist, LGBTQ & Ethnic Studies Programs Are Being Exposed

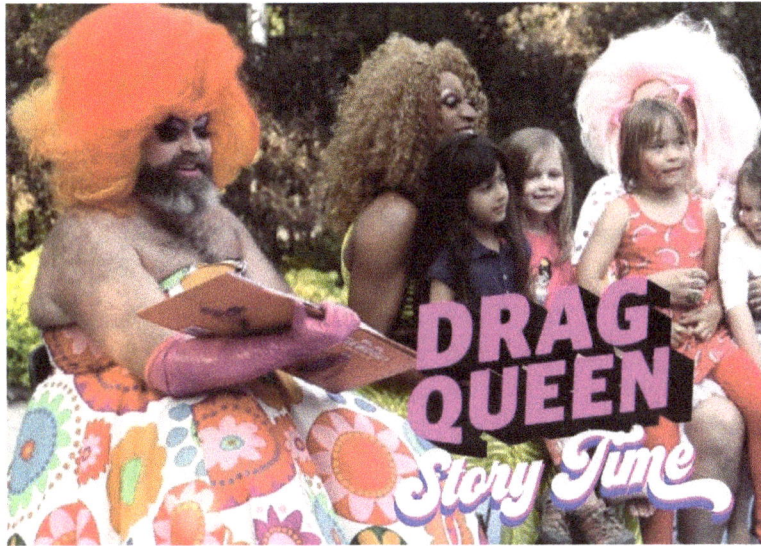

Credit: Feminist Current.

From the Robert Leroux "Woke Madness and the University" National Association of Scholars article in the Winter of 2021:

On college and university campuses, from where it emerged, the woke ideology has become a powerful instrument of censorship, a particularly clear manifestation of the intellectual terrorism that has reigned there for about half a century. In some cases, such as at Evergreen College in the State of Washington , it even encourages violence. In fact, woke culture is the intellectual plague of our times.

We must say that what we now call the woke culture or movement is nothing new. It is part of a long tradition, influenced by Marxism, feminism, relativism, etc. It is not a scientific approach to reality, but essentially an ideological posture, an attitude, a social movement. The situation is getting worst because most academics are now activists.

As early as the 1980s, in his seminal book *The Closing of the American Mind*, Allan Bloom analyzed this phenomenon in its first manifestations before the word woke was coined.

It became almost impossible to question the radical orthodoxy without risking vilification, classroom disruption, loss of the confidence and respect necessary for teaching, and the hostility of colleagues. Racist and sexist were, and are, very ugly labels—the equivalents of atheist or communist in other days with other prevailing prejudices—which can be pinned on persons promiscuously and which, once attached, are almost impossible to cast off. Nothing could be said with impunity. Such an atmosphere made detached, dispassionate study impossible."

For Bloom, it became almost impossible to question extremist orthodoxy without running the risk of being vilified as an intolerant person. The situation today is not really different.

New generations of professors have been hired not because they are concerned with and dedicated to science and objective knowledge, but because they are mainly political activists. Everything is wrong with the woke ideology: extreme paranoia, a mistaken view of social life, free speech, and the common man. Listening to the doctrinaires of the woke movement, we see that we are entering an unreal world, based on exaggerations, resolutely closed to dialogue and debate.

With wokeness, we cannot have a better example of the extreme radicalization of the left. The left which was once devoted to the fate of the working class and its struggles belongs to a bygone past. At the University of Ottawa, on a job posting one can read this:

The Institute of Feminist and Gender Studies at the University of Ottawa, located on the traditional and unceded territory of the Anishinabe-Algonquin people, is accepting applications for one tenure-track position in Afro-feminist studies. Applications from people who work with an intersectional framework on Islamophobia and anti-black racism, solidarities between Black and Indigenous people, transnational feminisms, Black feminist methodologies and practices, queer of colour or black trans studies and/or the history and impacts of slavery in Francophone contexts, are particularly welcome. Community experience is an asset, as is bilingualism . . . Qualified Black applicants from Africa or the African diaspora (descended from the Caribbean, North America, Europe, Latin America, etc.) are invited to apply for this position.

The description is ridiculous!

Wokeness views the world today with great disdain, indeed hates it bitterly. Not only must social distinctions disappear, it is, above all, important that politicized racial, sexual, and gender groups impose their interests and their vision on the world.

Like Marxism, this doctrine delivers the individual to servitude: we flout him, we censor him, we impose a new vocabulary on him, even a new way of thinking. It is clear that many universities have become liberticidal.

How Public Schools Went Woke—and What to Do About It

As per the Daniel Buck and Garion Frankel "How Public Schools Went Woke—and What to Do about It" *National Review* report in March 2022:

A radical theory of education—one that sees the classroom as the locus of societal change, not academic training—dominates our colleges of education. Thus, like a drainage pipe into a common supply, teacher-prep programs around the country dump a politicized approach to education into our schools, and it is here where our reform efforts must focus.

This outsized influence of the university on K–12 schools occurs not without precedent. Once before, our nation's dominant philosophy of education universally altered. Prior to the 20th century, American education was almost universally classical in nature—great books, grammar and rhetoric, direct teacher guidance, a healthy patriotism. However, the establishment of teacher colleges began to change that. Between 1910 and 1930, 88 normal schools—local institutions to train teachers—associated with universities and became teacher colleges.

At the most influential of these, Columbia's Teachers College, John Dewey and William Kilpatrick trained 35,000 students and wrote popular essays that influenced countless more. With such an influence, the progressive pedagogy of Dewey and Kilpatrick—which rejects liberal notions of knowledge worth knowing and direct teacher guidance to instead center a student's personal interests and exploration—supplanted classical education in American schools. The theory's association with colleges of education legitimated progressive education and so flooded American schools with proclamations of "best practices" and "expertise."

The influence of teacher colleges hasn't changed, only the theory within. Today, Teachers College, still one of the most prestigious teacher-prep programs in the country with 90,000 alumni, continues its significant role in determining what occurs in K–12 classrooms. A quick scroll through Columbia's course catalog reveals that teacher-prep programs now look toward "liberation" rather than virtue. A popular curriculum from Teachers College encourages children to read through critical-race lenses and acknowledges its dependence on critical race theory.

The college offers a class in "Black, Latina, and Transnational Feminisms," which seeks to "engage in an interdisciplinary exploration of feminist scholarship located at the intersections of race, class, and culture." In addition, the school offers a class in "Anti-Racist Curriculum, Pedagogy, Leadership and Policy." This trend continues across the college's course offerings, with frequent mentions of gender, race, class, and inclusivity.

Notably, course descriptions rarely if ever mention instruction, curriculum, assessment, or anything having to do with educating children. It amounts to a program in "proper" political opinions, not the practicalities of classroom instruction.

And Teachers College is no outlier

An education-policy course at the also influential University of Wisconsin-Madison "[focuses] on the ideas of transformative educators such as Paulo Freire and bell hooks (and yes, her name is all lower case!)." Freire's *Pedagogy of the Oppressed*, an incoherent attempt to explore the parasitic relationship between oppressor and oppressed in the context of the classroom, is considered a seminal work by many teacher-prep programs. References to Freire and other advocates of critical pedagogy appear on the syllabi of Harvard, UC Berkeley, California State-Long Beach, and the University of North Texas.

A UW professor, Gloria Ladson-Billings, is considered one of the single most influential thinkers in education. In 1998, she synthesized CRT and K–12 education, and in 2021, Indianapolis Public Schools hosted her at a racial-equity training for teachers.

Simply look through the DEI offerings at local schools to see that references to Freire, Billings, hooks, and other radical theorists abound. The organization Teachers Without Borders encourages their educators to understand and implement Freire's theory of "peace education"—ironic, considering that Freire cites Che Guevara and Lenin as exemplary teachers.

After the passing of bell hooks in 2021, countless testimonials appeared online of how teachers implemented her ideas in their classrooms.

Woke ideas about race and power did not form ex nihilo in the minds of DEI consultants at K–12 schools. They stem from a decades-long process that saw a noteworthy shift in the research interests of education faculty. As the DEI fad caught on, its teachings made their way to both university and K–12 classrooms. Moreover, the transformation of the university's pedagogical environment is not an unprecedented event. Once again, Columbia and universities like it are acting like a superspreader event of critical pedagogy and other radical ideas.

That our teaching force requires their credentials ensures that the drainage pipe will flow on. Even if we ban explicit instruction in something like CRT, its ideas can still influence policy, curricula, behavior plans, and teaching. Even if school-choice bills passed in every state today, the same teaching force trained in the precepts of Freire and other pedagogues would staff our schools tomorrow. We must decouple the colleges of education and schools by ending teacher-licensing requirements.

Thankfully, schools don't seem to need these schools of education. Research into the efficacy of such programs finds "little difference in the average academic achievement impacts of certified, uncertified and alternatively certified teachers." More like a degree in business than medicine, official teacher-training may assist in initial hiring but is no guarantee of effectiveness. In fact, many successful charter schools run on a model that relies on well-educated but untrained recent graduates who then undergo rigorous on-the-job training and constant professional development.

There are other potential knock-on benefits of ending our licensing racket. Burdensome processes that require years of training and financial investment create an opportunity cost that dissuades talented would-be candidates from other professions. Furthermore, fewer regulatory hoops to jump through could encourage entry into the profession and thereby mitigate the teacher-shortage crisis that our schools currently face.

Any attempt at reform—reestablishing classical and liberal conceptions of education in these institutions—would take a 50-year Gramscian countermarch of our universities. As such, our only recourse is to sever the control they have over teacher training.

CRT: The Monster Is in the Classroom

Per the Erika Sanzi "The Monster Is in the Classroom" *City Journal* report in April 2021:

Many American parents may assume that culture-war battles over critical race theory and "wokeness" are fought on legitimate terrain, involving such matters as how high school students can best grapple with our nation's complex past. Perhaps they think that the suddenly ubiquitous topics of gender identity and preferred pronouns rankle only those parents who are old-fashioned in their thinking. If only. America's youngest students are being bombarded with classroom activism and indoctrination that is inappropriate not only developmentally but for public school systems in general.

The contemporary obsession with identity has made its way into elementary school policy, curricula, and standards approved by state boards. While we continue to see poor reading and math scores, schools spend money and time confusing and shaming other people's children. Many educators and elected leaders have good intentions; they believe deeply that they are part of a necessary and long-overdue movement to teach racial literacy, social justice, equity, and antiracism.

But as virtuous as these terms may sound on their face, they mean something else in far too many classrooms. American schools are teaching young children race essentialism: reducing them to identity groups, putting them in boxes labeled "oppressor" and "oppressed," and often inflicting emotional and psychological harm.

If this sounds extreme, that's because it is

Schools indoctrinate children as young as eight in race and gender essentialism.

It is not happening everywhere—but it is happening enough to have juiced a multibillion-dollar, nationwide industry. Sometimes the source is a rogue teacher whom the principal and superintendent admit they are trying to rein in; but increasingly, it is simply public officials implementing approved policies.

- Consider Bellevue, Washington, home to Cherry Crest Elementary School. The school website indicates that students "will have explicit conversations about race, equity, and access" and "will identify culture and begin to recognize and identify white culture through storytelling, sharing, and conversation." The school promises to hold monthly assemblies that focus on culture, identity, and race, and has created a group called SOAR (Students Organized Against Racism) for fourth- and fifth-graders. These children, who range from ages nine to 11, are tasked with "implementing learning and stratimplementation of school-wide learning and strategies for being anti-racist." Left unclear is whether these students have been made aware that modern antiracism requires discrimination on the basis of race.

- Or take Lexington, Massachusetts, where, in October 2019, fourth-graders were taught to "articulate what gender identity is and why it's important to use nonbinary language in describing people we don't know yet." According to photos shared on Twitter by the district's Director of Equity and Student Supports, students learned about "gender identity," "gender expression," "sexual orientation," and "sex assigned at birth" by examining sticky notes on a "Gender Snowperson" who was drawn in magic marker on a large sheet of paper. The students were also taught that their pronouns had been "assigned at birth."

- In Oregon, teachers can use new state standards in "ethnic studies" starting in September 2021; the standards will become a mandatory part of the curriculum in 2025. The Oregon Department of Education released an update on the standards in 2020. While most Americans may not consider gender an essential component of ethnic studies, the Oregon Department of Education does. The revised recommendations for the standards require kindergartners to "understand their own identity groups, including but not limited to race, gender, family, ethnicity, culture, religion and ability." First-graders will be able to "describe how individual and group characteristics are used to divide, unite, and categorize racial, ethnic and social groups."

- In Rockwood, Missouri, a fifth-grade teacher recently gave students a handout with written excerpts by Alicia Garza, co-founder of Black Lives Matter. The writings included the claim that "Michael Brown was murdered just steps from his mother's home in Ferguson, Missouri." (They did not mention Attorney General Eric Holder's conclusion that "the facts did not support the filing of criminal charges against Officer Darren Wilson.") The handout goes on: "Disruption is the new world order. It is the way in which those denied power assert power. And in the context of a larger strategy for how to contend for power, disruption is an important way to surface new possibilities." When I asked the school principal about the assignment, he said: "This was used by a teacher and is not a Rockwood approved resource. I am working with the teacher to ensure that only Rockwood curricular resources are used when teaching lessons."

- This past February 2021, students in Evanston, Illinois, listened to the book *Not My Idea: A Book About Whiteness*. Parents were asked to discuss the book with their children at home. The book says that "whiteness is a bad deal" and "always was," and that "you can be white without signing on to whiteness." As Conor Friedersdorf reports in *The Atlantic*, Evanston schools ask kindergarten parents to quiz their five- and six-year-olds on whiteness and to give them examples of "how whiteness shows up in school or in the community."

- In Cupertino, California, third-graders at R. I. Meyerholz Elementary School were required to deconstruct their racial identities and then rank themselves according to their "power and privilege." The teacher asked all students to create an "identity map," which required them to list their race, class, gender, religion, family structure, and other characteristics. The teacher explained to students that they live in a "dominant culture" of "white, middle class, cisgender, educated, able-bodied, Christian, English speaker[s]," who, according to the lesson, "created and maintained" this culture in order "to hold power and stay in power." Students were then asked to deconstruct these intersectional identities and "circle the identities that hold power and privilege" on their identity maps, ranking their traits based on the hierarchy the teacher had just explained to them.

Some parents may agree with such content. But public institutions funded with public dollars do not exist to groom activists for particular causes, shame children for their immutable traits, or deny them their agency or their childhood. We are talking about eight- and nine-year-old kids who believe in Santa Claus, hide their lost teeth under their pillow for the tooth fairy, and curl up in their parents' laps for comfort and love. It is immoral—at least—to reduce them to confected racial and gender categories and to teach them to do the same to others. Parents around the country need to understand what is happening in a growing number of elementary classrooms.

"Banging Beyond Binaries"

Per the Christopher F. Rufo "Banging Beyond Binaries" *City Journal* article in May 2022:

In early July 2021, the district's Office of Diversity, Equity, and Inclusion sent invitations to the Philadelphia Trans Wellness Conference to teachers and staff on the SDP Connect mailing list, promoting the conference as a way to "learn more about the issues facing the trans community." The School District of Philadelphia encouraged teachers to attend a conference on "kink," "BDSM," "trans sex," and "banging beyond binaries."

The conference was organized by the Mazzoni Center, an LGBTQ activist organization that has worked with the district on sexual-education programs. (When reached for comment, the School District of Philadelphia described its promotion of the conference as part of its commitment to "creating equitable and inclusive environments," and said it did "not have any information" on the number of teachers who attended the event. The Mazzoni Center did not return request for comment.)

I have obtained videos from a publicly accessible website that show that the conference went far beyond the school district's euphemism about "issues facing the trans community." The event included sessions on topics such as "The Adolescent Pathway: Preparing Young People for Gender-Affirming Care," "Bigger Dick Energy: Life After Masculinizing [Gender Reassignment Surgery]," "Prosthetics for Sex," "The Ins and Outs of Masturbation Sleeves," and "Trans Sex: Banging Beyond Binaries."

The conference attendees included educators, activists, adults, and adolescents. There were graphic sessions on prosthetic penises, masturbation toys, and artificial ejaculation devices, which some hosts explicitly promoted to minors. As one session host explained, "there's no age limit, because I feel like everybody should be able to access certain information."

The conference began with presentations promoting puberty blockers, hormone treatments, breast removals, and genital surgeries. In one session, "The Adolescent Pathway Preparing Young People for Gender-Affirming Care," Dr. Scott Mosser, the principal at the Gender Confirmation Center in San Francisco, explained that he has performed "over two thousand top surgeries," which involve removing girls' breasts, and that there is no age limit for beginning the "gender journey."

"I do not have a minimum age of any sort in my practice," he said, explaining that he would be willing to consult with children as young as ten years old with parental consent. In another session open to children, "Gender-Affirming Masculine and Feminizing Hormones for Adolescents and Adults," Dane Menkin, divisional director of LGBTQ services at Main Line Health, endorsed treatments ranging from puberty-blocking hormones to manual breast-binding for "masculinizing" adolescent girls. "I'm a strong proponent that you can bind for as many hours a day as you can tolerate binding," he said.

Other presentations at the Trans Wellness Conference involved explicit sexual themes

Two female-to-male trans activists, Kofi Opam, a graduate student at the University of Iowa, and Sami Brussels, a medical illustrator, hosted a presentation called "Bigger Dick Energy," in which they explained the process of phalloplasty and using an artificial penis for "navigating cruising and anonymous/casual sex life."

Chase Ross, a transgender activist and YouTuber, hosted a series of sessions on "packers," "masturbation sleeves," and "prosthetics for sex," demonstrating various devices from his collection of more than 500 genital prosthetics. "I have tried and touched many dicks, right—prosthetics, real dicks, all dicks. This is one of the most realistic feeling in terms of like the inside of a penis," he said during one demonstration. "It's a big boy, this is, like, gigantic. Alright, give me two hours alone and I'll get this in my butt," he said during another.

The most extreme presentation at the three-day conference was "Trans Sex: Banging Beyond Binaries." Jamie Joy, a self-described "kinky," "polyamorous," "pretty big slut," and Lucie Fielding, a self-described "white, queer, kinky, polyamorous, visibly able-bodied, Jewish, witchy, non-binary, trans femme" led the session.

The women led a presentation on politically correct anatomical language, including terms such as "front hole" and "back hole," and shared personal information about organizing orgies for participants to "explore their fantasies and their perversions in groups." The instructors then discussed various "kink" activities, including fetishes about puppies, Mary Poppins, and spanking. "I haven't gotten to explore a lot of my mommy kink. And I think for tonight I'm really wanting to feel cared for, but also get punished a little bit," said Joy.

It is important to remember that this conference is not a fringe activity

The Mazzoni Center, which organized it, received more than $5 million in government contracts in 2021 and runs sexuality programs in schools throughout the region. The School District of Philadelphia has partnered with the Center on sexual-health research and student sexual-education programs, and the district's director of teacher leadership, Amy Summa, sits on Mazzoni's board of directors. Despite the school district's euphemisms about "wellness" and "self-esteem," the conference materials reveal a sexual ideology steeped in radical queer theory, not commonsense sex education. Parents and taxpayers should ask why the district's Office of Diversity, Equity, and Inclusion encouraged teachers to participate in such programming.

Radical Gender Lessons for Young Children

Per the Christopher F. Rufo "Radical Gender Lessons for Young Children" *City Journal* article in April 2022:

Evanston–Skokie School District 65 has adopted a radical gender curriculum that teaches pre-kindergarten through third-grade students to celebrate the transgender flag, break the "gender binary" established by white "colonizers," and experiment with neo-pronouns such as "ze," "zir," and "tree.

Rufo has obtained the full curriculum documents, which are part of the Chicago-area district's "LGBTQ+ Equity Week," which administrators adopted in 2021. The curriculum begins in pre-kindergarten, with a series of lessons on sexual orientation and gender identity. The lesson plan opens with an introduction to the rainbow flag and teaches students that "Each color in the flag has a meaning."

The teacher also presents the transgender flag and the basic concepts of gender identity, explaining that "we call people with more than one gender or no gender, non-binary or queer." Finally, the lesson plan has the teacher leading a class project to create a rainbow flag, with instructions to "gather students on the rug," "ask them to show you their flags," and "proudly hang the class flag where they can all see it."

In kindergarten, the lessons on gender and trans identity go deeper

"When we show whether we feel like a boy or a girl or some of each, we are expressing our GENDER IDENTITY," the lesson begins. "There are also children who feel like a girl AND a boy; or like neither a boy OR a girl. We can call these children TRANSGENDER."

Students are expected to be able to "explain the importance of the rainbow flag and trans flag" and are asked to consider their own gender identity.

The kindergartners read two books that affirm transgender conversions, study photographs of boys in dresses, learn details about the transgender flag, and perform a rainbow dance. At the end of the lesson, the students are encouraged to adopt and share their own gender identities with the class. "Now you have a chance to make a picture to show how YOU identify," the lesson reads. "Maybe you want to have blue hair! Maybe you want to be wearing a necklace. Your identity is for YOU to decide!"

In first grade, students learn about gender pronouns

The teachers explain that "some pronouns are gender neutral" and students can adopt pronouns such as "she," "tree," "they," "he," "her," "him," "them," "ze," and "zir."

The students practice reading a series of scripts in which they announce their gender pronouns and practice using alternate pronouns, including "they," "tree," "ze," and "zir." The teacher encourages students to experiment and reminds them: "Whatever pronouns you pick today, you can always change!" Students then sit down to complete a pronouns workbook, with more lessons on neo-pronouns and non-binary identities.

In third grade, Evanston–Skokie students are told that white European "colonizers" imposed their "Western and Christian ideological framework" on racial minorities and "forced two-spirit people to conform to the gender binary."

The teacher tells students that "many people feel like they aren't really a boy or a girl" and that they should "call people by the gender they have in their heart." Students are encouraged to "break the binary," reject the system of "whiteness," and study photographs of black men in dresses and a man wearing lipstick and long earrings.

"It is a myth that gender is binary," the lesson explains

"Even though we are all given a sex assigned at birth, you are NOT given your gender. Only you can know your gender and how you feel inside." At the end of the lesson, students are instructed to write a letter to the future on how they can change society. "Society right now is very unfair," reads a sample letter. "I see a lot of marches on the T.V and I even went to a march last summer."

The curriculum in Evanston–Skokie School District 65 is the perfect illustration of college-level queer theory translated into early-elementary pedagogy. For weeks, as the nation has debated Florida's Parental Rights in Education Act, which prohibits public schools from teaching gender identity and sexual orientation in grades K–3, commentators on the political left have claimed that public schools do not teach this material and have accused conservatives of instigating a "moral panic."

This claim is demonstrably false, and the Evanston–Skokie lesson plans offer additional proof for parents and legislators concerned about gender ideology in American public schools. Queer theory has made its way into public school curriculums for children as young as four. This development should be subject to robust political debate, not denial and dismissal from the political Left.

The Very Intersectional Caterpillar

Like most boys their age, Dave Seminara's sons would much rather play video games than read for pleasure, which they consider an oxymoron. From the Dave Seminara "The Very Intersectional Caterpillar" *City Journal* article in October 2021. I still buy them books, but every year it gets harder to find titles where the focus is on storytelling rather than politics. Per Seminara:

Recently, I perused three emails from bookstores offering children's book recommendations from a national "Indie Next" program organized by the American Booksellers Association (ABA). Amid 93 new books, all published since May, I couldn't find one that would appeal to my boys.

The choices included a "feel-good contemporary romance" about a young trans athlete fighting against a "discriminatory law targeting trans athletes"; a book about a young lesbian with pansexual and nonbinary friends who denounced her white privilege; a "queer coming of age story" about a young lesbian who joins the boy's football team; a young-adult novel about genderfluidity by a non-binary writer who is the mother of a transgender child; a "tale of self-discovery" about a bisexual love triangle; a book about a transgender witch named Wyatt; and a "fabulously joyful" novel about "drag, prom, and embracing your inner queen" that featured "a fat, openly gay boy stuck in a small West Texas town."

Other titles included the tale of a Puerto Rican eighth-grader who "navigates . . . the systemic pressures of toxic masculinity and housing insecurity in a rapidly gentrifying Brooklyn;" a young-adult thriller with a bisexual protagonist that explores the "politics of systemic racism;" and Don't Hate the Player, a novel about gamers I thought would appeal to the boys until I realized it was about a young feminist battling misogyny from the "male-dominated gaming community."

A host of new children's books available on Amazon appeals to the same set.

These included a new release for 8–12-year-olds about a young Muslim living in a xenophobic town in Texas where "hostile" townspeople protest the construction of a new mosque; a "swoony" gay pirate adventure story heralded by NPR; a queer ghost story featuring a bisexual teenage paranormal podcaster; and a polemic for 7–12 year-olds called Palm Trees at the North Pole: the Hot Truth About Climate Change.

The protagonists in these books included pigs, porcupines, dogs, cats, dinosaurs, mice, Navajos, immigrants from Vietnam and Pakistan, transgender witches, a lonely raccoon named Grub, gay pirates, lots of young feminists, and very, very few straight, white males.

If a story is a page-turner, the complexions and identities of the characters are irrelevant; my priority is to give my children good books. But the focus of many of these woke new children's titles appears to be identity politics and indoctrination, not storytelling. Moreover, the lack of representation for one group in particular is striking.

As a recent analysis in the *Wall Street Journal* recently illustrated, men now make up just 40 percent of college students. Enrollment rates for poor and working-class white men are now lower than those of young black, Latino, and Asian men from the same economic backgrounds. Given that reality, and the fact that boys read for pleasure far less than girls, shouldn't there be a push to get underprivileged white boys reading at an early age?

Literary agents serve as the gatekeepers for the publishing industry. Many explicitly advertise that they're looking for books by and for "marginalized and underrepresented communities." A nonprofit called We Need Diverse Books also strives to help authors publishing books with "diverse characters."

But diversity of thought and opinion isn't a priority in the publishing world; neither are poor white kids who live in gross exurbs or in the sticks and have parents who voted for Donald Trump.

I asked a representative from the ABA about the left-wing slant in their recommendations and was told that they represented "the titles (booksellers across the nation) are most excited about recommending to customers." As for conservative books, when I asked for such titles at my local Barnes & Noble, a bookseller looked at me as if I'd asked her for child pornography and replied, "There could be some on our website but without knowing the name of the book you want, I have no idea."

Sexual Liberation in Public Schools

Per the Christopher F. Rufo "Sexual Liberation in Public Schools" *City Journal* article in July 2022:

Los Angeles Unified School District has adopted a radical gender-theory curriculum encouraging teachers to work toward the "breakdown of the gender binary," to experiment with gender pronouns such as "they," "ze," and "tree," and to adopt "trans-affirming" programming to make their classrooms "queer all school year."

Rufo has obtained a trove of publicly accessible documents from Los Angeles Unified that illustrates the extent to which gender ideology has entered the mainstream of the nation's second-largest school district. Since 2020, the district's Human Relations, Diversity, and Equity department has created an infrastructure to translate the basic tenets of academic queer theory into K-12 pedagogy. The materials include a wide range of conferences, presentations, curricula, teacher-training programs, adult-driven "gender and sexuality" clubs, and school-sponsored protests.

In a week-long conference last fall, titled "Standing with LGBTQ+ Students, Staff, and Families," administrators hosted workshops with presentations on "breaking the [gender] binary," providing children with "free gender affirming clothing," understanding "what your queer middle schooler wants you to know," and producing "counter narratives against the master narrative of mainstream white cis-heteropatriarchy society."

The narrative follows the standard academic slop: white, cisgender, heterosexual men have built a repressive social structure, divided the world into the false binary of man and woman, and used this myth to oppress racial and sexual minorities. Religion, too, is a mechanism of repression. During the conference, the district highlighted how teachers can "respond to religious objections" to gender ideology and promoted materials on how students can be "Muslim and Trans."

In another training program, titled "Queering Culture & Race," the Human Relations, Diversity, and Equity office encouraged teachers to adopt the principle of intersectionality, a key tenet of critical race theory, and apply it to the classroom.

First, administrators asked teachers to identify themselves by race, gender, and sexual orientation, and to consider their position on the identity hierarchy. The district then encouraged teachers to "avoid gendered expressions" in the classroom, including "boys and girls" and "ladies and gentlemen," which, according to queer theory, are vestiges of the oppressive gender binary.

Administrators also warned teachers that they might have to work against the families of their minority students, especially black students, regarding sexuality. "The Black community often holds rigid and traditional views of sexual orientation and gender expression," the presenters claimed. "Black LGBTQ youth experience homophobia and transphobia from their familial communities."

Finally, Los Angeles Unified has gone all-in on "trans-affirming" indoctrination

The Human Relations, Diversity, and Equity department has flooded the district with teaching materials, including, for example, videos from the consulting firm Woke Kindergarten encouraging five-year-olds to experiment with gender pronouns such as "they," "ze," and "tree" and to adopt nonbinary gender identities that "feel good to you." The district requires teachers to use a student's desired name and pronoun and to keep the student's gender identity a secret from parents if the student so desires.

In other words, Los Angeles public schools can facilitate a child's transition from one gender to another without notifying parents. And the district is far from neutral: it actively celebrates sexual identities such as "pansexual," "sexually fluid," "queer," "same-gender-loving," and "asexual," and gender identities such as "transgender," "genderqueer," "agender," "bigender," "gender nonconforming," "gender expansive," "gender fluid," and "two-spirit."

The problem with creating a "trans-affirming" culture is obvious

In one of the district's own materials, "Mental Health Among Transgender Youth," the Human Relations, Diversity, and Equity department cites a survey by Mental Health America pointing out that, among 11-to-17-year-old transgender youth who were screened for mental health issues, 93 percent were at risk for psychosis, 91 percent exhibited signs of posttraumatic stress disorder, 90 percent likely used drugs and alcohol, 90 percent experienced moderate-to-severe anxiety, and 95 percent experienced moderate to severe depression. Additionally, according to a Trevor Project study, 71 percent of transgender youth have been diagnosed with eating disorders, with the ratio even higher for female-to-male transgender children.

These numbers are deeply alarming. But rather than provide a sober assessment of these risks and seek to mitigate them, Los Angeles Unified has adopted a year-round program glamorizing transgender identity and promoting an uncritical, "trans-affirming" culture in the classroom. It is, of course, a noble goal for schools to provide a safe environment for minority groups and to affirm the basic dignity of all children regardless of their sexuality. But Los Angeles Unified's program goes much further, promoting the most extreme strains of transgender ideology, which almost certainly contributes to the "social contagion" effect documented by Abigail Shrier and others.

The Los Angeles Unified School District governs the educational life of more than 600,000 children, the majority of whom are racial minorities from poor families. The implicit cynicism of the district's gender-ideology instruction is sickening: highly educated, well-paid bureaucrats promote fashionable academic programming that will do nothing to provide a basic education for these children or help them move up the economic and social ladder. It will only keep them trapped in a morass of confusion, fatalism, and resentment—while the bureaucrats keep collecting their paychecks.

Bonfire of the Sanities: California's Deranged Revival of the Aztec Gods

As noted in the Cameron Hilditch "Bonfire of the Sanities: California's Deranged Revival of the Aztec Gods" *National Review* story in March 2021:

The Board of Education in California recently voted unanimously to approve an Ethnic Studies Model Curriculum for use in all of the state's public schools. This curriculum is "probably the most radical, polemical, and ideologically loaded educational document ever offered up for public consideration in the free world."

Credit: Parts of an Aztec tower of human skulls – INAH/Reuters.

It's a purpose-built program of indoctrination into the worst kind of tribal politics—a project of social engineering designed to erase the unique personal distinctiveness of the human being and remake each of us into avatars of our immutable characteristics. The knowledge that entire generations of Californians will soon be catechized in the dogmas of such a bleak and thoroughly political gospel is almost too grievous to bear.

The most astonishing part of the curriculum is the section that deals with religion

Students are to be taught that white Christian settlers committed "theocide" against indigenous tribes when they arrived in the New World by murdering Native American gods and replacing them with the Christian God. According to the curriculum, this replacement ushered in a regime defined by "coloniality, dehumanization, and genocide," and the "explicit erasure and replacement of holistic Indigeneity and humanity."

But all is not lost, we are told. For students will learn that they have the power and the responsibility to build a social order defined by "countergenocide," which will eventually supplant the last vestiges of colonial Christianity and pave the way for the "regeneration of indigenous epistemic and cultural futurity."

The curriculum presents the pagan gods of the Aztec empire as worthier objects of study and veneration than Jesus of Nazareth. This presentation does not rest at the level of theory or academic inquiry. As Christopher F. Rufo has observed, teachers are encouraged by the authors of the curriculum to lead their students in an "ethnic studies community chant," which takes the form of worship offered up to these deities:

Students first clap and chant to the god Tezkatlipoka—whom the Aztecs traditionally worshipped with human sacrifice and cannibalism—asking him for the power to be "warriors" for "social justice." Next, the students chant to the gods Quetzalcoatl, Huitzilopochtli, and Xipe Totek, seeking "healing epistemologies" and "a revolutionary spirit." Huitzilopochtli, in particular, is the Aztec deity of war and inspired hundreds of thousands of human sacrifices during Aztec rule. Finally, the chant comes to a climax with a request for "liberation, transformation, [and] decolonization," after which students shout "Panche beh! Panche beh!" in pursuit of ultimate "critical consciousness."

5 – Social Justice, Woke Schooling & Critical Pedagogies Are Ruining U.S. Education

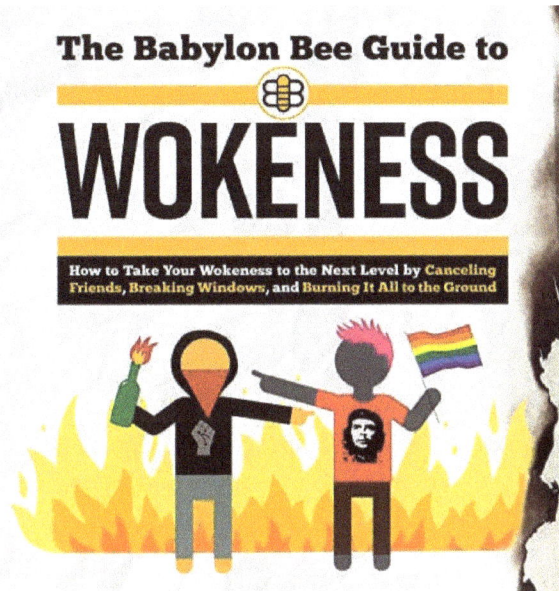

Credit: Babylon Bee.

Social-justice ideology is turning higher education into an engine of progressive political advocacy, according to a new report by the National Association of Scholars. Left-wing activists, masquerading as professors, are infiltrating traditional academic departments or creating new ones—departments such as "Solidarity and Social Justice"—to advance their cause.

They are entering the highest rung of college administration, from which perch they require students to take social-justice courses, such as "Native Sexualities and Queer Discourse" or "Hip-hop Workshop," and attend social-justice events—such as a Reparations, Repatriation, and Redress Symposium or a Power and Privilege Symposium—in order to graduate.

But social-justice education is merely a symptom of an even deeper perversion of academic values: the cult of race and gender victimology, otherwise known as "diversity." The diversity cult is destroying the very foundations of our civilization. It is worth first exploring, however, why social-justice education is an oxymoron.

Why shouldn't an academic aspire to correcting perceived social ills? The nineteenth-century American land-grant universities and the European research universities were founded, after all, on the premise that knowledge helps society progress. But social justice is a different beast entirely.

When a university pursues social justice, it puts aside its traditional claim to authority: the disinterested search for knowledge. We accord universities enormous privileges. Their denizens are sheltered from the hurly-burly of the marketplace on the assumption that they will pursue truth wherever it will take them, unaffected by political or economic pressures.

The definition of social justice, however, is deeply political, entailing a large number of contestable claims about the causes of socioeconomic inequality. Social-justice proponents believe that those claims are settled, and woe to anyone who challenges them on a college campus. There are, however, alternative explanations—besides oppression and illegitimate power—for ongoing inequalities, taboo though they may be in academia—they are fully covered in *Education Madness*.

The Cost of America's Cultural Revolution

From the Heather Mac Donald "The Cost of America's Cultural Revolution" *City Journal* report in December 2019:

Social-justice pedagogy is driven by one overwhelming reality: the seemingly intractable achievement gap between whites and Asians on the one hand, and blacks and Hispanics on the other. Radical feminism, as well as gay and now trans advocacy, are also deeply intertwined with social-justice thinking on campus and off, as we have just seen. But race is the main impetus. Liberal whites are terrified that the achievement and behavior gaps will never close. So they have crafted a totalizing narrative about the racism that allegedly holds back black achievement.

What are the "white norms" and "culture" that "race talk" seeks to deconstruct? Objectivity, a strong work ethic, individualism, a respect for the written word, perfectionism, and promptness, according to legions of diversity trainers and many humanities, social sciences, and even STEM faculty. Any act of self-discipline or deferred gratification that contributes to individual and generational success is now simply a manifestation of white supremacy.

The *New York Times* recently singled out parents who had queued up hours early to visit a sought-after public school in New York City. "Why were white parents at the front of the line for the school tour?" asked the *Times* headline. The article answered: their white privilege, not their dedication to their children's schooling.

The test for whether a norm is white and thus illegitimate is whether it has a disparate impact on blacks and Hispanics. Given the behavioral and academic skills gaps, every colorblind standard of achievement will have a disparate impact.

The average black 12th-grader currently reads at the level of the average white eighth-grader. Math levels are similarly skewed. Truancy rates for black students are often four times as high as for white students. Inner-city teachers, if they are being honest, will describe the barely controlled anarchy in their classrooms—anarchy exacerbated by the phony conceit that school discipline is racist.

In light of such disparities, it is absurd to attribute the absence of proportional representation in the STEM fields, say, to bias. And yet, STEM deans, faculty, and Silicon Valley tech firms claim that only implicit bias explains why 13 percent of engineering professors are not black. The solution to this lack of proportional representation is not greater effort on the part of students, according to social-justice and diversity proponents.

Instead, it is watering down meritocratic standards

Professors are now taught about "inclusive grading" and how to assess writing without judging its quality, since such quality judgments maintain white language supremacy. The social-justice diversity bureaucracy has constructed a perpetual-motion machine that guarantees it eternal life.

Minority students who have been catapulted by racial preferences into schools for which they are not academically prepared frequently struggle in their classes. The cause of those struggles, according to the social-justice diversity bureaucracy, is not academic mismatch; it is the lack of a critical mass of other minority students and faculty to provide refuge from the school's overwhelming bigotry. And so, the school admits more minority students to create such a critical mass.

Rather than raising minority performance, however, this new influx of diverse students lowers it, since the school has had to dig deeper into the applicant pool. The academic struggles and alienation of minority students will increase, along with the demand for more diversity bureaucrats, more segregated safe spaces, more victimology courses, more mental health workers, more diverse faculty, more lowered standards, and of course, more diversity student admits.

And the cycle will start all over again

The only precedent for our current resentment-driven war on the West's magnificent achievements is the Chinese Cultural Revolution, and that didn't turn out well. The Cultural Revolution, however, was waged mostly by the less educated against the more educated.

The oddest feature of today's social-justice crusade is that it is being prosecuted by the elites against themselves. Every college president, law firm managing partner, and Fortune 500 CEO would rather theatrically blame himself and his colleagues for phantom bigotry than speak honestly about the real causes of ongoing racial inequality: family breakdown and an underclass culture that mocks learning and the conformity to bourgeois values as acting "white."

Anti-racism has become the national religion, with the search for instances of racism to back up that religion becoming ever more desperate.

In fact, America is among the least racist countries on the planet

There is not a single mainstream institution not trying to hire and promote as many underrepresented minorities as possible. Conservative philanthropists and corporations spend billions each year on social-uplift programs to close the achievement gap. Taxpayer dollars are as liberally distributed from government coffers. We so take these efforts for granted that we don't even see them; they have no effect on the dominant narrative about white indifference and exploitation.

We are in uncharted territory. How a civilization survives with so much contempt for itself is an open question.

Social Justice Education in America

Per the David Randall "Social Justice Education in America" National Association of Scholars report in November 2019:

American universities have drifted from the political center for fifty years and more. By now scarcely any conservatives or moderates remain, and most of them are approaching retirement. The radical establishment triumphed on campus a generation ago. What they have created since is an even more disturbing successor to the progressive academy of the 1990s.

In the last twenty years, a generation of academics and administrators has emerged that is no longer satisfied with using the forms of traditional scholarship to teach progressive thought. This new generation seeks to transform higher education itself into an engine of progressive political advocacy, subjecting students to courses that are nothing more than practical training in progressive activism. This new generation bases its teaching and research on the ideology of social justice.

What we may call radical social justice theory, which dominates higher education, adds to broader social justice theory the belief that society is divided into social identity groups defined by categories such as class, race, and gender; that any "unfair distribution" of goods among these groups is oppression; and that oppression can only— and must—be removed by a coalition of "marginalized" identity groups working to radically transform politics, society, and culture to eliminate privilege.

A rough, incomplete catalogue of the social justice movement's political goals includes increased federal and state taxation; increased minimum wage; increased environmental regulation; increased government health care spending and regulation; restrictions on free speech; restrictions on due process protections; maximizing the number of legislative districts that will elect racial minorities; support for the Black Lives Matter movement; mass release of criminals from prison; decriminalizing drugs; ending enforcement of our immigration laws; amnesty for illegal aliens; open borders; race and sex preferences in education and employment; persecution of conscientious objectors to homosexuality; advocacy for "transgender rights"; support for the anti- Israeli Boycott, Divest, and Sanction movement; avowal of a right to abortion; and mob violence to enforce the social justice policy agenda.

Social justice advocates' emphasis on words such as justice, equity, rights, and impact all register social justice's fundamental goal of acquiring governmental power. Social justice advocates tend to dedicate any activity in which they engage to the effort to achieve the political ends of social justice.

Activism is the exemplary means to forward social justice

This word signifies the collective exertion of influence via social justice nonprofit organizations. Activism may take the form of organization-building (staff work, fundraising, membership recruitment), publicity, lobbying, and actions by responsible officials in pursuit of social justice. It may also take the form of "protest"— assembling large numbers of people on the streets to "persuade" responsible officials into executing the preferred policies of social justice advocates. Social justice activism formally eschews violence, but far too many social justice advocates are willing to engage in all "necessary" violence.

Social justice activists in the university are subordinating higher education toward the goal of achieving social justice. Social justice education takes the entire set of social justice beliefs as the predicate for education, in every discipline from accounting to zoology. Social justice education rejects the idea that classes should aim at teaching a subject matter for its own sake, or seek to foster students' ability to think, judge, and write as independent goods.

Social justice education instead aims directly at creating effective social justice activists, ideally engaged during class in such activism. Social justice education transforms the very definitions of academic disciplines—first to permit the substitution of social justice activism for intellectual endeavor, and then to require it.

Social justice advocates' most important curricular tactic within higher education is to insert one or more social justice requirements into the general education requirements. They give these requirements different names, including Diversity, Experiential Learning, Sustainability, Global Studies, and, forthrightly, Social Justice. This tactic forces all college students to take at least one social justice course, and thereby maximizes the effect of social justice propaganda.

The common practice of double counting a social justice requirement so that it also satisfies another requirement powerfully reinforces the effect of social justice requirements. These requirements also effectively reserve a large number of teaching jobs and tenure-track lines for social justice educators. No one but a social justice advocate, after all, is really qualified to teach a course in social justice advocacy. The direct financial burden of social justice general education requirements is at least $10 billion a year nationwide, and rising fast.

The direct financial burden of social justice general education requirements is at least $10 billion a year nation- wide, and rising fast.

Social justice advocates also have taken over or created a substantial portion of the academic departments in our universities. The departments most likely to advertise their commitment to social justice are those most central to the social justice educators' ideological vision, political goals, and ambition for employment. The heaviest concentrations of social justice departments are the Identity Group Studies, Gender Studies, Peace Studies, and Sustainability Studies pseudo-disciplines; the career track departments of Education, Social Work, and Criminology; and the departments dedicated to activism such as Civic Engagement, Leadership, and Social Justice.

Social justice's dizziest success has been its takeover of the university administration

While social justice education has made great strides among university professors, its dizziest success has been its takeover of the university administration. Higher education administration is now even more liberal than the professoriate. The training of higher education administrators, especially within the labyrinth of "co-curricular" bureaucracies, increasingly makes commitment to social justice an explicit or an implicit requirement. These administrators insert themselves into all aspects of student life, both outside and inside the classroom. Overwhelmingly, they exercise their power to promote social justice.

Social justice administrators catechize students in social justice propaganda; select social justice advocates as outside speakers; funnel students to off-campus social justice organizations that benefit from free student labor; and provide jobs and money for social justice cadres among the student body. The formation of social justice bureaucracies also serves as an administrative stepping stone to the creation of social justice departments. Perhaps most importantly, university administration provides a career for students specializing in social justice advocacy.

Higher education's administrative bloat has facilitated the growth of social justice bureaucracies—among them, Offices of Diversity and Multicultural Affairs; Title IX coordinators; Offices of First-Year Experience and Community Engagement; Offices of Student Life and Residential Life; Offices of Service-Learning and Civic Engagement; Offices of Equity and Inclusion; Offices of Sustainability and Social Justice; and miscellaneous institutes and centers.

These bureaucracies focus on co-curricular activities, which consist largely of social justice activities such as Intersectionality Workshops and Social Justice Weekend Retreats. Social justice administrators aim to subordinate the curriculum to the co-curriculum, as the practical way to subordinate the pursuit of truth to social justice advocacy.

Social justice administrators have set up institutions that make social justice advocacy inescapable

Offices of Residential Life have turned large amounts of housing into venues for social justice advocacy. The most intensive advocacy proceeds through Living Learning Communities—housing units dedicated to themes such as Global Citizenship, Gender and Social Justice, and Social Justice Action.

Bias Incident Response Teams, which rely on voluntary informers ("active bystanders") throughout campus, dedicate themselves to gathering reports of "bias incidents"—which, practically speaking, can include any word or action that offends social justice advocates. Bias Incident Response Teams act as enforcers of social justice orthodoxy on campus. Break and Study Abroad programs have also been largely taken over by social justice advocates, and are now frequently exercises in service-learning and social justice advocacy.

Offices of Residential Life subject students to social justice education even while they are eating and sleeping, Bias Incident Response Teams monitor every private social interaction, and Study Abroad and Break programs subject students to social justice education even while they are away from campus.

The social justice bureaucracies sponsor a large number of social justice events on campus

These events are the actual substance of social justice education on campus. The varieties of social justice events include activism programs, commencements, community mobilizations, conferences, dialogues, festivities, films, fine arts performances, hunger banquets, lectures, projects, residence hall programs, resource fairs, retreats, roundtables, student education, student training, workshops, and youth activities.

The subjects of these events have included activism, ally education, Black Lives Matter, civic engagement, community organizing, diversity, food, gender identity, health care, illegal aliens, implicit bias, leadership, LGBTQ, mental illness, policing, power, prisons, racial identity, social justice, and sustainability.

The social justice bureaucracies also engage in large amounts of student training.

This student training identifies, catechizes, and provides work experience for the next generation of social justice advocates. This student training is especially useful for training the next generation of social justice educators. By scholarships, the provision of student jobs, and linking social justice cadres to careers, social justice educators ensure that social justice education is linked to social justice jobs for graduates. The Diversity Peer Educator of today is the Dean of Diversity of tomorrow. Today's Social Justice Scholar will become tomorrow's Dean of Student Affairs. Student training provides the cadres for social justice activism.

"During a Hunger Banquet, each group experiences the wealth or poverty of their representative group. The very rich dine on a meal that most North Americans would consider standard: meat, vegetables, side dishes and clean water. The middle class receives a small bowl of rice and beans, typical of the meal that middle-class households often consume around the world. The poorest group sits on the floor, receiving only a communal pot of rice that leaves them all hungry

The Diversity Peer Educator of today is the Dean of Diversity of tomorrow. Today's Social Justice Scholar will become tomorrow's Dean of Student Affairs.

Social justice education, in addition, prepares students for positions in private industry (human resources, diversity associates), progressive nonprofit organizations, progressive political campaigns, progressive officials' offices, government bureaucracies, K-12 education, social work, court personnel, and the professoriate. University administration and faculty directly provide a massive source of employment for social justice advocates: the total number of social justice advocates employed in higher education must be well above 100,000.

Soon all of higher education may be reserved for social justice advocates

Before we know it, all of higher education may be reserved for social justice advocates since university job advertisements have begun explicitly to require affirmations of diversity and social justice. These ideological loyalty oaths will effectively reserve higher education employment to the 8% of Americans who are progressive activists.

Since social justice educators have to publish a minimum amount of peer-reviewed academic research to receive tenure, they have also created an apparatus of journal and book publication as cargo-cult scholarship—an imitation of the form of academic research, largely consisting of after-action reports on social justice activism on campus.

The core of this cargo-cult apparatus is a network of hundreds of academic journals dedicated to social justice scholarship, whose editors and peer reviewers are also social justice educators.

Their specializations mirror the range of social justice education—ethnic studies and gender studies, education journals and sustainability journals, journals devoted to critical studies, dialogue, diversity, equity, experiential education, inclusive education, intercultural communication, multicultural education, peace, service-learning, social inclusion—and, of course, social justice.

The bureaucracy of accreditation plays an important role in forwarding social justice advocacy at America's colleges and universities. Some accreditation bureaucracies require diversity, or other keywords that can be used to justify the creation of social justice requirements, programs, or assessments. Where accreditation bureaucracies do not explicitly require social justice advocacy, college bureaucrats often justify social justice advocacy as a way to fulfill other accreditation requirements. In both cases, social justice advocates within colleges and universities twist accreditation to advance their own agenda.

Education reformers must disrupt higher education's ability to provide stable careers for social justice advocates. These reforms cannot be aimed piecemeal at individual campuses. Social justice education is a national initiative, which has taken over entire disciplines and professions. Social justice's capture of higher education must be opposed on a similarly national scale. Above all, the opposition must aim at cutting off the national sources of funding for social justice education. A priority should be to deny public tax dollars for social justice education.

Nine general reforms would severely disrupt social justice education:

1) eliminate experiential learning courses;

2) remove social justice education from undergraduate general education requirements;

3) remove social justice education from introductory college courses;

4) remove social justice requirements from departments that provide employment credentials;

5) remove social justice positions from higher education administration;

6) restrict the power of social justice advocates in higher education administration;

7) eliminate the "co-curriculum;"

8) remove social justice requirements from higher education job advertisements; and

9) remove social justice criteria from accreditation.

Most importantly of all, college students must cease cooperating with social justice requirements. A mass coordinated campaign of civil disobedience, in which students simply stop taking social justice classes, attending social justice events, or obeying social justice administrators, would deal a body-blow to social justice education.

Woke Schooling: A Toolkit for Concerned Parents

Shared by the Manhattan Institute in their June 2021 guide "Woke Schooling: A Toolkit for Concerned Parents:"

An appropriate name for this phenomenon has proved elusive: "wokeness," "the successor ideology," or "neo-racism" have all been floated. In the context of schooling, sometimes critics allude to "critical race theory" (CRT), a school of thought in law schools that has been adapted into the educational domain. But because CRT is both overinclusive (it includes concepts not used in schools) and underinclusive (not all the ideas emergent in schools come from CRT), it is not the most apt name for what's going on.

Critical Pedagogy

Rather, what we are interested in here might be termed "critical pedagogy." "Critical pedagogy" names—without exhaustively defining—the host of concepts, terms, practices, and theories that have lately taken hold in many public and private schools. This term alludes to a connection to CRT—it might be thought of as critical race theory as applied to schooling—but also to "critical studies" and "critical theory," a broader set of contemporary philosophical ideas that have been particularly influential in certain circles of the modern Left.

In the American context, ideas espoused by proponents of critical pedagogy are the product of an influential group of thinkers in the 1970s and 1980s who were disappointed with the progress made on racial equality in America after the end of the civil rights movement. Given persistent racial disparities of wealth, health, and educational outcomes, critical pedagogy advocates argue that ostensible advances in racial relations are, in fact, a cover for persistent white supremacy that, they say, is inextricably entwined with the very fabric of American society.

Given this outlook, any particular racial inequality is taken to be evidence—indeed, a product—of racism. In an educational context, proponents of critical pedagogy claim that lower academic achievement and test scores among black or Hispanic students, higher dropout rates, school discipline, and nonrepresentative racial composition in admissions to selective private and public high schools are all evidence of persistent, systematic white supremacy.

This theory is behind many changes taking place in our schools. Constant conversation about race, including compelling students to identify and sort themselves along racial lines, is meant to resist "colorblindness." Endless workshops teach students to overcome their "white fragility" and embrace "antiracism." Efforts to end standardized testing are taken to be a blow against the "myth of meritocracy"—the presumption that educational outcomes reflect an individual's natural talent and hard work. Most important, students must be repeatedly reminded that theirs is a racist, white supremacist, nation, in whose crimes they are daily complicit.

Fighting Back

If all this makes you uncomfortable, you are not alone. Parents across the country are increasingly worried about the extremism spreading in their children's schools. These parents are not bigots and racists—they endorse tolerance, respect for all people, and believe in equal justice under the law. They believe, as Martin Luther King, Jr., said, that people should be judged not by the color of their skin but by the content of their character. This is precisely why they are ill at ease with critical pedagogy, with its emphasis on teaching children that their skin color does matter—and that it is perhaps the only thing that matters.

Critical pedagogy has been germinating in our schools for decades, but its recent explosion has galvanized many parents to action. If you are with them—if you, like them, believe that the solution to racism and intolerance is not the further entrenching of ethnic stereotypes and division by race—then this toolkit is for you and a link to it can be found in the Appendix.

If you are a parent worried about your child's miseducation but afraid to speak up for fear of being called a "bigot" and a "racist," recognize this: you are not alone, and thousands of parents like you are preparing to fight back.

The Racial Achievement Gap

The "achievement gap" is at the root of the controversy about race and schooling. This term "refers to the disparity in academic performance between groups of students," particularly between black and Hispanic students, compared with white and Asian students. For example, on the National Assessment of Educational Progress (the "nation's report card"), white eighth-graders outscored black eighth-graders by an average of 32 points on a 500-point scale in math and 28 points in reading.[9] The high school dropout rate among black students is 24% higher than the white rate, while the Hispanic dropout rate is nearly twice the white rate.

The source of this gap, its persistence, and how to close it are all subjects of debate. The Obama administration identified key goals for closing the gap, including requiring a high, uniform standard for academic instruction, using statewide measures of student progress, increasing access to high-quality preschools, and holding schools that do not show progress accountable.

Critical pedagogy advocates, however, see the achievement gap as proof of the persistence of racism and white supremacy. Gloria Ladson-Billings—a former professor of education at the University of Wisconsin who helped introduce critical race theory to education—rejected the idea of an "achievement gap" in her 2006 presidential address to the American Educational Research Association. Instead, she called disparities in test scores an "education debt" that comprised accrued injustices done to black and Hispanic students and that is enshrined in school funding disparities. (Complicating this narrative, research shows that poor school districts receive slightly more funding than rich, and within districts, poor and minority students receive slightly more funding—1%–2% on average—than non-poor, white students.)

More recent commentators have put it in blunter terms. Bettina Love, a professor of education at the University of Georgia, has written that "the achievement gap is not about White students outperforming dark students; it is about a history of injustice and oppression," identifying it entirely with "racism and White rage," which has left students as metaphorical "sharecroppers" unable to escape the debt.

In addition to the achievement gap definition, there are another dozen relevant critical pedagogy glossary terms and organizational strategies are listed below, whose definitions are explained in detail in the Appendix link.

- Affinity Group
- Antiracism
- Colorblindness
- Critical Race Theory
- Culturally Responsive Teaching
- Equity
- Implicit Bias
- Meritocracy
- Microaggression
- Restorative Justice
- White Fragility

- White Supremacy
- Proportionality
- The Minority Rule
- Effective Persuasion
- Solving the Problem Yourself
- Getting Organized
- Responding as a Group
- Offering a Positive Vision
- Working with the Media
- Taking Legal Action

Whom Can I Ask for Help?

The organizations listed below (and there are many more not listed) are meant to be a starting point for parents looking to fight back against critical pedagogy in their school, but it's far from the only resource. Many national organizations—many brand-new—are interested in fighting various manifestations of critical pedagogy at every level of education, from kindergarten through college. They can help you connect to other parents, give you advice on organizing in your school, offer tips on talking to the media, and even help with lawsuits. Here are a few organizations:

- Foundation Against Intolerance and Racism (FAIR) is a nonpartisan, centrist organization focused on responding to radicalism with a "compassionate anti-racism" dedicated to equal dignity and equality under the law. FAIR runs a membership organization, including local chapters, to help connect people from all parts of society skeptical of "woke" approaches that they term "neo-racism." It can also help connect parents like you to other parents and to professional and legal aid and can be contacted using the link in the Appendix.

- Parents Defending Education is a "national grassroots organization working to reclaim our schools from activists promoting harmful agendas," PDE is a school-focused group working to connect parents and provide resources to respond to critical pedagogy. It can help you find other parents in your local area and offer resources on how to respond effectively to your administration's agenda and can be contacted using the link in the Appendix.

- Foundation for Individual Rights in Education (FIRE) has historically focused on repressive speech policing at the college level, and is now expanding its work to K–12 education. Its high school network offers a free-speech curriculum, as well as resources for parents and students concerned about their voices being silenced and can be contacted using the link in the Appendix.

- Pacific Legal Foundation is a national nonprofit public-interest law firm focusing on civil rights issues. It has recently taken an interest in critical pedagogy discrimination in public schools, organizing the lawsuit against Thomas Jefferson High School. If you are considering legal action, or if you believe that you have a test case, this organization may be a useful resource and can be contacted using the link in the Appendix.

The Art of Teaching and the End of Wokeness

Per the Adam Ellwanger "The Art of Teaching and the End of Wokeness" National Association of Scholars paper in the Winter of 2021:

Any enthusiast of classical liberal education will be much dismayed at the current state of education in America, both in K-12 schools and our colleges and universities. In addition to the schools' incessant propagation of the modern leftist worldview, there is the new war against standardized means of assessing student performance—and even a growing conviction that any formal measure of academic success is a way of perpetuating the injustices of the "status quo."

For over thirty years, when surveying the unfolding crisis in the nation's schools, conservatives and their allies have centered their critique on matters of curriculum. Almost without exception their arguments revolve around the conviction that we are teaching the wrong things, and the solutions that they propose usually consist of recommitting ourselves to teaching the right things.

These critics aren't wrong. American students are being taught the wrong things. History has been reduced to a cataloguing of Euro-American failure, injustice, and violence. Literature serves as a springboard from which to launch attacks on "uninterrogated" traditional values and "assumptions." Social studies are now a vehicle for gender ideology and Critical Race Theory, which teaches a moralistic race essentialism where whites are de facto bigoted oppressors and minorities are virtuous victims of "systemic" brutality and hatred. In the wake of the racial unrest in the summer of 2020, some public schools have abandoned advanced mathematics courses on the grounds that they marginalize minorities.

Suffice it to say, then, that there are many ways in which the curriculum can be improved. Nevertheless, focusing on curricular concerns as a way to "reclaim" the schools is a deeply misguided approach. The conservative fetishization of the whats of American education (i.e., considerations of what is being taught) is largely responsible for the success of the left in conquering these institutions.

Put simply, an exclusive focus on the whats has been self-defeating, because the left's successes in turning schools into houses of political indoctrination were largely achieved by ignoring the question of content: their victory was secured through an elevation of style over substance, of form over content. Their conquest was achieved through a resolute dedication to the hows of schooling; that is, the methods by which content is conveyed to students and how teaching techniques and strategies can be instrumentalized to serve ideological ends.

They also devoted themselves to changing how the schools are run at the administrative and procedural levels. This elevation of the hows over the whats allowed the political left to take over education at a time when their activists were a minority within what was then a culturally conservative institution. This hostile takeover was consolidated mainly throughout the 1980s.

Sounding the alarm that American schools were in intellectual decline

By the time that educational reformer William Bennett was appointed to the post of Secretary of Education by Ronald Reagan in 1985, many were sounding the alarm that American schools were in intellectual decline. But by then, the left's alternate model of education had already substantially dislodged the older model that had been defined by strict standards and rigorous monitoring of student performance. By the mid-1990s, the new educational order had received the tacit (if oft-unspoken) approval of administrators and school boards.

If we are to redirect the trajectory of American education, there is only one viable form of recourse: we must temporarily abandon the concern with content and dedicate ourselves to developing teaching techniques that might cultivate a disposition and style of thinking that will encourage students to view current institutional politics and official ideology with skepticism and hostility.

This reorientation will require dissident teachers to give significant thought to "mundane" aspects of teaching that were previously viewed as frivolous and subordinate to the issue of curricular content. Some progress can be made simply by refusing the innovations and commonplaces of modern education. Re-centralize the classroom, for example. Give lectures (rather than holding open-ended "discussions"). Stand at the front of the room when lecturing. Maintain an attendance policy and insist upon punctuality. Penalize plagiarism. Insist upon the existence of objective truth: maintain that there are correct and incorrect answers and that knowledge is not contingent upon the "lived experience" of the individual.

The left's annexing of the schools was achieved by attending to the hows of education more than to the whats. Formulating a complete pedagogical model for reclaiming American education will be an involved process that will require sustained dialogue and collaboration between dissident teachers across the country. This dialogue—which demands a focus on tactics rather than texts—is our most urgent task. Together, we must develop strategies to form a much different sort of citizen than the schools are now producing. Nothing less will be sufficient for our aims.

Taking Off the Mask

As per the Max Eden "Taking Off the Mask" *City Journal* article in April 2021:

Last month, Stanley Kurtz accused two Republicans, Senator John Cornyn and Representative Tom Cole, of being "hornswoggled" into backing the Civics Secures Democracy Act, which would appropriate $1 billion for federal grants to support curriculum development and teacher training in K-12 civics education. Kurtz and others argued that the key words in the bill all but assured the Department of Education would use the money to promote critical race theory (CRT).

We no longer need to take Kurtz's word for it. This week, the Department of Education proposed a regulation that eliminates all plausible deniability, directing civics grant programs to prioritize applications that "support the development of culturally responsive teaching and learning."

"Culturally responsive" is one of CRT's favorite terms. For many, it might sound like the melting-pot pedagogy that centrists have long held dear: finding elements in students' diverse backgrounds that could be used as hooks to bring them closer to the spirit of E pluribus unum. But the creators of "culturally responsive" education actually mean the opposite.

According to New York University professor David Kirkland, author of "Culturally Responsive Education: A Primer for Policy and Practice" and key architect of New York State's culturally responsive framework, the old approach to diversity facilitated "assimilation by dominant systems and ideologies which centered Anglo-European-Christian-Judeo-cis-hetero-male whiteness as the normative reference point." Culturally responsive education, he says, "challenges this doxa." How far does that anti-assimilationist challenge go? Kirkland has declared that expecting class to be conducted in American standard English reinforces "narratives of white supremacy."

The Department of Education just made it clear that it will promote critical race theory.

The Department of Education's proposed rule does not go quite that far, but it does put what it wants in remarkably plain language. As an example of a work showcasing the "vital role of diversity in our Nation's democracy," the Department of Education lauds the "landmark" 1619 Project, which scholars have heavily criticized for its factual and interpretive distortions.

The proposed rule also applauds that "schools across the country are working to incorporate antiracist practices into teaching and learning," and invokes Ibram X. Kendi, author of *How to Be an Anti-Racist*, which declares, "The only remedy to racist discrimination is antiracist discrimination. The only remedy to past discrimination is present discrimination. The only remedy to present discrimination is future discrimination."

The proposed rule would also prioritize civics programs that foster "an 'identity-safe' learning environment." But what, according to the rule, puts students in danger? The idea that teachers should treat them equally, regardless of race. Teachers who "try to be colorblind," explain the authors of a book cited in the proposed rule, "inadvertently [are] creating an unsafe environment."

No one paying close attention should be surprised to see the Department of Education turning its grantmaking apparatus into an engine to promote CRT and foster "anti-racist" racial discrimination in the classroom. Unfortunately, moderates and conservatives in Congress typically don't pay that much attention.

Or perhaps they really do believe that our country was founded as a "slavocracy;" that our schools should engage in "antiracist" racial discrimination, and that "colorblindness" endangers student safety.

Whatever the case may be, the Department of Education has done Americans a favor by making its intentions clear: it will use any money Congress gives it for civics education to promote critical race theory.

Inside the Woke Indoctrination Machine

From the Andrew Gutmann and Paul Rossi "Inside the Woke Indoctrination Machine" *The Wall Street Journal* report in February 2022:

Last spring, we exposed how two elite independent schools in New York had become corrupted by a divisive obsession with race, helping start the national movement against critical race theory. Schools apply this theory under the guise of diversity, equity and inclusion programming. Until now, however, neither of us fully grasped the dangers of this ideology or the true motives of its practitioners. The goal of DEI isn't only to teach students about slavery or encourage courageous conversations about race, it is to transform schools totally and reshape society radically.

Over the past month we have watched nearly 100 hours of leaked videos from 108 workshops held virtually in 2021 for the National Association of Independent Schools' People of Color Conference. The NAIS sets standards for more than 1,600 independent schools in the U.S., driving their missions and influencing many school policies. The conference is NAIS's flagship annual event for disseminating DEI practices, and more than 6,000 DEI practitioners, educators and administrators attended in 2022. Intended as professional development and not meant for the public, these workshops are honest, transparent and unfiltered—very different from how private schools typically communicate DEI initiatives. These leaked videos act as a Rosetta Stone for deciphering the DEI playbook.

The path to remake schools begins with the word "diversity," which means much more than simply increasing the number of students and faculty of color—referred to in these workshops as "Bipoc," which stands for "black, indigenous and people of color." DEI experts urge schools to classify people by identities such as race, convince them that they are being harmed by their environment, and turn them into fervent advocates for institutional change.

In workshops such as "Integrating Healing-Centered Engagements Into a DEIA School Program" and "Racial Trauma and the Path Toward Healing," we learned how DEI practitioners use segregated affinity groups and practices such as healing circles to inculcate feelings of trauma. Even students without grievances are trained to see themselves as victims of their ancestors' suffering through "intergenerational violence."

The next step in a school's transformation is "inclusion." Schools must integrate DEI work into every aspect of the school and every facet of the curriculum must be evaluated through an antibias, antiracist, or antioppressive lens. In "Let's Talk About It! Anti-Oppressive Unit and Lesson Plan Design," we learned that the omission of this lens—"failing to explore the intersection of STEM and social justice," for instance—constitutes an act of "curriculum violence."

All school messaging must be scrubbed of noninclusive language, all school policies of noninclusive practices, all libraries of noninclusive books

Inclusion also requires that all non-Bipoc stakeholders become allies in the fight against the systemic harm being perpetuated by the institution. In "Small Activists, Big Impact—Cultivating Anti-Racists and Activists in Kindergarten," we were told that "kindergartners are natural social-justice warriors."

It isn't enough for a school to be inclusive; it also must foster "belonging." Belonging means that a school must be a "safe space"—code for prohibiting any speech or activity, regardless of intent, that a Bipoc student or faculty member might perceive as harmful, as uncomfortable or as questioning their "lived experience." The primary tool for suppressing speech is to create a fear of microaggressions.

In "Feeding Yourself When You Are Fed Up: Connecting Resilience and DEI Work," we learned techniques, such as "calling out," that faculty and students can use to shut down conversations immediately by interrupting speakers and letting them know that their words and actions are unacceptable and won't be tolerated. Several workshops focused on the practice of "restorative justice," used to re-educate students who fall afoul of speech codes.

The final step to ensure belonging is to push out families or faculty who question DEI work. "Sometimes you gotta say, maybe this is not the right school for you... I've said that a lot this year," said Victor Shin, an assistant head of school and co-chairman of the People of Color Conference, in "From Pawns to Controlling the Board: Seeing BIPOC Students as Power Players in Student Programming."

With the implementation of diversity, inclusion and belonging, schools can begin to address the primary objectives of DEI work: equity and justice. National Association of Independent Schools (NAIS) obligates all member schools to commit to these aims in their mission statements or defining documents. Equity requires dismantling all systems that Bipoc members of the community believe to cause harm. Justice is the final stage of social transformation to "collective liberation." The goal is to remake society into a collective, stripped of individualism and rife with reparations.

6 – SPLC/NEA & Leftists Writing Your Child's History, Science & Social Studies Curriculum

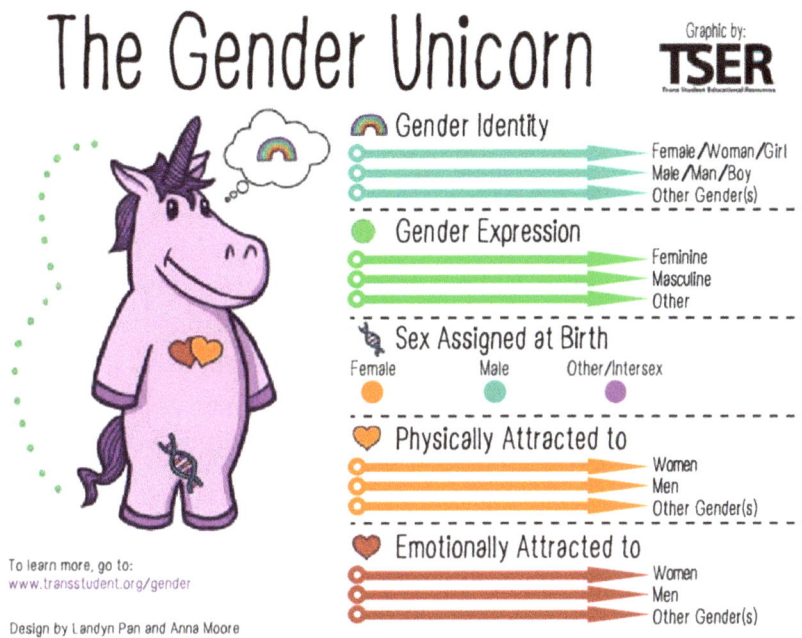

Credit: Trans Student Educational Resources (TSER).

As noted by the S.A.P.I.E.N.T. Being, something alarming has happened to the academy since the 1990s that shows, it has been transformed from an institution that leans to the left, which is not a big problem, into an institution that is almost entirely on the left, which is a noticeably big problem.

If you've spent time in a college or university any time in the past quarter-century you probably aren't surprised to hear that professors have become strikingly more liberal. In 1990, according to survey data by the Higher Education Research Institute (HERI) at UCLA, 42 percent of professors identified as "liberal" or "far-left." By 2014, that number had jumped to 60 percent and represents a much higher percentage as opposed to the student body they teach.

Over the same period, the number of academics identifying as "moderate" fell by 13 percentage points, and the share of "conservative" and "far-right" professors dropped nearly six points. In the academy, liberals now outnumber conservatives by roughly 5 to 1. Among the general public, on the other hand, conservatives are considerably more prevalent than liberals and have been for some time.

Nowadays there are no conservatives or libertarians in most academic departments in the humanities and social sciences. The academy has been so focused on attaining diversity by race and gender (which are valuable) that it has created a hostile climate for people who think differently.

The American academy has—arguably—become a politically orthodox and quasi-religious institution. When everyone shares the same politics and prejudices, the disconfirmation process breaks down. Political orthodoxy is particularly dangerous for the social sciences, which grapple with so many controversial topics (such as race, gender, poverty, inequality, immigration, and politics).

Can a Social Science that Lacks Viewpoint Diversity Produce Reliable Findings?

America needs innovative and trustworthy research on all these topics, but can a social science that lacks viewpoint diversity produce reliable findings?

But the folks that first put these numbers together, a group of academic faculty calling themselves Heterodox Academy, argue that homogeneity in higher education is a bigger problem than it is in other areas. "With relatively few right-leaning voices in the professoriate, particularly in the humanities and the social sciences where ideas matter most, many college students receive less than the intellectually rigorous education they deserve," some of the group's members recently wrote.

Dr. Samuel Abrams explored how the left-to-right ratio has increased over the past 25 years, particularly at colleges and universities in New England. He also reviewed work by Honeycutt and Freberg (2016) which suggested that conservatives experience a more hostile climate in academia than moderates or progressives.

A quarter-century ago, college professors were about 16 percentage points more likely to identify as "liberal" or "far-left" than their first-year students. By 2014, professors were close to 30 percentage points more likely than freshmen to call themselves liberal.

Among the college class of 2009, 39.1 percent identified as liberals, 38.5 percent called themselves moderates, and 22.5 percent said they were conservatives. While more liberal and less conservative than the general public, the seniors were also considerably less liberal and more conservative than the people who taught them.

Marxism in the Classroom, Riots in the Streets

Per the Clare M. Lopez "Marxism in the Classroom, Riots in the Streets" Front Page Magazine story in July 2020:

The explosion of lawless rioting on American streets was only a matter of time. Sixty-two years ago, former FBI agent W. Cleon Skousen wrote "The Naked Communist" to warn Americans about how communists planned to destroy our system from within, not by means of sudden revolution as envisioned by Karl Marx, but through a version of Italian communist Antonio Gramsci's "cultural Marxism." With a nod to the Chinese Communist Party (CCP) and its People's

Liberation Army (PLA), it has been a "long march through the institutions" that has brought us to the brink of catastrophe—and much of it began in our schools.

Chapter 13 of Skousen's book lists 45 goals of communism in America. Number 17 reads: "Get control of the schools. Use them as transmission belts for socialism and current Communist propaganda. Soften the curriculum. Get control of the teachers' associations. Put the party line in textbooks." And so they did.

While American parents were busy working to sustain their families and achieve a piece of the American dream, their children were at schools with teachers and textbooks that taught them to hate America, the Judeo-Christian foundations of our national identity, and the remarkable individuals who built this country on the principles of the Declaration of Independence, our Constitution, the Federalist Papers, and more.

As a result, the brainwashed generations of automatons marching in lockstep out of such schools possess neither critical thinking nor the intellectual ability to appreciate the brilliance and opportunity bequeathed to them by the great philosophers of Western Civilization. But, as Gramsci envisioned, they enter the ranks of art, film, music, literature, faith communities, government, media, and of course, academia, in droves. There will be no need for gulags or firing squads—or at least, not much.

As KGB defector Yuriy Bezmenov told us, subversion is a far more destructive weapon than violence. Today, we face a situation perhaps only slightly exaggerated in this recent quote from Jeff Nyquist: "The Constitution of the United States is something alien to most of the persons who occupy the actual government formed under it." [Emphasis in the original.]

Schools Using Fake 'History' to Kill America

From the Alex Newman "Schools Using Fake 'History' to Kill America" *Epoch Times* article in September 2020:

Americans educated by government today are, for the most part, hopelessly ignorant of their own nation's history—and that's no accident. They're beyond ignorant when it comes to civics, too. On the history of the rest of the world, or the history of communism, Americans are generally clueless as well. This was all by design, of course.

The reason why history is being rewritten is hardly a mystery. In George Orwell's classic dystopian novel *Nineteen Eighty-Four*, the totalitarian ruling Party's motto explaining its strategy is "Who controls the past controls the future. Who controls the present controls the past." And it's very true—whoever controls the historical narrative will be able to shape the future. Liberty-minded Americans and truth are currently losing the battle—big time.

Totalitarians have long understood the power of historical narratives. Consider Chairman Mao Zedong's "Cultural Revolution" in communist China. Under the guise of purging remnants of the old ways of capitalism and tradition, Mao's communist storm troopers did their best to destroy the records and evidences of thousands of years of Chinese history. Books were burned and monuments destroyed in an orgy of destruction.

After true history was erased and disfigured, the Chinese Communist Party was able to rewrite history on a blank slate to suit its own agenda. Especially important to that effort was the indoctrination of children in government schools. Everything ancient and traditional was portrayed as primitive or even evil, while the new party line surrounding the supposed glories and progress of communism was force-fed to China's youth.

America's ongoing cultural revolution hasn't been quite as dramatic, violent, or thorough—so far. But if left unchecked, the results of this long-term operation may turn out to be just as deadly. And there should be no doubt in anyone's mind about the effectiveness of the effort to rewrite the history of the United States, Western civilization, and even the world—has already started.

Howard Zinn: Radical Communist Party Member

By 1980, pseudo-historian Howard Zinn, a radical exposed in declassified FBI documents as a Communist Party member, had published his book *A People's History of the United States*. It's a favorite in public schools. More than 3 million copies have been sold so far, shaping the minds and attitudes of countless millions of Americans while turning them against their own nation and their own political institutions that guaranteed individual liberty for so long.

The propaganda "history" book was full of obvious lies, as exposed most recently by scholar Mary Grabar in her book *Debunking Howard Zinn*. The deception was strategic, too, and powerful. The lies begin right at the start of the book, portraying Columbus as a genocidal monster, and continue onward from there.

"We were really no better than the Nazis in the way Zinn presents it," Grabar told *The Epoch Times*.

It was carefully calculated. "Rewriting history is what communists do," continued Grabar, who also serves as a resident fellow at the Alexander Hamilton Institute for the Study of Western Civilization. "They don't want people to know about any other form of government or to remember a time when there was freedom and abundance. Like Zinn, the Marxists of today want young people to be so disgusted with their own country that they become inspired to overthrow it."

While demonizing the United States and Western civilization more broadly, Zinn and other communists work hard to conceal the history of communism—"the horrors of starvation, gulags, repression, and mass murder," Grabar said. Interestingly, there were clear parallels between Zinn's fake history and a history written by Communist Party USA chief William Z. Foster published in 1951 dubbed "Outline Political History of the Americas." Foster wrote openly about how crucial hijacking education would be for the Soviet-style communist regime he envisioned for America.

When starting the project, Grabar said she already knew Zinn's book was biased. "But even I was surprised by how blatantly and deliberately Zinn lied," she said, urging students, parents, and community members to use her book to refute the propaganda with facts.

More recently, *The New York Times* released its 1619 Project, the brainchild of Nikole Hannah-Jones. Like Zinn's book, it's essentially fake history, as historians from across the political spectrum—and even The New York Times' own fact-checker—publicly confirmed. Like Zinn's book, it seeks to "reframe" America's history as one based on oppression, slavery, and racism rather than liberty. And like Zinn's fake history, the 1619 Project is now being used in public schools across America.

Perhaps most alarming about Hannah-Jones's false narrative is the notion that racism and evil are embedded "in the very DNA" of America. In other words, there's nothing short of the complete annihilation of the United States' very foundations and essence that could possibly resolve the real and imagined shortcomings. The message of the project was obvious and clear: Death to America!

In reality, the truth about American history is almost exactly the opposite of what the project presents. The principles upon which the nation was founded—"all men are created equal," for instance, and are "endowed by their Creator with certain unalienable rights"—paved the way for abolishing slavery worldwide while facilitating the greatest expansion of human freedom and prosperity in world history.

Despite the obvious lies and deception, Hannah-Jones received a Pulitzer Prize for her work on the 1619 Project. Ironically, though, *New York Times* writer Walter Duranty also won a Pulitzer Prize for peddling lies and communist propaganda. In Duranty's case, he infamously parroted Stalin's obvious propaganda and covered up the Soviet genocide in Ukraine that killed by some estimates up to 10 million people.

Effects of Fake History

This strategic rewriting of history in public schools across America has led to dramatic shifts in Americans' attitudes, values, beliefs, and worldview. For example, national pride among Americans, who arguably live in the richest and freest nation in human history, has reached historic lows, according to a Gallup poll released in 2020. Among younger Americans, just 1 in 5 are extremely proud to be American, while among those 65 and older, just over half are extremely proud.

But the real dangers are becoming clear, too. A 2019 survey by the Victims of Communism Memorial Foundation found that 7 in 10 millennials said they are likely to vote for a socialist. Fully 36 percent of millennials support communism, the survey found. And just 57 percent of them believe the Declaration of Independence guarantees freedom and equality better than the Communist Manifesto. A generation ago, these numbers would have been inconceivable.

"When we don't educate our youngest generations about the historical truth of 100 million victims murdered at the hands of communist regimes over the past century, we shouldn't be surprised at their willingness to embrace Marxist ideas," explained Victims of Communism (VOC) Memorial Foundation Executive Director Marion Smith.

"We need to redouble our efforts to educate America's youth about the history of communist regimes and the dangers of socialism today."

In comments to *The Epoch Times*, VOC Director of Academic Programs Murray Bessette explained that American public schools simply don't teach the true history of communism. Part of the reason for that, he said, is the "ideological character of many involved in developing and delivering curricula for American schools." Parents must insist on a full account of history, and teachers must seek out programs and materials that teach the whole truth, added Bessette.

The effects of these false narratives pushed on children in government schools are becoming more and more obvious. Just think of the brainwashed armies of young Americans rampaging through the streets rioting, looting, killing, protesting, and destroying. Funded by rich and powerful individuals, companies, and foundations, their goal is to "fundamentally transform" what they view as an evil America. And because they don't know the truth about their own nation or its history, many genuinely believe in what they're doing.

Speaking at an Independence Day celebration in 2020, then President Donald Trump hit the nail on the head. "The violent mayhem we have seen in the streets of cities that are run by liberal Democrats, in every case, is the predictable result of years of extreme indoctrination and bias in education, journalism, and other cultural institutions," Trump explained. "Against every law of society and nature, our children are taught in school to hate their own country, and to believe that the men and women who built it were not heroes, but that they were villains."

Their Goal is Not to Improve America, But to Destroy It

Fortunately, now that the problem has been identified, steps are being taken to address it. And at the core of that process will be ensuring that young Americans understand the truth about their own nation's history. During remarks made on Constitution Day, Trump blasted the left's distortion of American history with lies and deception.

"There is no better example than The New York Times' totally discredited 1619 Project," said Trump, calling it "toxic" propaganda that would "destroy" America. "This project rewrites American history to teach our children that we were founded on the principle of oppression, not freedom."

In reality, as Trump correctly pointed out, "nothing could be further from the truth.

"America's founding set in motion the unstoppable chain of events that abolished slavery, secured civil rights, defeated communism and fascism, and built the most fair, equal, and prosperous nation in human history," the president declared.

Trump also promised action to reverse the progress of the history destroyers and rewriters. "We must clear away the twisted web of lies in our schools and classrooms, and teach our children the magnificent truth about our country," he said. "We want our sons and daughters to know that they are the citizens of the most exceptional nation in the history of the world."

To accomplish that, grants are being awarded by the National Endowment for the Humanities to help develop a pro-American curriculum that "celebrates the truth about our nation's great history," Trump said. He also said he would soon sign an executive order to create a national "1776 Commission" (which he did by executive order, only to be rescinded by Joe Biden his first day in office) that will promote patriotic education that will "encourage our educators to teach our children about the miracle of American history."

Skewed History: Textbook Coverage of Early America and the New Deal

As noted in the Preface and Acknowledgments section by Peter W. Wood of the "Skewed History: Textbook Coverage of Early America and the New Deal" National Association of Scholars article in April 2021:

America cannot survive if its children do not learn the history of their country. That's because, in America, our history is the foundation of our public life and civic participation. We are a

self-governing republic, and every bit of that depends on our knowing who we are and how we came to be that way.

Even those who hate America realize that our history is the key to our strength. That's why they try so hard to erase, distort, and corrupt that history. Many others, who do not hate America but who nurse grievances against American society, look to the telling of history to advance their claims to redress.

All of this plays out in the textbooks that American schools use to teach history. Some of those textbooks have, in the past, been mere celebrations of America's achievements. Others, unfortunately, have been mere diatribes concentrating on America's faults—real and fancied. The majority of American history textbooks today fall between patriotic panegyric and cynical denunciation. They often edge, however, closer to the latter. America's faults tend to loom very large in contemporary textbooks, while its accomplishments are writ small.

Our history told well should never omit America's faults, but it should also serve as more than just a record of 'what happened.' The deeper purpose of teaching our history is to teach affection for our country. Learning the truth and developing affection for America are not at cross-purposes. That's because our history is a history of overcoming great obstacles and, taught accurately, inspires love and delight. There is no more important component to American education.

Unfortunately, it has become increasingly difficult for American students to learn proper American history. As the 1776 Commission correctly noted in its The 1776 Report, a coterie of radicals has seized control of much of American history and civics instruction. They seek to use American history and civics to teach social justice ideology and identity-group politics; American history and government are either ignored or tendentiously rewritten so as to present American history in the worst possible light. The rewriting of American history and government extends to state history standards, College Board Advanced Placement history examinations—and textbooks.

A Short History of Slavery From Candice Owens 'Not Being Told'

From the Candace Owens "A Short History of Slavery" Prager U video in August 2021:

Below is a brief history of slavery and its salient points for Prager U that every American needs to know, titled "A Short History of Slavery" by renowned conservative newscaster and escapee from the Democratic Party plantation, Candice Owens, author of *Blackout*. In less than two-pages, she succinctly refutes the false narratives, lies, and bigotry of The 1619 Project. Per Owens:

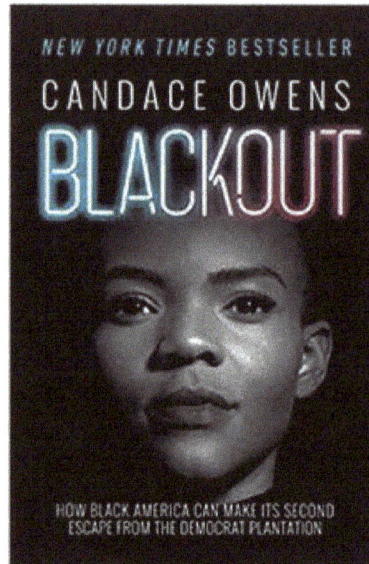

Credit: Candice Owens - Blackout.

Here's the first thing you need to know: Slavery was not "invented" by white people.

It did not start in 1619 when the first slaves came to Jamestown. It existed before then. It did not start in 1492 when Columbus discovered the New World.

In fact, when the intrepid explorer landed in the Bahamas, the native Taino tribe hoped he could help them defeat their aggressive neighbors, the Caribs. The Caribs enslaved the Taino and, on occasion, served them for dinner.

Slavery existed when the Roman Empire controlled the Mediterranean and most of Europe from the 1st through the 5th centuries. Slavery existed when Alexander the Great conquered Persia in the 4th century BC. It was so common that Aristotle simply considered it "natural." The slave/master model was just how the world operated in the great philosopher's day. Slavery existed during the time of the ancient Egyptians five thousand years ago. As far back we can go in human history, we find slavery.

Slavery existed in Africa, Asia and the Middle East. The word "slave" actually comes from the Slavs of Eastern Europe. Millions of them—all white by the way—were captured and enslaved by Muslims in the ninth century and later by the Ottoman Turks.

As renowned historian John Steele Gordon notes, from time immemorial, "slaves were a major item of commerce...As much as a third of the population of the ancient world was enslaved."

Here's the second thing you need to know: White people were the first to formally put an end to slavery

In 1833, Britain was the first country in the history of the world to pass a Slavery Abolition Act. They were quickly followed by France, who in 1848 abolished slavery in her many colonies. Then, of course, came the Thirteenth Amendment to the United States Constitution. After centuries of human slavery, white men led the world in putting an end to the abhorrent practice. That includes the 300,000 Union soldiers, overwhelmingly white, who died during the Civil War.

Am I saying that this makes white people better than anyone else? Of course not. My purpose here is to simply tell the truth, and the truth is that human history is complicated; no one, regardless of skin color, stands guiltless.

Yet today we are never told to consider the murderous Persian Empire or the cannibalism of indigenous tribes of North and South America, or the heinous actions under the imperialistic Muslim, Chinese, Mongol, or Japanese Empires, to name just a few.

Instead, we're told that slavery is a white phenomenon. Like all persistent (progressivism) lies, this lie spawns a bunch of other lies. On social media I come across extraordinary depictions about how Africans lived liked pharaohs before Europeans came and laid waste to their paradise.

I wish any of this were true. But it's not. It's a fantasy.

The truth is that Africans were sold into slavery by other black Africans. And in many cases, sold for items as trivial as gin and mirrors. Whites didn't go into the interior and round up the natives. They waited on the coast for their black partners to bring them black bodies.

The stark reality is that our lives had very little value to our ancestors.

Here's the third thing you need to know: If you think slavery is a relic of the past, you're wrong

There are some 700,000 slaves in Africa today. Right now. That's the lowest estimate I could find. Other sources say there are many more.

For context, that's almost twice as many slaves as were ever brought to the United States. Child soldiers, human trafficking, forced labor—these are the conditions that currently exist within the same sub-Saharan region where the transatlantic slave trade originated.

African bodies are being sold today like they were sold then—and no, they are not being purchased by any country of white men. In fact, slavery, by any traditional definition, is exclusively practiced today within nonwhite countries.

But we hear almost nothing about this. Just like we hear nothing about how slavery was universal until good people in Europe and America ended it two centuries ago. Why? Because our so-called "leaders"—black and white—wouldn't profit from it. Black victimhood is nothing if not profitable. It elects politicians and funds racial grievance groups.

And if black Americans began to view themselves as partners in the American dream…If we embraced the patriotic spirit that holds all men are created equal, the patriotic spirit that is our real heritage…Then the race hustlers would soon be out of business.

And who wants that?

The NEA/SPLC's Radical "Learning For Justice" Program

Per the in depth Meg Kilgannon "The SPLC's Radical 'Learning For Justice' Program: What Parents, Teachers, and Administrators Need to Know" Family Research Council report in 2021:

When America's public schools went virtual in 2020 on account of the COVID-19 pandemic, many parents had a front-row seat to observe their children's education. These parents gained a clearer understanding of what their children are being taught— and how divisive and dangerous some of it is.

Family Research Council (FRC) has created this resource to help parents, teachers, school administrators, and concerned citizens identify and monitor a particular threat to our values and religious freedom: divisive identity politics inserted into school curricula. Often portrayed as "inclusive," "anti-racist," or "social justice" education, disputed ideologies like Critical Race Theory (CRT) and gender identity are increasingly being presented as fact in curricula, professional development trainings for teachers, and even policies at the school board level. These ideologies were originally forced upon American schools, but now are seemingly being embraced by public schools across the country.

One of the organizations most responsible for this trend is the highly partisan and left-wing Southern Poverty Law Center (SPLC) and its Learning for Justice (LFJ) initiative. Formerly called "Teaching Tolerance," Learning for Justice is a special project run by the SPLC. It is designed to infiltrate schools through radically progressive education resources.

Prompted by a newly stated mission, "to reach our goal of justice for all," the SPLC rebranded "Teaching Tolerance" to "Learning for Justice" (LFJ). We know that for the SPLC, the objective is not "justice for all" but rather indoctrinating our children with their progressive worldview. According to an executive at the SPLC, "[w]e are focused, whether people like it or not, on the radical right." A former Senior Fellow at the SPLC describes their purpose as not just a "hate monitoring" organization, but in reality, "[o]ur aim in life is to destroy these groups, completely destroy them."

Parental rights and Christian values about marriage and family are in the crosshairs of Learning for Justice materials and resources. This booklet outlines the content within the LFJ project and empowers parents to protect their children against indoctrination if such "resources" are discovered in your local school.

The "critical conversations" Learning for Justice seeks to "navigate" with children have less to do with the acquisition of knowledge and much more to do with shaping a worldview in line with the SPLC's progressive agenda, inculcating voting habits informed by identity politics, and advancing a "social justice" mission to protest and disrupt political structures. By inserting their radical notions into the American education system, they defy the rights of parents to direct their children's education and determine what is best for them. To "counteract injustice and encourage togetherness," LFJ relies on ideologies that reject the notion of American exceptionalism and promote their subjective views and definitions of "diversity, equity, and inclusion," along with all the administrative bureaucracy it requires.

The SPLC'S Access to Schools Through the NEA

Learning for Justice and the Southern Poverty Law Center enjoy direct access to schools that flows from a longstanding working relationship with the National Education Association (NEA).

The NEA has endorsed and even collaborated on developing the SPLC's teacher indoctrination programs. NEA cites SPLC executives as experts.48 The NEA has embraced the SPLC and empowered them to prioritize activism over academics in our public schools. The NEA even presented its 2016 NEA President's Award for Human and Civil Rights to (the now- fired) SPLC co-founder Morris Dees. The powerful teacher's union, which has an iron grip on the nation's schools, flexes its muscle to foist LFJ on unsuspecting teachers and innocent students.

The National Education Association has embraced the SPLC and empowered them to prioritize activism over academics in our public schools. In her book *Standing Up to Goliath*, former teacher and education advocate Rebecca Friedrich explains:

NEA's 2017 New Business Item (NBI) 30 states: "In partnership with the Southern Poverty Law Center, NAACP, ACLU, GLSEN [Gay Lesbian Straight Education Alliance], National Center for Trans-Equality, Human Rights Campaign, and any other legal and human rights groups of related concerns, NEA will track incidents of discrimination, racism, homophobia, and transphobia, as well as anti-Semitism, Islamophobia, and all other forms of religious discrimination, and bigotry in our public schools.

The data will be shared with districts to educate and eradicate hate through the development of programs that include, but are not limited to, training on unconscious bias, culturally responsive instruction, and the anti-defamation league."

... The unions, as usual, are complicating matters because their real motives are not to combat the bullying of all students; instead, their motivations are to push their social and political agenda onto every single child, parent, and educator in every single school across America.

Friedrich also notes that education unions "initiate, condone, and promote bullying when the victims are teachers, parents, students, or Christians who dare to question the union agenda." The group's radical agenda was on full display at the 2021 NEA annual meeting and representative assembly. Several business items on the calendar focused on punishing conservative groups and promoting CRT and other left-leaning ideologies and groups. When media coverage exposed this bias, the NEA scrubbed its website of those biased entries.

Enter the nonprofit educational industrial complex, dominated by national left-wing and progressive organizations, which seek to influence our education system. Infiltrating educational systems on the local level means access to both minds and money. Education nonprofits want to shape the thinking of the next generation and direct the schools' resources to that end.

There are hundreds of such groups—all with a progressive agenda to shape the worldview of the next generation of adults while they are still children. Groups with enough funding to offer schools "free" resources enjoy the advantage of means and can fly under the radar of public accountability. But their influence is profound.

Groups like the American Civil Liberties Union, the National Education Association, the Human Rights Campaign, and the Southern Poverty Law Center seek to influence or control the material and messaging aimed at America's students today.

The Unsapient and Illiberal Challenge from Action Civics

From the "The Challenge from Action Civics" National Association of Scholars website in 2022:

American civics education is under sustained assault by radical activists. Their New Civics uses the pedagogy of service-learning to teach action civics, also known by names such as civic engagement, civic learning, community engagement, global civics, and project-based civics.

In recent years, some educators saw an opportunity to replace the old civics. It was first called "new civics," but gained other names as it grew, including "action civics." The basic idea was to rush students into "doing" stuff rather than just learning.

Civics could be a perpetual field trip spiced with exciting forms of "advocacy." Students could learn about government by jumping right into lobbying legislators, protesting injustices, and volunteering their time for public projects. When the "new civics" first received federal endorsement in *A Crucible Moment: College Learning & Democracy's Future* (2011), commissioned by the Obama administration, it called for "civics education" defined by a combination of diversity, multiculturalism, sustainability, and becoming "a citizen of the world." New civics has become steadily more radical. By 2021, the U.S. Education Department defined civics education as The 1619 Project and Ibram X. Kendi's "anti-racism".

New civics or action civics puts the cart before the horse. Young children have no basis to judge the merits of the political causes to which action civics recruits them. They have no understanding of what our government is or how it works. What action civics gives them is the excitement of identity politics and the thrill of pleasing their teachers. This provides a foundation of the bigger thrill to come of expressing one's identity through protest and alienation from all that came before.

At bottom, new civics is an "I hate America" curriculum, though it is typically dressed up in a red-white-and blue costume. To judge by superficial appearances, new civics is a "I love America so much, I want to fix it" curriculum. Only when you look closely at the proposed repairs do you discover that it is really about destroying the basis of American self-government.

The New Civics Indoctrination:

- Teaches students how to organize and take part in mob intimidation and calls it "civic engagement."

- Treats America's founders—Washington, Jefferson, Madison—as hypocrites and power-hungry oppressors.

- Treats the Declaration of Independence as a lie and the Constitution as pro-slavery.

- Looks on American history as mainly a story of rich white men exploiting the poor, women and minorities.

- Treats American prosperity as grounded in rapacious treatment of the environment, the dispossession of Native peoples, and the subordination of immigrants.

- Treats the free market as a tool of systematic abuse.

- Teaches students the American republic isn't worth preserving and that civic virtue consists of tearing it down.

The New Civics threatens to replace all of America's civics education with Neo-Marxist "social justice" propaganda, vocational training for left-wing activism, and Alinsky-style community organizing techniques adapted for use in the classroom.

Not every advocate of the New Civics consciously works for all these goals. The true radicals enlist many Americans who think these pedagogies and subject matters are more innocuous. Some New Civics advocates even consciously steer clear of entanglements with initiatives such as the 1619 Project Curriculum. But the radicals will provide the programmatic details that put the New Civics' vague rhetoric into practice.

The New Civics, which instills utopian visions grounded on national self-hatred, will have a revolutionary effect, regardless of the good intentions of some of its advocates.

Report Finds that America's Leading Science Curriculum Fails Students

Analyzing the "Report Finds that America's Leading Science Curriculum Fails Students" National Association of Scholars report in April 2021, we see that:

America's most popular science curriculum, the Next Generation Science Standards (NGSS), fails students. A new report, *Climbing Down: How the Next Generation Science Standards Diminish Scientific Literacy*, details how the popular curriculum omits basic tenets of science, including the scientific method. *Climbing Down* was authored by Jennifer Helms, James Nations, and David Randall and states:

"The NGSS are an underwhelming set of standards that condemn American students to a misunderstanding of various science concepts, fields, and methodology. Instead of raising the bar to instruct students to be ready for colleges and careers, the NGSS lower it in the name of equity," said report author David Randall. "How are America's students supposed to compete in a global marketplace when their own schools anticipate their failure by watering down curriculums to exclude a wealth of scientific knowledge?"

The NGSS's most extraordinary omission is the scientific method itself. The absence of an explicit articulation of the scientific method means that students will never learn the theoretical foundations for proper research techniques that seek to produce verifiable and reproducible evidence. Students cannot learn scientific research's rational processes without learning the scientific method.

Randall added: "The NGSS further damage science instruction by replacing what students must learn with how students must learn. Worse, the NGSS require one teacher to somehow teach and integrate the physical sciences, life sciences, engineering, and earth and space sciences within a single class."

Climbing Down extensively documents the failures of the NGSS, but also provides eleven steps parents, teachers, and school boards should take to correct the deficiencies in this curriculum. They include using the Fordham Institute's A-graded science standards as a template; allowing, encouraging, or requiring students to begin algebra in 8th grade rather than 9th; replacing Common Core State Standards (CCSS) mathematics with higher-level standards, such as the excellent and highly rated pre-CCSS California mathematics standards; and ensuring that science standards steer students toward the full range of scientific careers, especially those that serve the American national interest.

America's students deserve better than the NGSS. Our nation's education systems should encourage and adopt the best curriculums that challenge and equip students with the skills and knowledge to bring about innovation, but also to sustain rational and objective scientific discovery.

7 – Campus Illiberalism & Intolerance vs. Freedom of Speech & Viewpoint Heterodoxy

Credit: A Moment Symposium.

From the David Randall "Charting Academic Freedom" National Association of Scholars (NAS) report in January 2018:

This is the situation that confronts us today. Decades of progressive orthodoxy in hiring, textbooks, syllabi, student affairs, and public events have created campus cultures where legitimate intellectual debates are stifled and where dissenters, when they do venture forth, are often met with censorious and sometimes violent responses.

Student mobs, egged on by professors and administrators, now sometimes riot to prevent such dissent. The idea of "safe spaces" and a new view of academic freedom as a threat to the psychological well- being of disadvantaged minorities have gained astonishing popularity among students.

Most college students in the United States should be able to expect that freedom of expression will be upheld on their campuses. After all, public institutions are legally bound by the First Amendment, and the vast majority of private colleges and universities promise their students commensurate free speech rights.

In spite of this legal landscape, far too many colleges across the country fail to live up to their free speech obligations in policy and in practice. Often, this occurs through the implementation of speech codes: university policies that restrict expression that is protected under First Amendment standards.

University censorship regimes are teaching some students not only to live with but to embrace the conformism of thought inculcated through university speech codes, speaker dis-invitations, "safe spaces," "trigger warnings," and campus shout-downs of invited speakers.

Too many students feel afraid to speak honestly on campus for fear of offending someone, a new national survey of college students says. Furthermore, the Foundation for Individual Rights in Education (FIRE) surveyed the written policies of 466 colleges and universities, evaluating their compliance with First Amendment standards and their college rankings are disturbing.

More college students than ever claim to have reservations about free expression and this bleak view of open speech is not merely the reserve of a dismissible fringe. Forty-four percent of surveyed students told the Brookings Institution that they do not believe that the First Amendment protects free speech, compared with the 39 percent who believe that it does. A full 20 percent of respondents maintained it acceptable to inflict physical harm on those deemed to have made "offensive and hurtful statements."

The rights that James Madison worked to preserve in the name of reason and humanity now yield to the dictatorship of "culture." Professors, students, and their intellectual allies act as though our country were a tribe rather than a republic, in which any unapproved remark becomes an illicit defection from the mandated social order.

The New Campus Illiberalism is More Than Intolerance

Webster's Dictionary defines illiberalism as "opposition to or lack of liberalism." In popular usage, the word is used to describe an attitude that is close-minded, intolerant, and bigoted. Furthermore, from *Free Speech Madness: A SAPIENT Being's Guide to the War Against Truth, Conservative Ideals & Freedom of Speech*:

The pursuit of knowledge and the maintenance of a free and democratic society require the cultivation and practice of the virtues of intellectual humility, openness of mind, and, above all, love of truth. These virtues will manifest themselves and be strengthened by one's willingness to listen attentively and respectfully to intelligent people who challenge one's beliefs and who represent causes one disagrees with and points of view one does not share.

That's why all of us should seek respectfully to engage with people who challenge our views. And we should oppose efforts to silence those with whom we disagree—especially on college and university campuses. As John Stuart Mill taught, a recognition of the possibility that we may be in error is a good reason to listen to and honestly consider—and not merely to tolerate grudgingly—points of view that we do not share, and even perspectives that we find shocking or scandalous.

All of us should be willing—even eager—to engage with anyone who is prepared to do business in the currency of truth-seeking discourse by offering reasons, marshaling evidence, and making arguments. The more important the subject under discussion, the more willing we should be to listen and engage—especially if the person with whom we are in conversation will challenge our deeply held—even our most cherished and identity-forming—beliefs.

Intolerance as Illiberalism

"We live in intolerant times" notes Dr. Kim R. Holmes of The Heritage Foundation from his 2014 article in Public Discourse "Intolerance as Illiberalism." All across America, this illiberal mindset is spreading, corrupting our culture and our politics. It is evident in the mendacity with which opposing opinions are attacked and in the way that state and federal governments conduct their business.

This mindset turns ideas like tolerance and liberalism on their heads. It weakens the checks and balances that have long protected our rights and freedoms. As a result, illiberalism threatens not only the social peace of our country, but the very future of freedom and democracy in America. We ignore this growing phenomenon at our peril.

It's all-too-common these days for people to try to immunize from criticism opinions that happen to be dominant in their particular communities. Sometimes this is done by questioning the motives and thus stigmatizing those who dissent from prevailing opinions; or by disrupting their presentations; or by demanding that they be excluded from campus or, if they have already been invited, disinvited.

Sometimes students and faculty members turn their backs on speakers whose opinions they don't like or simply walk out and refuse to listen to those whose convictions offend their values. Of course, the right to peacefully protest, including on campuses, is sacrosanct. But before exercising that right, each of us should ask: Might it not be better to listen respectfully and try to learn from a speaker with whom I disagree? Might it better serve the cause of truth-seeking to engage the speaker in frank civil discussion?

The Culture of Illiberalism

The S.A.P.I.E.N.T. Being's *Free Speech Madness: A SAPIENT Being's Guide to the War Against Truth, Conservative Ideals & Freedom of Speech* has shown the roots of modern American illiberalism lie in the trauma experienced by liberals in the 1960s. The rise of the New Left and its sister movement, the Counter-Culture, changed how liberals viewed not only culture but also politics. As described in *Rebound: Getting America Back to Great*, by Dr. Kim R. Holmes, rebellion for New Left liberals moved beyond mere economic class issues to ones involving gender, sex, and race.

Politics became cultural, and Marxist assumptions about the irreconcilability of class conflict were transferred to the culture wars over gender, race, and sexual identity. Channeling the ideas of philosopher Herbert Marcuse, the New Left dismissed old-fashioned liberalism that preached individualism and moral responsibility as "repressive tolerance." Liberation focused now on groups, not on individuals, and dissent was seen not as an individual right of conscience, but as a political weapon to overthrow traditional morality.

Since the 1960s, the radical egalitarianism of the New Left has fused with traditional progressive ideas about state and society. Feminism is no longer about giving women equal political and legal rights—it's about confronting the male power structure and the "rape" culture. Fighting racism is no longer about ensuring that African-Americans and minorities are treated equally

95

before the law—it's about eradicating "systemic" racism and promoting affirmative action. Environmentalism is no longer about conserving natural resources—it's about "saving" the planet from overpopulation and climate change.

With such utopian causes, it seems perfectly acceptable to "break a few eggs" to make a new liberal omelet.

Traditional American Liberalism Has Changed in Three Important Ways

The first change involves the understanding of tolerance. The old Jeffersonian notion, rooted in debates over religious freedom, holds that individual conscience is sacrosanct. This has given way to the notion that certain ideas (e.g., racism or sexism) are so heinous that no one should be allowed to hold, much less express, any idea about race or women or sexuality that proponents believe is socially oppressive. In other words, intolerance is now seen as a good thing—if it serves the purpose of a certain definition of social liberation.

The second change involves the idea of dissent. Historically, respect for dissent had its roots in debates over religious freedom and freedom of conscience. But the New Left took an entirely different view of dissent. Rather than an expression of individual conscience, dissent was now seen as a weapon to overthrow the old order. The end justified the means. It was perfectly justifiable, according to the New Left, to shut out the views of the ruling class, defined now along race, gender, and sexual orientation lines.

The third idea that has undergone a radical change is our conception of virtue. Historically, virtue has been understood as a positive habit that forms one's personal character. In this view, one acquires virtue by repeatedly choosing to treat others well and act in accord with objective standards of morality, even when it is difficult.

Today, people who see themselves as "liberal-minded" have come to justify the most illiberal of ideas—namely, curbing freedom of expression and using the power of the state to deny equal rights to Americans with whom they disagree.

Modern liberalism thus does not merely flirt with intolerance. It is now fundamentally based on it. And that is largely because it has become accepted by the culture as a good thing to employ in the service of a cause you believe in. Whatever you may call this new American culture, you cannot call it liberal, for tolerance is the acid test of true liberalism.

This is where the culture stands today. The thinkers of the New Left infect it with illiberal values consciously designed to destroy classic liberalism. It may be true that illiberalism always lurked on the edges of American progressivism in the various ideologies associated with socialism.

But for most of history, progressives had tried to keep their distance from the more blatantly illiberal values of the far Left. That resistance started breaking down in the sixties. As a result, American liberalism today has a decidedly illiberal wing eating away at its purported core values.

Free Speech Zone Policies

Free speech zones have repeatedly been struck down by courts or voluntarily revised by colleges as part of settlements to lawsuits brought by students. The FIRE's Stand Up For Speech Litigation

Project has included successful challenges to free speech zone policies at eight colleges and universities and includes an ongoing challenge to a free speech zone policy at Pierce College in Los Angeles.

Additionally, state legislatures have continued to take action to prohibit public colleges and universities from maintaining free speech zones. Currently, twelve states have enacted laws prohibiting these restrictive policies: Virginia, Missouri, Arizona, Kentucky, Colorado, Utah, North Carolina, Tennessee, Florida, Georgia, Louisiana and Alabama.

Based on the Campus Free Expression (CAFE) Act model legislation from the FIRE, Florida's bill, which was signed into law in March 2018, states:

A person who wishes to engage in an expressive activity in outdoor areas of campus may do so freely, spontaneously, and contemporaneously as long as the person's conduct is lawful and does not materially and substantially disrupt the functioning of the public institution of higher education or infringe upon the rights of other individuals or organizations to engage in expressive activities ... A public institution of higher education may not designate any area of campus as a free-speech zone or otherwise create policies restricting expressive activities to a particular area of campus ...

The law also provides a right to sue a public institution of higher education in Florida if the institution violates the expressive rights guaranteed by the law.

Furthermore, the Student Press Law Center (SPLC) has worked to support, promote and defend the First Amendment and freedom of expression rights of student journalists at the high school and college level, and the advisers who support them. Working at the intersection of law, journalism and education, SPLC runs the nation's only free legal hotline for student journalists.

Universities Must Choose One Telos: Truth or Social Justice

On the Heterodox Academy website, Dr. Jonathan Haidt explains eloquently why universities must choose one telos: truth or social justice. Furthermore, he elaborates that Aristotle often evaluated a thing with respect to its "telos"—its purpose, end, or goal. The telos of a knife is to cut. The telos of a physician is health or healing. What is the telos of university?

The most obvious answer is "truth"—the word appears on so many university crests. But increasingly, many of America's top universities are embracing social justice as their telos, or as a second and equal telos. But can any institution or profession have two teloses (or teloi)? What happens if they conflict?

Haidt believes that the conflict between truth and social justice is likely to become unmanageable. Universities will have to choose, and be explicit about their choice, so that potential students and faculty recruits can make an informed choice. Universities that try to honor both will face increasing incoherence and internal conflict.

To further illuminate his point, consider two quotations:

The philosophers have only interpreted the world, in various ways; the point is to change it.— Karl Marx, 1845

He who knows only his own side of the case knows little of that. His reasons may be good, and no one may have been able to refute them. But if he is equally unable to refute the reasons on the opposite side, if he does not so much as know what they are, he has no ground for preferring either opinion…– John Stuart Mill, 1859

As Haidt puts it: Marx is the patron saint of what he calls "Social Justice U," which is oriented around changing the world in part by overthrowing power structures and privilege. It sees political diversity as an obstacle to action.

Mill is the patron saint of what he calls "Truth U," which sees truth as a process in which flawed individuals challenge each other's biased and incomplete reasoning. In this process, all become smarter. However, Truth U dies when it becomes intellectually uniform or politically orthodox.

One Telos: Truth or Social Justice?

Truth is paramount to sapience, and the antithesis to sapience is modern progressivism. Not only does progressivism deny commonly held truths across all cultures of the world, today's progressivism has evolved to many degrees into a twentieth century version of Marxism lite— without the horrific calories of human sacrifice, failed regimes, and economic ruin.

When progressivism madness is incubated in the right condition on campus, illiberalism will follow, and when illiberalism follows, so do social justice warriors and campus radicals. Put simply enough by Haidt, "no university can have Truth and Social Justice as dual teloses. Each university must pick one.

The Leftist Roots of Campus Rage

A 2017 issue of *The Wall Street Journal* ran an interview article featuring New York University professor Dr. Jonathan Haidt by Bari Weiss with an article titled "The Cultural Roots of Campus Rage," and in it, Haidt shares his insights into what's happening on many a college campus across the nation. An unorthodox professor explains the 'new religion' that drives the intolerance and violence at places like Middlebury and Berkeley.

Haidt, a psychologist and professor of ethical leadership, along with Jordan Peterson at the University of Toronto, have become inspirations to writers like Scott Allen, who share with us the Left's new religion of progressivism, and his analysis of its very disturbing cultural trends is a chapter of focus in *The SAPIENT Being*.

"What I think is happening," Haidt says, is that "as the visible absurdity on campus mounts and mounts, and as public opinion turns more strongly against universities—and especially as the line of violence is crossed—we are having more and more people standing up saying, 'Enough is enough. I'm opposed to this.'

In introducing the leftist roots of campus rage, the fundamentalists may be few, Haidt says, but they are "very intimidating" since they wield the threat of public shame. On some campuses, "they've been given the heckler's veto, and are often granted it by an administration who won't stand up to them either."

The Berkeley episode illustrates the Orwellian aspect of campus orthodoxy. A scheduled February 2017 appearance by right-wing provocateur Milo Yiannopoulos prompted masked agitators to throw Molotov cocktails, smash windows, hurl rocks at police, and ultimately cause $100,000 worth of damage. The student newspaper ran an op-ed justifying the rioting under the headline "Violence helped ensure safety of students." Read that twice!

The Left Has Undergone an Ideological Transformation

Dr. Jonathan Haidt has observed: In the recent past, important social matters were settled though free and open discussion and debate using logic and reason. Our American civil order is predicated on this. It works well when those engaged share a conviction that universal truth exists—regardless of one's beliefs, feelings, and opinions.

For today's campus radicals, feelings have largely replaced logic and reason. A generation ago, social justice was understood as equality of treatment and opportunity. Per Haidt, "… If black people are getting discriminated against in hiring and you fight that, that's justice."

Today justice means equal outcomes. "There are two ideas now in the academic left that weren't there 10 years ago," Haidt says. "One is that everyone is racist because of unconscious bias, and the other is that everything is racist because of systemic racism." That makes justice impossible to achieve: "When you cross that line into insisting if there's not equal outcomes then some people and some institutions and some systems are racist, sexist, then you're setting yourself up for eternal conflict and injustice."

Haidt is right. If the goal of this new social justice is equality of outcome, you are setting yourself up for eternal conflict, injustice, and ultimately social disintegration. Equal outcomes can only be achieved through the tyrannical imposition of power and coercion, with a resulting loss of individual freedom. It results in human beings being objectified, manipulated, and otherwise treated unjustly.

Where it has been attempted—in places like Maoist China and the Soviet Union—the outcomes were utterly destructive. Millions were imprisoned and murdered. Millions more lost their families, livelihoods, and freedoms. These are the facts!

Say NO to Campus Mob Fascism With the Chicago Statement

In response to the Berkeley riot incident in 2017, the Foundation for Individual Rights in Education (FIRE) issued this statement:

No university may be considered "safe" if speakers voicing unpopular ideas on its campus incur a substantial risk of being physically attacked. A university where people or viewpoints are likely to be opposed with fists rather than argumentation is unworthy of the name. Granting those willing to use violence the power to determine who may speak on campus is an abdication of UC Berkeley's moral and legal responsibilities under the First Amendment.

Strong-arming one's belief onto others is just a form of mob fascism—no matter what side of a political spectrum you are coming from. If the Chicago Principles support allowing any invited speaker, as the statement does, then great. We must value our wonderful educational space, framed by laws and policies on one side and supported by documents like the Chicago Principles on the other. We need students to feel free to offer any viewpoint and likewise to offer any challenge, both within the context of our curriculum and on campus, to open up a discourse, and to learn from the engagement.

Let's underscore that point at the beginning: the Chicago Principles envision and protect both controversial viewpoints and protests against those viewpoints, with the proviso that protesters "may not obstruct or otherwise interfere with the freedom of others to express views they reject or even loathe."

Any statement or policy that supports students' freedom of speech rights is welcomed. Below is an excerpt from the Chicago Statement as a reference if there is ever a question or push-back about allowing a controversial speaker on campus because someone finds some topic of inquiry distasteful.

"Because the University is committed to free and open inquiry in all matters, it guarantees all members of the University community the broadest possible latitude to speak, write, listen, challenge, and learn . . . . [I]t is not the proper role of the University to attempt to shield individuals from ideas and opinions they find unwelcome, disagreeable, or even deeply offensive."

The "Chicago Statement" refers to the free speech policy statement produced by the Committee on Freedom of Expression at the University of Chicago. In July of 2014, University of Chicago President Robert J. Zimmer and Provost Eric D. Isaacs tasked the Committee with "articulating the University's overarching commitment to free, robust, and uninhibited debate and deliberation among all members of the University's community." The Committee, which was chaired by esteemed University of Chicago Law School professor Geoffrey Stone, released the report in January of 2015.

Here are several tips for ensuring that your university will be the next institution to stand in solidarity with the Chicago Statement's principles:

- Work to pass a student government resolution calling on the university to adopt its own version of the Chicago Statement.

- Reach out to faculty members and work with faculty governing bodies on campus.

- Build a broad coalition of students and groups, particularly across the ideological spectrum, to support the Chicago Statement and raise awareness on campus.

- Publish articles and op-eds in student newspapers and other outlets.

- Host events on campus, such as debates, speakers, and panels to discuss the principles supported by the Chicago Statement.

- Communicate and collaborate with members of your university's administration.

- Host a petition drive, asking students to pledge their support for the Chicago Statement's principles in a petition that will go to the administration.

Viewpoint Diversity on Campus is Essential

As noted in *The S.A.P.I.E.N.T. Being: Enhancing Viewpoint Diversity and Intellectual Humility to Make Free Speech Again on Campus*, viewpoint diversity refers to the state of a community or group in which members approach questions or problems from multiple perspectives.

When a community is marked by intellectual humility, empathy, trust, and curiosity, viewpoint diversity gives rise to engaged and civil debate, constructive disagreement, and shared progress towards truth. Viewpoint diversity enables colleges and universities to realize their twin goals of producing the best research and providing the best education.

As citizens who are counting on students' and researchers' future contributions to our shared social, civic, moral, and scientific endeavors, we all suffer when orthodoxies distort and limit understanding of the social, aesthetic, and natural world—or when institutions of higher learning are unable to draw in perspectives from the whole of society. To help solve this problem we need heterodox academies.

To make headway on solving the world's most complex problems, scholars and policy makers must deploy the best ideas. This typically requires consulting a wide range of perspectives.

While a community of inquiry defined by intellectual humility, curiosity, empathy, and trust may hold many beliefs in common, few ideas will be beyond discussion, revision, or good-faith debate.

The Surest Sign of an Unhealthy Scholarly Culture is the Presence of Orthodoxy

Orthodoxies are most readily apparent when people fear shame, ostracism, or any other form of social or professional retaliation for questioning or challenging a commonly held idea.

The best way to defend against orthodoxies—or to neutralize them—is to foster commitment to open inquiry, viewpoint diversity and constructive disagreement. When these elements are missing, orthodoxies can take root and thrive.

Viewpoint diversity occurs when members of a group or community approach problems or questions from a range of perspectives. Institutions of higher learning face several interrelated viewpoint diversity deficits including:

- Racial/Ethnic
- Socioeconomic
- Geographical
- Religious
- Political
- And in many fields, Gender

Academic freedom demanded a respect for a diversity of views. During the Vietnam War years, college campuses were alive with debates about the war and a host of other subjects. There was no effort to silence diverse points of view.

Per Haidt, the future of liberal democracy depends in no small measure on empathy—the ability to humanize and understand others and tolerance. Students need to see those with whom they disagree politically as people—or else they risk alienating and demonizing the other side, which only leads to further conflict and highly-limited understanding.

A culture that will not tolerate divergence of opinion harms students, but academic research is also at risk when dominant theories and opinions no longer encounter counterclaims that test their validity.

Viewpoint Diversity Deficits Can Lead to Intolerance

When environments lack sufficient viewpoint diversity, problematic assumptions can go unchallenged, promising ideas and methods can go underexplored, and it can be difficult to effectively understand or engage with others who have different backgrounds, priors, and commitments.

For instance, to the extent that institutions of higher learning lack viewpoint diversity (and are thus not representative of the broader societies in which they are embedded), scholars may struggle to communicate the value and relevance of their work to people outside the academy in an accessible and compelling way.

Well-intentioned social programs can fail in their stated aims—or even cause harm—when the people designing policies are too far removed from the populations their interventions are intended to serve. Meanwhile, young people from underrepresented groups may come to feel as though they don't belong in the academy—and decline to apply to college, drop out midway through, or pursue non-academic paths if they push through to graduation.

In short, we would have reasons to recruit and retain a more diverse pool of faculty, staff, and students even if the lack of viewpoint diversity were purely the result of differences in interests and priorities among members of various groups.

However, we know that many disparities are also—at least in part—the result of a hostile atmosphere, discrimination, a lack of access or institutional dynamics that tend to privilege certain groups for reasons other than the quality of their research or ideas. It seems important to rectify these imbalances for moral as well as practical reasons.

Why Today's Students Are Less Tolerant Than Before

From *The S.A.P.I.E.N.T. Being: Enhancing Viewpoint Diversity and Intellectual Humility to Make Free Speech Again on Campus*:

The resurgence of influence of Herbert Marcuse's New Left, who argued in the 1960s that true "liberating" tolerance requires suppressing all non-progressive voices is problematic with Millennials and college students. April Kelly-Woessner shows the big split in American opinion on matters of free speech:

Millennials, Zillennials and college students embrace Marcusian ideals much more than did previous generations, and it is this moralistic illiberalism that leads to the witch-hunts and ultimatums that are sweeping across American college campuses since Halloween 2015.

Millennials Are Less Politically Tolerant Than Their Parents

First, Kelly-Woessner makes the case that young people are less politically tolerant than their parents' generation and that this marks a clear reversal of the trends observed by social scientists for the past 60 years. Political tolerance is generally defined as the willingness to extend civil liberties and basic democratic rights to members of unpopular groups.

Second, Kelly-Woessner argues that youthful intolerance is driven by different factors than old fashioned intolerance, and that this change reflects the ideology of the New Left. Herbert Marcuse considered "The Father of the New Left," articulates a philosophy that denies political expression to those who would oppose today's progressive social agenda. In his 1965 essay "Repressive Tolerance," Marcuse (1965) writes:

"Tolerance is extended to policies, conditions, and modes of behavior which should not be tolerated because they are impeding, if not destroying, the chances of creating an existence without fear and misery. This sort of tolerance strengthens the tyranny of the majority against which authentic liberals protested… Liberating tolerance, then, would mean intolerance against movements from the Right and toleration of movements from the Left."

The Orwellian Argument of Liberating Tolerance

The idea of "liberating tolerance" then is one in which ideas that the left deems to be intolerant are suppressed. It is an Orwellian argument for an "intolerance of intolerance" and it appears to be gaining traction in recent years, reshaping our commitments to free speech, academic freedom, and basic democratic norms.

If we look only at people under the age of 40, intolerance is correlated with a "social justice" orientation. That is, I find that people who believe that the government has a responsibility to help poor people and blacks get ahead are also less tolerant. Importantly, this is true even when we look at tolerance towards groups other than blacks. For people over 40, there is no relationship between social justice attitudes and tolerance. I argue that this difference reflects a shift from values of classical liberalism to the New Left.

For older generations, support for social justice does not require a rejection of free speech. Thus, this tension between leftist social views and political tolerance is something new.

Third, Kelly-Woessner states that intolerance itself is being reclassified as a social good. For six decades, social scientists have almost universally treated intolerance as a negative social disease. Yet now that liberties are surrendered for equality rather than security, the Left seems less concerned about the harmful effects of intolerance. In fact, they have reframed the concept altogether. For example, political scientist Allison Harell (2010) uses the term "multicultural tolerance," which she defines as the willingness to "support speech rights for objectionable groups" but not for "groups that promote hatred."

In other words, multicultural tolerance allows individuals to limit the rights of political opponents, so long as they frame their intolerance in terms of protecting others from hate. This is what Marcuse refers to as "liberating tolerance."

In fact, the idea that one should be "intolerant of intolerance" has taken hold on many college campuses, as exemplified through speech codes, civility codes, and broad, sweeping policies on harassment and discrimination. Students now frequently lead protests and bans on campus speakers whom they believe promote hate.

While this may have the effect of creating seemingly more civil spaces, it has negative consequences. In fact, tolerance for all groups is positively correlated. It is not simply the fact that leftists oppose the expression of right-wing groups. Rather, those who are intolerant of one group tend to be intolerant of others and of political communication in general.

When colleges fail to represent the full measure of political ideas, students are less likely to learn to tolerate those unlike themselves. This combined with the New Left's legacy of "liberating tolerance," creates an environment that values anger and orthodoxy over inquiry, debate and viewpoint diversity.

When College Students Self-Censor, Society Loses

Colleges—the intended training ground for the sort of creative and integrative thinking such problem-solving requires—have become increasingly characterized by orthodoxy in what types of questions can be asked and what sort of comments can be shared in the classroom and around campus.

As a result, many students and even some faculty elect to self-censor. As citizens who are counting on students' future contributions to our shared social and civic endeavors, we all suffer when students elect to sit on the sidelines of their own learning or opt-out of scholarship because they feel they do not "belong" at institutions of higher learning.

Also from *The S.A.P.I.E.N.T. Being: Enhancing Viewpoint Diversity and Intellectual Humility to Make Free Speech Again on Campus:* Indeed, it is vital for America's future to encourage a diversity of opinions on college campuses. But what will it take to achieve that goal?

Academic stakeholders must create campuses eager to welcome professors, students and speakers who approach problems and questions from different points of view, explicitly valuing the role such diversity plays in advancing the pursuit of knowledge, discovery, and innovation.

Rather than merely tolerating fellow learners whose views are wildly different from one's own, all should seek out and cherish that difference. Because we see things differently, we will be better able to explore the nuances of the topics we study, deepening our understanding and thus equipping us to be better able to move the needle on those issues we care about most.

This is Not a Left-Right Issue

This is about creating intellectual institutions where learners can come together, humbled by their incomplete knowledge, curious what they can learn from others, able to share their own ideas and perspectives and eager to think together with nuance, open minds, respect and goodwill—all in service to understanding the complexities of our world more deeply.

The concept of constructive disagreement centers around creating a dynamic where key stakeholders in an organization can and are compelled to disagree. The word constructive alludes to the need to raise issues, debate, and resolve them. In the academy, this no longer or rarely happens--but it does in the corporate world.

To achieve that goal in academia where it's sorely lacking, academic stakeholders must enact policies and practices that support heterodox classrooms and campuses. This requires three ingredients:

First, stakeholders must value open inquiry and constructive disagreement. The good news is the available data suggest students, faculty and administrators overwhelmingly do value these things (in principle).

Second, stakeholders must have access to, or be willing to create, effective strategies for enacting these values. For students, this could mean forming or participating in freedom of speech organizations or related initiatives.

For professors, it could be about strategies they deploy in the classroom to create an environment conducive to open inquiry and constructive disagreement or signaling a desire for viewpoint diversity in job ads during faculty searches.

In other cases, it's as simple as the chief academic officer being a vocal and visible cheerleader for the role constructive disagreement across lines of difference plays in realizing the very mission of the institution.

Other interventions are a heavier lift, like actually following through on the consequences stated in an existing policy even when there's tremendous social pressure to do otherwise. Organizations like Heterodox Academy, OpenMind and Village Square continue to design and distribute tools and resources to support these efforts of administrators and faculty.

Third, stakeholders must perceive social permission to act on these values. This is a tougher nut to crack. For instance, even if professors set a good tone, students could be concerned about social sanction from peers.

Many of America's colleges and universities have fallen into a narrow orthodoxy in what is acceptable to say and to think on campus. Now is the time for all of us who value the pursuit of knowledge to support a new heterodoxy that welcomes, supports, and encourages a diversity of viewpoints.

The concept of constructive disagreement centers around creating a dynamic where key stakeholders in the faculty and student body are compelled to disagree. The word constructive alludes to the need to raise issues, debate, and resolve them reasonably. In the academy, this no longer or rarely happens--but it does so in the corporate world.

Report Finds Title IX Offices are Sex Monitors, not Education Monitors

From the "Report Finds Title IX Offices are Sex Monitors, not Education Monitors" National Association of Scholars report in October 2020:

Title IX, the federal law banning sex discrimination at schools receiving federal funds, has been weaponized by campus administrators and is now used to persecute students accused of sexual misconduct, concludes a new report from the National Association of Scholars (NAS). Dear Colleague: The Weaponization of Title IX calls for a total overhaul of the broken Title IX regime.

Dear Colleague explains how sexual assault came to be seen as a form of sex discrimination and surveys the regulatory path that Title IX administrators took to make this word-play a reality. The report also presents interviews with students, with Title IX staff, and with other school personnel in charge of campus Title IX proceedings to detail the price students pay for running afoul of the campus "sex police."

"Most Title IX offices are exclusively female, ardently feminist, and have no one on staff with courtroom experience, even though they are running a parallel quasi legal system on campus," said the report's author, NAS Policy Director Teresa R. Manning. "Given the prevalence of feminist and gender ideology in Title IX offices, alongside their lack of relevant legal experience, it is no wonder that so many students accused of sexual misconduct are not getting due process in campus Title IX cases."

The sex lives of young men and women have become pawns in a larger ideological game played by Title IX administrators. Their actions, as detailed in the report, amount to malpractice and abuse of power, as they've become sex monitors rather than education monitors. To date, over 600 wrongly accused students have sued their schools in court over unfair Title IX proceedings; almost half have received favorable rulings.

"How many lives have been disrupted and ruined by higher education's 'sex monitors'?" asked Peter Wood, President of the NAS. "This report details the abuses of Title IX by campus ideologues and shows the path to reform, ensuring equal access to education for both sexes."

The report recommends a full reform of Title IX by:

- Sidelining ideologues and abandoning the hysteria of the "campus rape epidemic" to follow the data;

- Prioritizing and publicizing due process protections for students;

- Requiring Title IX offices to hire staff with criminal defense experience; and

- Stopping sexual misconduct before it happens by educating students on the benefits of healthy relationships that exist outside the "frat scene" or the "hook up" culture.

"Title IX is broken, but its purpose remains sound," explains Manning. "Equal access to education is essential. This is why we recommend a full reform of Title IX and recommend the firing and dismissal of all Title IX administrators who abuse their power by punishing students for conduct the administrators themselves likely encouraged and who then refuse these same students due process and fundamental fairness."

8 – Critical Race Theory (CRT), Illiberal Diversity Programs, 1619 Fiction vs. 1776 Facts

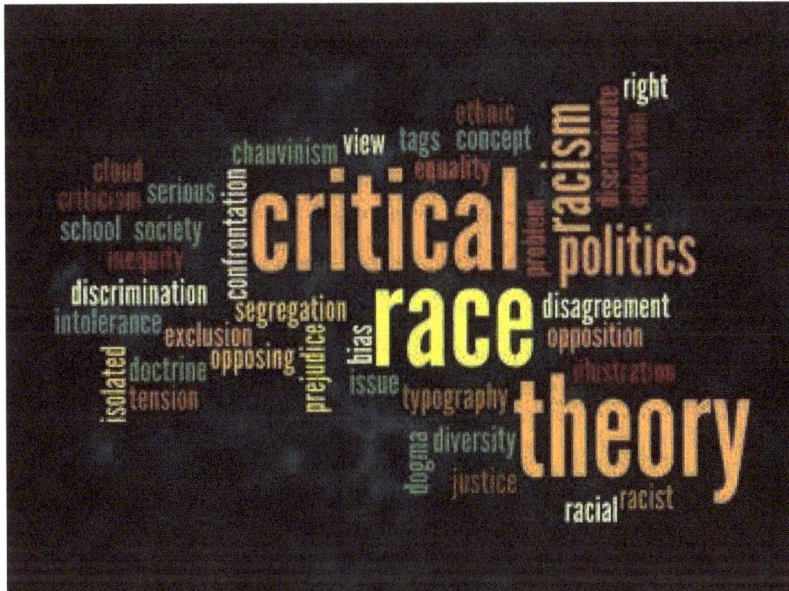

shutterstock.com · 2016916802

As responded to in the Wilfred Reilly "What Is Critical Race Theory, Really?" *City Journal* article in October 2021:

This debate over the semantics of critical theory might provide an interesting basis for a panel at a scholarly conference, but it's of little use or interest for parents concerned that their children are being taught partisan nonsense. While technical differences exist between the various critical paradigms, virtually all of them share three baseline assumptions:

1) that racism is "everywhere," and supposedly neutral systems, such as policing or standardized tests, are set up to oppress minorities;

2) that to prove the existence of this oppression one need only note that large groups perform at different levels;

3) and that the solution to this problem is equity—or proportional representation of all groups across all endeavors.

None of this is an exaggeration. The quote about racism being "everyday" and constant comes from Richard Delgado, one of the founders of critical race theory. The claim that group differences must indicate racism or other prejudice comes from no less a critical eminence than

Ibram X. Kendi, who has famously said that the only possible explanations for such gaps are either oppression or literal genetic inferiority. Kendi has also proposed a federal-level Department of Anti-Racism.

Along with these core ideas of "systemic racism" generally come a basket of other woke concepts like white privilege, "cultural appropriation," "intersectionality," the Black Lives Matter take on policing, and the idea of constant interracial conflict and crime.

Parents reject most of this CRT package not because they are bigots or too complacent in suburbia but because they believe it is wrong. As analysts like Thomas Sowell have pointed out for more than 40 years, the idea that gaps in performance between large groups must be due either to racism or to genetics is absurd.

Groups of people who vary in race and religion also often vary across other cultural and situational traits. For example, the most common age for a black American, which could be fairly called the modal average, is 27; the most common age for a white American is 58. Simply adjusting for these differences in age (and thus work experience), and for a few other traits like the regions people live in and their scores on standard aptitude tests, closes black-white gaps in income to almost nothing. In fact, either seven or eight—depending on how you count South Africans—of the top ten income-earning groups in the United States these days are made up of "people of color."

Most of the ideas associated with the major critical paradigms collapse as easily and totally as their core concepts

After years of flattering mainstream media coverage of Black Lives Matter, a large recent study revealed that the majority of "very liberal" Americans believes that in a typical year police kill anywhere from "about 1,000" to "more than 10,000" unarmed black men. In 2020, the year of the Floyd Riots, the actual number of blacks killed in this manner was 18.

Yes, the number is a mere 18!

A serious look at the data on interracial crime and conflict reveals similar patterns. Major papers run nonstop stories about cruel whites or mobs attacking minorities. Meantime, figures from the U.S. National Crime Victimization Study reveal that only about 3 percent of all serious crimes in a normal year, like 2019, are violent crimes involving a white perpetrator and a black victim or a black perp and a white victim. Further, 70 percent to 90 percent of these incidents are generally black-on-white, rather than the reverse.

Facts matter, but so does context. Critical theorists say some things that are essentially true, but meaningless—and likely to mislead unless one has a nuanced understanding of history or other disciplines. For example, it is undeniably true that slavery once existed in the United States. However, it is also undeniably true that almost every other powerful nation in history held slaves as well.

A trans-African slave trade run largely by Muslim merchants lasted far longer than even the trans-Atlantic slave trade, and it subjected far more people (about 18 million) to human bondage. The same amoral traders didn't hesitate to sell battle captives or shipwrecked sailors with pale skin: the conveniently forgotten Barbary slave trade shipped more than 1 million Caucasian slaves to Arab and black masters for centuries. Focusing lesson plans and curricula on the horrors of slavery without ever mentioning the universal nature of the practice or the fact that it was ended by Western countries is hardly "just being honest."

Just being honest: that phrase really sums up what parents demand—not, generally, a jingoistic system of education, but also not a reflexively critical one. Parents want an honest, fair, and reasonably apolitical curriculum that depicts the United States as it was and is, warts and all.

Yes, Critical Race Theory Is Being Taught in Schools

As pr the Zach Goldberg and Eric Kaufmann "Yes, Critical Race Theory Is Being Taught in Schools" *City Journal* report in October 2022:

To what extent, if at all, are critical race theory (CRT) and gender ideology being taught or promoted in America's schools? With little data previously available, and no agreement about what constitutes the teaching of critical social justice (CSJ) ideas, the answer up to now has remained open to political interpretation—but a new survey of young Americans vindicates the fears of CRT's critics.

Motivated by the work of Manhattan Institute senior fellow and *City Journal* contributing editor Christopher F. Rufo, many on the right allege that CRT-related concepts—such as systemic racism and white privilege—are infiltrating the curricula of public schools around the country. Educators following these curricula are said to be teaching students that racial disparities in socioeconomic outcomes are fundamentally the result of racism, and that white people are the privileged beneficiaries of a social system that oppresses blacks and other "people of color."

On gender, they are being taught that gender identity is a choice, regardless of biological sex. But are the cases Rufo and others point to representative of American public schools at large— or are they merely outliers amplified by right-wing media?

The response to these charges from many on the left has been to deny or downplay them. CRT, they contend, is a legal theory taught only in university law programs. Therefore, what conservatives are up in arms about is not the teaching of CRT, but the teaching of America's uncomfortable racial history.

But strong connections exist between the cultural radicalism of CRT and the one-sided, decontextualized portrayal of American history and society that Democratic activists endorse. And these ideas have also influenced many Democratic voters. Indeed, according to a 2021 YouGov survey, large majorities of Democratic respondents support public schools' teaching many of the morally and empirically contentious ideas to which opponents of CRT object.

These include the notions that racism is systemic in America (85 percent support), that all disparities between blacks and whites are caused by discrimination (72 percent), that white people enjoy certain privileges based on their race (85 percent), and that they have a responsibility to address racial inequality (87 percent).

Whatever one thinks of these ideas, they are hardly "settled facts" on the same epistemic plane as heliocentrism, natural selection, or even climate change. To the contrary, they are a moral-ideological just-so theory of group differences, an all-encompassing worldview akin to a secular religion, whose claims can't be measured, tested, or falsified.

They treat an observed phenomenon (disparate group outcomes) as evidence of its cause (racism), while specifying causal mechanisms that are nebulous, if not magical. Their advocates have not refuted counterarguments; they've merely asserted empirically unverified statements about the nature of group differences.

Publicly funded schools that teach and pass off left-wing racial-ideological theories and concepts as if they are undisputed factual knowledge—or that impart tendentiously curated readings of history—are therefore engaging in indoctrination, not education. The question before us, then, is not whether or to what extent public schools are assigning the works of Richard Delgado, Kimberlé Crenshaw, and other critical race theorists. It is whether schools are uncritically promoting a left-wing racial ideology.

To answer this and other related questions, we commissioned a study on a nationally representative sample of 1,505 18- to 20-year-old Americans—a demographic that has yet to graduate from, or only recently graduated from, high school. A complete Manhattan Institute report of all the findings from this study will be published in the coming months; what follows is a preview of some of them. Our analysis here focuses mainly on the results for the sample overall rather than for various subgroups.

Perhaps it's wrong to assume that the teaching of these CSJ concepts necessarily amounts to ideological indoctrination. After all, such concepts are salient on social and other media, and have also been uttered or invoked by prominent politicians. Perhaps, then, most teachers are merely using them as fodder for healthy classroom debate or presenting them as perspectives among other competing ideas.

If this isn't indoctrination—unwitting or otherwise—then what is?

The prevalence of students' classroom exposure to left-wing ideological concepts raises the question of its attitudinal effect. Are students who report receiving such instruction more "woke" than those who do not? Given the many other sources of attitudinal influence with which any effect of exposure must compete, there is ample reason for skepticism. At the same time, our respondents are in a phase of life in which, by some accounts, social and political attitudes are malleable.

The potential for exposure to shape related attitudes is plausible. In fact, in a dissertation chapter, one of us found that having white respondents read a short "racially woke" op-ed article led to eight- to 12-point increases (mostly via increases in collective shame and guilt) in support for race-based affirmative action, government assistance, and reparations to African-Americans. If attitudinal shifts of this magnitude can be produced over a span of just minutes, what might be the effects of more protracted exposure?

It's also fair to say that many educators incorporating such concepts into their instruction expect, or at least hope, that doing so makes a difference in the minds of students. Indeed, the notion that concepts like "white privilege" and "systemic racism" are solely taught for knowledge's sake strains credulity, especially when such instruction usually entails the omission or delegitimization of competing arguments.

The hope instead seems to be that students will come to see white people as ultimately responsible for the creation and persistence of racial inequality; and that this realization will inspire support for race-conscious, "equity"-oriented policies.

Perhaps this hope is ill-founded, but our data indicate otherwise. As an initial test, we examined whether those who report being taught a given concept are more likely to endorse it.

For instance, relative to those who reported they were not taught the related concept, those who indicated they were taught it were 14 points more likely to agree that the black-white pay gap is mainly due to discrimination, 15 points more likely to agree that "being white is one of the most important sources of privilege in America," 23 points more likely to agree that "white people have unconscious biases that negatively affect non-white people," and 29 points more likely to agree that "America is built on stolen land."

These differences, all statistically significant at the 99.9 percent level, persist after adjustments for a host of theoretically plausible alternative explanations, including race, political orientation, county rurality, county partisanship, county racial liberalism, and county school segregation.

Biden Criminalizes CRT Dissent

As noted in the Christopher F. Rufo "Biden Criminalizes CRT Dissent" *City Journal* article in October 2021: In an official memo, Attorney General Merrick Garland has pledged to mobilize the FBI against parents protesting critical race theory in public schools, citing unspecified "threats of violence" against school officials.

Garland's memo follows a National School Boards Association (NSBA) request that the Biden administration investigate threats to school board members and classify sometimes-heated parent protests as "domestic terrorism." The NSBA suggested that some of these parents should be prosecuted under the PATRIOT Act and federal hate-crimes legislation.

The school board association letter, however, is riddled with falsehoods, errors, and exaggerations. It begins with the claim that "critical race theory is not taught in public schools," despite a vast body of evidence, including my own reporting, showing that the teaching of CRT is widespread in public schools. Even the national teachers' union has admitted as much and called for CRT's implementation in all 50 states.

The NSBA deliberately misrepresents debates at school board meetings as "threats" and sometimes-vociferous and angry speech as "violence." The letter refers to dozens of news stories alluding to "disruptions," "shouts," "argument," and "mobs," but, contrary to its core claim, cites only a single example of actual violence against a school official: a case of aggravated battery in Illinois, which is obviously condemnable, but hardly the justification for a national "domestic terrorism" investigation.

The association even fabricated entire storylines to support its political objectives. For example, the NSBA claims that a Tennessee school board official named Jon White resigned due to "threats and acts of violence;" the linked source, however, reports that White resigned for "concerns about too much time away from his family," with no mention of threats or violence. (In another local report, White complains about parents calling him a "child abuser" and other epithets, which, while harsh, are hardly the equivalent of an "act of violence.")

The administration has mobilized the FBI against parents who oppose critical race theory.

Still, despite the school board association's flimsy pretext, the Biden administration appears to be doing its bidding. Garland's memo instructs the FBI to coordinate with "federal, state, local, Tribal, and territorial law enforcement" to develop plans to "discourage these threats, identify them when they occur, and prosecute them when appropriate." NSBA director Chip Slaven and national teachers' union president Randi Weingarten immediately praised Garland's aggressive actions.

This is a deeply politicized and dangerous escalation in the debate about critical race theory in public schools. For months, critical race theory proponents, including teachers' unions, have struggled to respond to critics, and new survey data show that strong majorities among all racial categories oppose teaching CRT in public schools. But as its standing in polls has plummeted, the education establishment has turned to more heavy-handed tactics.

The purpose of mobilizing the FBI is not only to monitor dissent but also to subdue it. The suggestion that parents might be engaging in "domestic terrorism" is designed to suppress speech and assembly and to justify further federalization of education policy. In congressional testimony, Education Secretary Miguel Cardona refused to say that parents are the "primary stakeholders" in their children's education; this week, Attorney General Garland is attempting to drive an even bigger wedge between parents and public schools.

Parents should not let this overreach deter them from speaking out against critical race theory in schools. The Biden administration has raised the stakes, and the fight is no longer only about CRT; it is also about protecting the basic rights of free speech, assembly, and constituent control over the nation's public institutions. The grassroots revolt against critical race theory is proof that Americans still have the instinct for self-rule. They must not let the Biden administration crush it.

Disingenuous Defenses of Critical Race Theory

As revealed in the Christopher F. Rufo "Disingenuous Defenses of Critical Race Theory" *New York Post* article in July 2021:

In July 2021, *The New York Times* published an opinion piece by commentators David French, Kmele Foster, Thomas Chatterton Williams and Jason Stanley, who presented themselves as a heroic "cross-partisan group of thinkers."

They derided as "un-American" laws passed by states such as Texas, Florida, Idaho, Oklahoma, Arkansas and New Hampshire that prohibit public schools from promoting the core principles of critical race theory, including race essentialism, collective guilt and state-sanctioned discrimination.

These authors imagine themselves the steady hand in a grandiose morality play, defending liberal-democratic freedoms against the threat of illiberalism, wherever it comes from.

But in practice, they are enablers of the worst ideologies of the Left and would leave American families defenseless against them. Their three core arguments—that critical race theory restrictions violate "free speech," that state legislatures should stay out of the "marketplace of ideas," and that citizens should pursue civil-rights litigation instead—are all hollow to the core.

In reality, they would usher in the concrete tyrannies of critical race theory, which explicitly seeks to subvert the principles of individual rights and equal protection under the law. Despite the superficial ideological differences between the four authors, they serve a single function: to prevaricate, stall and run interference for critical race theory's blitz through American institutions.

Teaching Hate: An Example

As uncovered by the Christopher F. Rufo "Teaching Hate" *City Journal* story in December 2020:

Seattle Public Schools recently held a training session for teachers in which American schools were deemed guilty of "spirit murder" against black students. The United States is a "race-based white-supremist society," the training instructed, and white teachers must "bankrupt [their] privilege in acknowledgement of [their] thieved inheritance."

The Seattle school district claims that the U.S. education system is guilty of "spirit murder" against black children.

The central message is that white teachers must recognize that they "are assigned considerable power and privilege in our society" because of their "possession of white skin." Consequently, to atone for their collective guilt, white teachers must be willing to reject their "whiteness" and become dedicated "anti-racist educator[s]."

The trainers acknowledge that this language might meet resistance from white teachers. They explain that any negative emotional reaction to being denounced for "whiteness" is an automatic response from the white teachers' "lizard-brain," which makes them "afraid that [they] will have to talk about sensitive issues such as race, racism, classism, sexism, or any kind of 'ism.'" The trainers insist that the teachers "must commit to the journey," regardless of their emotional or intellectual hesitations.

In the most disturbing portion of the session, the teachers discussed "spirit murder," which, according to Bettina Love, is the concept that American schools "murder the souls of Black children every day through systemic, institutionalized, anti-Black, state-sanctioned violence." Love, who originated the concept, declares that the education system is "invested in murdering the souls of Black children," even in the most ostensibly progressive institutions.

The goal of these inflammatory "racial equity" programs is to transform Seattle schools into activist organizations. At the conclusion of the training, teachers must explain how they will practice "anti-racist pedagogy," address the "current social justice movements taking place," and become "anti-racist outside the classroom." They are told to divide the world into "enemies, allies, and accomplices," and work toward the "abolition" of whiteness. They must, in other words, abandon the illusion of neutral teaching standards and get in the trenches of race-based activism.

Unfortunately, this indoctrination is not an aberration—it reflects deep ideological currents within Seattle Public Schools. In recent years, the district has expanded its Department of Racial Equity Advancement and deployed "racial equity teams" in dozens of neighborhood schools. The stated goal is to "advance educational racial equity," but in practice, these programs often serve to introduce, perpetuate, and enforce a specific ideological agenda.

Subversive Education: An Example

Also uncovered by the Christopher F. Rufo "Subversive Education" *City Journal* story in March 2021: North Carolina's largest school district launches a campaign against "whiteness in educational spaces."

In 2020, the Wake County Public School System, which serves the greater Raleigh, North Carolina area, held an equity-themed teachers' conference with sessions on "whiteness," "microaggressions," "racial mapping," and "disrupting texts," encouraging educators to form "equity teams" in schools and push the new party line: "antiracism."

The February 2020 conference, attended by more than 200 North Carolina public school teachers, began with a "land acknowledgement," a ritual recognition suggesting that white North Carolinians are colonizers on stolen Native American land. Next, the superintendent of Wake County Public Schools, Cathy Moore, introduced the day's program and shuffled teachers to breakout sessions across eight rooms. Freelance reporter A.P. Dillon obtained the documents from the sessions through a public records request and provided them to *City Journal*.

At the first session, "Whiteness in Ed Spaces," school administrators provided two handouts on the "norms of whiteness." These documents claimed that "(white) cultural values" include "denial," "fear," "blame," "control," "punishment," "scarcity," and "one-dimensional thinking." According to notes from the session, the teachers argued that "whiteness perpetuates the system" of injustice and that the district's "whitewashed curriculum" was "doing real harm to our students and educators." The group encouraged white teachers to "challenge the dominant ideology" of whiteness and "disrupt" white culture in the classroom through a series of "transformational interventions."

Parents, according to the teachers, should be considered an impediment to social justice. When one teacher asked, "How do you deal with parent pushback?" the answer was clear: ignore parental concerns and push the ideology of antiracism directly to students. "You can't let parents deter you from the work," the teachers said. "White parents' children are benefiting from the system" of whiteness and are "not learning at home about diversity (LGBTQ, race, etc.)."

Therefore, teachers have an obligation to subvert parental wishes and beliefs. Any "pushback," the teachers explained, is merely because white parents fear "that they are going to lose something" and find it "hard to let go of power [and] privilege."

This isn't an aberration. In fact, the district's official Equity in Action plan encourages teachers to override parents in the pursuit of antiracism. "Equity leaders [should] have the confidence to take risks and make difficult decisions that are rooted in their values," the document reads. "Even in the face of opposition, equity leaders can draw on a heartfelt conviction for what is best for students and families." In other words, the school should displace the family as the ultimate arbiter of political morality.

The equity plan outlines this new ideology in chart format, announcing the district's commitment to a series of fashionable pedagogies, including "color consciousness," "white identity development," "critical race theory," "intersections of power and privilege," and "anti-racist identity and action."

What's Wrong With the 1619 Project?

Discussed in the Wilfred Reilly "What's Wrong With the 1619 Project?" Prager U video:

Have you heard of The 1619 Project? It was published by the *New York Times* in August of 2019. It won the Pulitzer Prize for Commentary in 2020. Its thesis: The United States was founded in 1619, when the first slave was brought to North America.

Wait—that brings up some questions…What happened to 1776? To July 4th? The Declaration of Independence? George Washington, Thomas Jefferson and James Madison?

According to The 1619 Project, the Founding Fathers pushed for all that "Life, Liberty and the Pursuit of Happiness" stuff to protect their slave holdings. Independence from England? That was just a smoke screen. To them, everything that's wrong with America is tied to her "original sin" of slavery: from segregation to traffic jams (yes—traffic jams!). For The 1619 Project authors, racism is not a part of the American experience; it is the American experience.

Is this true? Let's look at three of the project's major claims:

1. **Preserving slavery was the real cause of the American Revolution**

If you asked the Founders why they no longer wanted to be a British colony, they would have given you a long list of reasons: Taxation without representation, conflicts over debts from the French and Indian War, and the Stamp Act would be just a few. Probably most important was the burning desire to be free—to chart their own destiny as a sovereign nation.

Protecting slavery? Slavery was not under threat from the British. In fact, Britain didn't free the slaves in its overseas colonies until 1833—57 years later, after the Declaration of Independence. Yes, the subject of slavery was hotly debated at the Constitutional Convention, but that was after the war was won.

2. Slavery made America rich

Slavery made some Americans rich—true enough. Eli Yale, for example, made a fortune in the slave trade. He donated money and land for the university that is named after him. But the institution of slavery didn't make America rich. In fact, the slave system badly slowed the economic development of half the country.

As economist Thomas Sowell points out, in 1860, just one year before the Civil War began, the South had only one-sixth as many factories as the North. Almost 90% of the country's skilled, well-paid laborers and professionals were based in the North. Banking, railroads, manufacturing—all were concentrated in the North. The South was an economic backwater.

And the cost of abolishing slavery was enormous—not merely in terms of dollars (Lincoln borrowed billions to pay for it), but also in terms of human life: 360,000 Union soldiers died in order to free 4 million slaves. That works out to about one soldier in blue for every ten slaves freed. It's hard to look at that butcher's bill and conclude that the nation turned a profit from slavery.

And many things have happened since 1865. In the almost 200 years since the Civil War, the population of the country has grown almost 900% and our national GDP has increased 12,000%. Slavery did not make America rich.

3. Racism is an unchangeable part of America

This argument is more philosophical than scholarly, but it undergirds the entire 1619 Project. It's also pernicious because it suggests that the United States is an inherently racist country that can't overcome its flaws. Yet that's exactly what it's done.

Today, America is the most successful multi-racial country in history, the only white-majority country to elect a black President—twice. Of course, progress has not always been smooth. There have been terrible setbacks. But to compare American attitudes about race today to America a hundred years ago, let alone to 1619, is absurd.

Here's a fact that should be better known: Two million black Africans have come to America as legal immigrants—from countries like Nigeria—in the last 50 years, and have become one of the most successful groups in the country. Why would these folks move to what is often called an evil, racist country? Because, unlike many people lucky enough to be born here, they know that America is a land of opportunity for everyone.

It's also only fair to note that while blacks have heroically fought for our rights, often against great odds, we haven't done it alone. A vast number of decent whites have also advanced the cause of racial equality. To cite one of countless examples, the U.S. Senate that passed the landmark Civil Rights Act in 1964 contained 98 whites and two men of color (and they were Asian)

The great black leaders of the past—Harriet Tubman, Frederick Douglass, Booker T. Washington, Martin Luther King—never lost faith in America's promise that all people are created equal. None of them believed that racism was America's defining characteristic. They were right.

Shortly after The 1619 Project was published, a group of distinguished historians—almost all on the left—wrote a public letter condemning the work. They called it a "displacement of historical understanding by ideology."

They were right, too.

Kick the '1619 Project' Out of Schools

Per the David Randall "Kick the '1619 Project' Out of Schools" National Association of Scholars article in August 2020:

America needs to get the "1619 Project" curriculum out of its schools. Senator Tom Cotton (R-Ark.) has introduced a new bill that would go a long way toward that goal—the Saving American History Act of 2020 (SAHA 2020).

The *New York Times* introduced The "1619 Project" last August. The "1619 Project" mainstreamed the anti-American ideology of a new generation of woke activists, who have graduated from college radicalism to careers in progressive institutions such as the *Times*. The "1619 Project" seeks to rewrite American history with the claim that it is based on slavery and oppression, rather than on liberty and democracy, in order to delegitimize the American republic.

The "1619 Project" claims to be "revisionist" history—but many of the best scholars of American history swiftly demonstrated that it was nothing more than a shabby, fact-free polemic. Nikole Hannah-Jones, the Pulitzer Prize-winning mastermind of the "1619 Project," recently admitted that the effort never had a historical basis—and never even intended to be history.

"I've always said that the '1619 Project' is not a history," Hannah-Jones said in a series of tweets. "It is a work of journalism that explicitly seeks to challenge the national narrative and, therefore, the national memory. The project has always been as much about the present as it is the past."

Nevertheless, the "1619 Project" has had a profound impact on America's schools.

School districts in cities ranging from Buffalo to Chicago to Newark to Washington immediately announced that they would incorporate the "1619 Project" into their school history curriculums—using a "1619 Project" curriculum that the Pulitzer Center posted to the internet as soon as the *Times* published the special edition of its Sunday magazine. The Pulitzer Center claims more than 3,500 classrooms have adopted their curriculum.

Clearly, the project's creators of the "1619 Project" had coordinated with the Pulitzer Center and school district leaders to transform the nation's curricula immediately—without bothering to wait for input from parents, school boards, or historians.

The "1619 Project" was meant to be a revolution from above, imposed on America's children to teach them to despise their country.

But Cotton carefully tailored SAHA 2020 to avoid measures that would harm students who are the victims of woke administrators. No school lunch funding would be affected, nor would funding for students with disabilities—no funding would change except for these two specific funding streams.

Indeed, Cotton would be warranted in strengthening SAHA 2020 considerably, to deal effectively with the challenge posed by the 1619 Project curriculum. Cotton might amend SAHA 2020 to:

1. Define what is meant by the 1619 Project curriculum, by reference to the contents of the Pulitzer Center's the 1619 Project Curriculum.

2. Extend the federal government's financial sanctions to prohibit funding that supports any third-party organization or curriculum that incorporates substantial elements of the 1619 Project Curriculum, such as the Zinn Education Project or Facing History.

3. Extend the federal government's financial sanctions to prohibit funding that supports any state-level standardized assessment that incorporates substantial elements of the 1619 Project Curriculum.

4. Draft standard procedures by which individuals and organizations may report to the Department of Education that a school district has adopted some or all of the 1619 Project Curriculum.

5. Require the Department of Education to report annually to Congress which school districts have adopted some or all of the 1619 Project Curriculum.

6. Restrict eligibility for further carefully defined Department of Education grants and programs to school districts that the Department of Education certifies as free of the 1619 Project Curriculum.

Credit: America's founding in 1776 - The Heritage Foundation.

Legislation to restrict the 1619 Project Curriculum should be as rigorous as possible. America's future depends on knowing our true past. We must get rid of the 1619 Project Curriculum to save our children from the anti-American lies of the woke establishment.

The 1776 Commission Report Reinvigorates the American Mind

Per the Mike Sabo "The 1776 Commission Report Reinvigorates the American Mind" National Association of Scholars article in January 2021:

Former President Trump's 1776 Commission has issued a report that summarizes "the principles of the American founding and how those principles have shaped our country." It will be the only such report – President Biden swiftly dissolved the Commission by executive order after being sworn into office.

Biden's decision is regrettable because "The 1776 report calls for a return to the unifying ideals stated in the Declaration of Independence," as Chairman Larry P. Arnn, Vice Chair Carol Swain, and Executive Director Matthew Spalding said in a statement. "It quotes the greatest Americans, black and white, men and women, in devotion to these ideals."

The report rejects the teachings of historians such as Howard Zinn, the New York Times's 1619 Project, and other efforts aimed at fundamentally transforming how Americans view their country's history. Neither hiding America's flaws nor offering a triumphal account of American history, the 1776 Commission aimed to recover "our shared identity rooted in our founding principles" – which, its report argues, is "the path to a renewed American unity and a confident American future."

"Our country's founding principles are the key to a peaceful, self-governing people," Arnn stated, "and the 1776 Commission sets out to educate the American public about them. The Commission's report is an approachable introduction to the historical facts of the founding and the principles that animate it."

Beginning with an overview of American founding principles and the constitutional architecture that the Founders fashioned to secure them, the report then catalogues the various threats to republican government and proposes tools that Americans can use to recover a way of life conducive to republican citizenship.

Though not denying that America was founded by a particular people with a particular history, religion, and virtues, the report stresses that the nation was nevertheless founded on the universal principles enunciated in the Declaration. This is why Abraham Lincoln argued by implication in the Gettysburg Address that the United States celebrates its birthday on July 4th, 1776.

Appealing to both human reason and biblical revelation – for example, the Declaration's references to the Creator, Providence, and the Supreme Judge – the Founders justified the government on the basis of eternal, universal principles. Frederick Douglass once described them as "saving principles" that were the "ring-bolt to the chain of" America's "destiny."

The Progressive movement rejected the idea of permanent truths in favor of constantly evolving group rights meted out by the administrative state, a fourth branch of government composed of independent agencies staffed with experts insulated from political accountability.

Today, identity politics strikes at the heart of republican government by demanding "equal results and explicitly sorting citizens into 'protected classes' based on race and other demographic categories." Even worse, the purveyors of identity politics see people of certain races as evil not necessarily because of what they've done but simply because of their skin color. The 1776 Commission report states unequivocally that identity politics "makes it less likely that racial reconciliation and healing can be attained" because it rejects "Martin Luther King, Jr.'s dream for America."

In order to preserve the blessings of liberty for future generations, families should raise "morally responsible citizens who love America and embrace the gifts and responsibilities of freedom and self-government;" state and local governments should produce curricula that convey an "enlightened patriotism" through reading primary sources; and songwriters, filmmakers, and social influencers should create content that speaks "to eternal truths" that "embody the American spirit."

In the words of Commission member Charles Kesler, the 1776 report intends to rebaptize American citizens in the Declaration of Independence and the Constitution, reinvigorating the American mind in the twenty-first century. President Biden's move to dissolve the Commission does not change this imperative. Indeed, as Arnn, Swain, and Spalding have declared: "The Commission may be abolished, but these principles and our history cannot be. We will all continue to work together to teach and to defend them."

9 – Testing, Admissions, Training, DEI Programs, Escalating Costs, Tuition & Student Debt

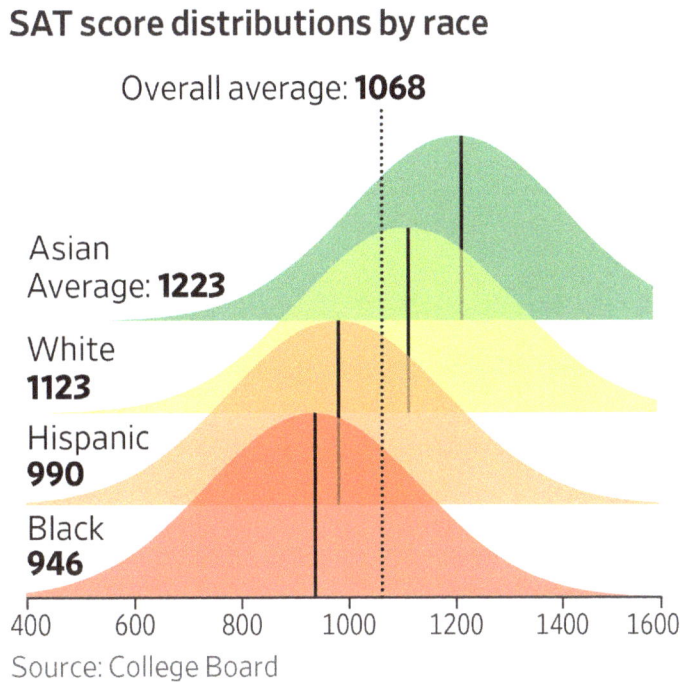

SAT score distributions by race

Overall average: **1068**

Asian
Average: **1223**

White
1123

Hispanic
990

Black
946

400   600   800   1000   1200   1400   1600

Source: College Board

Race and education data are from 2018 high school graduates.

From the Heather Mac Donald "Conformity to a Lie" *City Journal* article in the Summer of 2020:

It has been taboo to hint at the reason that the millions of dollars already expended on campus diversity initiatives have yet to engineer exact proportional representation of blacks in the student body and on the faculty: the vast academic skills gap. Now this truth will be even more professionally lethal to anyone who dares mention it.

The highest reaches of the university have declared as a matter of self-evident fact that systemic racism is the defining feature of American society, one that explains every inequality. Fighting against that racism has now officially become colleges' reason for being.

The prevalence of systemic racism in the U.S. is far from an established fact, however. Other credible explanations exist for ongoing racial disparities, including family structure, cultural attitudes, and individual behavior.

To declare from the highest reaches of the academy that racism is the defining and all-explaining feature of American society is to adopt a political position, not to state a scientific truth. That political position entails a host of unspoken assumptions about the world, themselves open to debate.

In aligning itself with one particular political position, the academy is betraying what Max Weber saw as its mission: to stay assiduously neutral and to teach "inconvenient" facts about the world that undercut received assumptions across the political spectrum. Political action was antithetical to scholarship, Weber argued.

SAT Math Scores Mirror and Maintain Racial Inequity

As per the Ember Smith and Richard V. Reeves "SAT Math Scores Mirror and Maintain Racial Inequity" Brookings Institute article in December 2020:

The race gap in test scores is far from a new phenomenon; Asian and white students consistently outperform their Black and Hispanic or Latino peers on the math and verbal sections of the SAT.

In 1996, the gap between the mean Black score and the mean white score was 0.91 standard deviations; by 2020, the gap had narrowed to 0.79 standard deviations. Despite a wide range of efforts to reduce inequality, the racial gap in SAT scores has scarcely narrowed during the lifetimes of the class of 2020. In 2002, the average white student's SAT math score was 106 points higher than the average Black student's (533 compared to 427); by 2020, the gap narrowed to 93 points. Still, nearly a third (31%) of white test takers scored above 600 on the math portion of the SAT, compared to just 7% of Black test takers.

Rising SAT participation and college enrollment

Test score gaps shrunk by a small margin in the last two decades, but other indicators show reason for optimism: the portion of students taking the SAT rose drastically over the last two decades, outpacing the increase in the number of public high school graduates from 2000-2020.

From 2000-2020, there was a 119% increase in the number of Black students taking the SAT and a 482% increase in Latino or Hispanic students, compared to a 36% and 185% increase in the number of Black and Hispanic or Latino students graduating from a public high school (reflecting, to a large extent, the increase in the size of the Hispanic population). SAT participation also rose dramatically among Asian and Pacific Islander students—136% compared to a 66% increase in the number of public high school graduates. By contrast, slightly fewer white students graduated from a public high school in 2020 than in 2000, but the number of white students taking the SAT increased by 28%.

As SAT participation gaps have shrunk, so have enrollment gaps. But significant gaps in graduation rates and test scores remain; representation is increasing, but success rates have yet to catch up. Half of Asian students and 45% of white students graduate college in 4 years compared to 21% of Black students, and 32% of Latino or Hispanic students. Default rates on student loans tell a similar story; Black and Latino or Hispanic students are much more likely to default within 12 years of graduation.

Beyond the score: effects of racial math score gaps

As our colleague Andre Perry has written, "Standardized tests are better proxies for how many opportunities a student has been afforded than they are predictors for students' potential." This is right. While attempting to measure college-readiness, the SAT both mirrors and maintains racial inequity. There is also evidence that test scores are a less accurate predictor of subsequent Black and Hispanic or Latino performance.

In 2019, the SAT developed an adversity score to contextualize students' scores to their school and neighborhood. Under pressure, the College Board then abandoned the single statistic in favor of an Environmental Context Dashboard, which provides information like the portion of students at a high school receiving free and reduced lunch, median family income, and advanced placement enrollment.

Nonetheless, SAT scores clearly capture important information about the academic position of the test taker; it is also clear that many fewer Black and Latino or Hispanic students are college ready, especially in math.

So, is it time to scrap the test? No. While unthoughtful use of standardized test scores certainly reproduces inequality, abandoning them altogether risks making matters even worse. Scrapping tests altogether in college admissions could result in colleges overemphasizing factors that privilege being rich just as much.

Furthermore, post pandemic, fewer than half of the students who applied early to college in the fall of 2022 submitted standardized test scores, according to an analysis by the nonprofit that publishes the Common Application.

How Admissions Officers Could be Setting Up Minority Students for Failure

Per the James Piereson and Naomi Schaefer Riley "Less Than Meets the Eye" *City Journal* story in May 2021:

Dropping the requirement that students submit SAT or ACT scores meant that admissions officers could rely only on grades, essays, and recommendations. Thus students with lower scores may have been more willing to apply to schools they otherwise would have considered a reach.

Despite the shift of public opinion against them, SAT scores remain fairly good predictors of not only how well students will perform in college but also the difficulty of the classes they'll take. "Students with high test scores are more likely to take the challenging route through college," University of Minnesota psychologists Nathan Kuncel and Paul Sackett maintain.

Too often, young people admitted to demanding colleges wind up switching to easier, less remunerative majors. According to researchers at the University of Texas–Austin, "More than a third of black (40%) and Latino (37%) [STEM] students switch majors before earning a degree, compared with 29% of white STEM students."

While the authors of that study suggest that the reasons for this discrepancy are social rather than academic, the truth, as Purdue University researcher Samuel Rohr discovered, is that "a higher aggregate score on the SAT helped predict the retention of science, technology, engineering, mathematics, and business students." He concluded: "For every point increase in SAT, there was 0.3% increase in retention."

In other words, admitting students with lower SAT scores to fulfill diversity quotas may prevent those students from achieving their academic and career goals—something they might have done at a lower-tier school. Indeed, it may prevent them from completing their degree at all. At the most elite schools, the likelihood is that students who didn't perform as well as their peers on the SATs will simply be shunted into easier but less remunerative majors. For schools farther down on the academic ladder, these efforts could mean lower overall graduation rates.

Admissions, Affirmative Action and Two Supreme Court Cases

As per the Andrew I. Fillat and Henry I. Miller "Diversity Smokescreen" *City Journal* report in March 2022:

The Supreme Court has agreed to hear two more cases challenging the use of race as a criterion in college admissions, as has allegedly happened at Harvard University (a private institution) and the University of North Carolina (public).

On the surface, the argument turns on whether the desire for a diverse student body trumps many laws and the Fourteenth Amendment to the U.S. Constitution, which prohibit discrimination and guarantee equal protection to all. The question applies to virtually all universities because they are either public or accept government money.

The main argument in favor of discrimination in admissions is that diversity enhances the educational experience. But is it true that a student body needs to parallel, even roughly, the demographics of the general population to ensure that students are exposed to people from diverse backgrounds?

In fact, we would argue that the very process of using affirmative action—read: "discrimination"—to enhance the numbers of designated identity groups can contribute to the tribalization of the student body rather than helping it cohere into a harmonious whole.

Furthermore, even after receiving an affirmative action boost, minority students sufficiently qualified for a given university are already likely to have similar backgrounds to non-minority students, thus limiting the diversity of viewpoints and experiences that affirmative action allegedly enhances.

Nevertheless, it has become an article of faith that affirmative action, by enhancing narrowly defined diversity, improves education.

Digging deeper into the issue raises a fundamental question about the mission of a university. We believe that universities—and especially the more selective ones—should prioritize the following, in order of importance: the development of critical reasoning skills; the acquisition of a greater knowledge base and certain professional skills; and socialization. These priorities reflect centuries of precedent, including at institutions of higher education throughout Europe and Asia. The net result should be to turn out more productive individuals who can both achieve personal success and contribute to social harmony and national prosperity.

Some schools shuffle the order of these priorities or even radically deemphasize some of them. Doing so can produce graduates overburdened with debt and with lower lifetime earning capacity—and uncertain what to do with their degrees in gender or ethnic studies or "Disruption." (Yes, such a major exists, at the University of Southern California, where the cost to attend is more than $77,000 per year.)

If universities stuck to their traditional priorities, the admissions criteria that matter most would be academic achievement and potential

Diversity of the student body would pertain only to socialization, the lowest of the educational priorities. Diversity of ideas and interests, however, contributes to higher-priority goals and thus deserves far more consideration than it gets. An applicant who designs robots or rockets, did an internship in an R&D lab, or wrote a published critical essay in high school should win extra points.

If racial preferences in admissions aren't furthering the mission of a university, what are they doing? They become, effectively, a form of reparations, providing the potential "ticket" of a diploma to individuals who would otherwise have been deprived of that benefit based purely on academic merit. After all, a degree, particularly from a prestigious university, confers a lifetime benefit in terms of economic and other factors.

Though the idea of reparations to persons who have been wronged, as in restitution for theft, may have some justification, current university practices are different. They are a form of compensation (to the less-qualified students admitted) for past injury, given at the expense of those who bear no responsibility for the injury (the more qualified but rejected candidates). This is not "social justice," or any kind of justice, which is correctly defined as the fair treatment of individuals.

The notion that a demographically representative college class makes for better education is a pretext for the real proposition: that certain people deserve reparations. The deeper question for the Supreme Court to decide in the battle over racial preferences is thus whether a university, private or public, should be allowed to dispense de facto reparations, even if existing law suggests that it is not permissible.

Modern Diversity Training Too Often Violates Martin Luther King's Vision of Racial Healing

From the Chloé Valdary "Reconciliation, or Grievance?" *City Journal* article in June 2019:

Diversity training has become a standard feature of American corporate culture. Its origins date to Title VII of the Civil Rights Act of 1964, which codified protecting employees against discrimination and resulted in numerous lawsuits filed with the Equal Employment Opportunity Commission, the agency created by the statute.

Underpinning Dr. Martin Luther King's philosophy was his belief in the sanctity of the individual and the "amazing potential for goodness" within human beings. "We do not wish to triumph over the white community," he wrote. "That would only result in transferring those now on the bottom to the top. But, if we can live up to nonviolence in thought and deed, there will emerge an interracial society based on freedom for all."

Unfortunately, most major institutions' diversity and inclusion programs ignore these lessons and betray King's vision. Robin DiAngelo, an academic and diversity consultant who counts Amazon, Unilever, the YMCA, and the City of Oakland, among others, as clients, coined the term "white fragility," calling it "inevitable" that whites are racist. "Racism," she states, "is the foundation of Western society." Though making such sweeping judgments would surely offend many whites, she concedes, this reaction is itself a "weaponized defensiveness that . . . functions as a kind of white racial bullying."

DiAngelo holds that all whites are complicit in racism by virtue of their skin color. To argue otherwise is racist; to object to the label proves that the label fits. This racial double bind negates King's belief in the capacity for human goodness. In "The Current Crisis in Race Relations," King wrote that "the important thing about a man is not the color of his skin or the texture of his hair but the texture and quality of his soul." For DiAngelo, no distinction exists between skin and soul. She and other purveyors of such thinking embrace a reductive and repellent vision of racial guilt.

So...what is the aim of diversity and inclusion training? Should it embrace the beloved community and its transcendent vision of human beings working through conflict—racial or otherwise? Or should it bring about a hierarchical inversion, in which one group of people is favored over another, which is perpetually castigated for sins, real or imagined? How we answer this question may shape our institutions, and the workplace, for decades to come.

Diversity Statements Can Determine Who Gets Hired at Universities

From the Mckenna Dallmeyer "Diversity Statements Can Determine Who Gets Hired at Universities" Campus Reform story in April 2022:

A 2021 study found that diversity statement requirements for applicants seeking university faculty jobs are common and on the rise. Campus Reform analyzed faculty job postings to evaluate their frequency. And they concluded:

According to a 2021 study, approximately one-fifth of university job postings require applicants to expound their dedication to diversity by submitting a diversity, equity, and inclusion (DEI) statement with their application materials.

The study conducted by the American Enterprise Institute (AEI) estimated the prevalence of requisite diversity statements in public higher education job postings. After analyzing 999 job postings, the study found that 19% required applicants to submit a diversity statement in the job application materials alongside the traditional requirements such as a resume and cover letter.

"We believe our coding schemes are conservative and, if anything, likely underestimate the prevalence of DEI statements," researchers James Paul and Robert Maranto conjecture. As a surprise to the researchers, STEM jobs were found to be just as likely to require a diversity statement from applicants as social science jobs.

"The most surprising finding of the paper is that these requirements are not just limited to the softer humanities. I would have expected these statements to be less common in math and engineering, but they're not," Paul told the *Washington Free Beacon*.

Offering an example, the study cites UC Berkeley's 2018-2019 Initiative to Advance Faculty Diversity, Equity and Inclusion in the Life Science Year End Summary Report. The report reveals that of the 893 job applicants who met basic qualifications, only 214 were able to advance to the subsequent round due to "contributions to diversity, equity and inclusion."

Paul and Maranto believe that DEI requirements have "grown rapidly in recent years" and will continue to become more prevalent in the future. "If policymakers do not intervene, DEI requirements are likely to grow substantially in the years to come," the authors state. Campus Reform analyzed several universities' job advertisements finding that diversity statements are, in fact, prevalent.

The Campus Diversity Swarm

Cultivating the imaginary grievances of an ever-growing number of "oppressed" groups, a costly administrative infrastructure threatens the goals of higher education. Per the Mark Pulliam "The Campus Diversity Swarm" report in the *City Journal* in October 2018, consider the following examples:

- The University of Michigan's diversity bureaucracy employs nearly 100 full-time employees, one earning more than $300,000 per year, at an annual cost of more than $11 million. More than a quarter of UM's diversocrats make more than $100,000 a year, far more than the average salary of assistant professors with doctorates. UM is not exceptional.

- The University of Texas at Austin employs a similar number of bureaucrats in its Division of Diversity and Community Engagement (boasting eight vice presidents), at an annual cost of $9.5 million. The head of UT's diversity bureaucracy makes over $265,000 a year, more than most tenured faculty.

- *The Economist* reports that UC Berkeley has 175 diversity bureaucrats, and nationwide, the trend is toward increased spending in this area. According to The Economist, "Bureaucrats outnumber faculty 2:1 at public universities and 2.5:1 at private colleges, double the ratio in the 1970s."

- Over the same period, tuition has soared. Ohio State's Richard Vedder estimates that more than 900,000 nonteaching administrators—most of them unnecessary—bloat university payrolls.

What do all these diversity administrators do? By one account, "Diversity officials promote the hiring of ethnic minorities and women, launch campaigns to promote dialogue, and write strategic plans on increasing equity and inclusion on campus." NADOHE Standard Six helpfully supplies examples of other "delivery methods" for diversocrats: "presentations, workshops, seminars, focus group sessions, difficult dialogues, restorative justice, town hall meetings, conferences, institutes, and community outreach."

Campus diversity officers also advocate progressive causes, which coincidentally justify an enlargement of their bureaucratic empire.

In this fashion, diversity bureaucracies—like a ratchet—grow ever larger. When laws or regulations impose new compliance requirements (sometimes at the urging of the diversity bureaucrats themselves), administrative ranks and budgets swell.

Diversity bureaucrats exist to service the grievances of an evolving—and potentially unlimited—number of supposedly oppressed groups recognized by postmodern identity politics. Thus, by promoting "social justice" and encouraging "marginalized" students to embrace victimhood, diversocrats ensure their own job security. The mission of campus diversity officers is self-perpetuating.

Unless the cycle of promoting and nursing imaginary grievances is ended, diversity bureaucracies will take over our colleges and universities, supplanting altogether the goal of higher education.

California Community Colleges System Proposes a DEI System Unique for its Ideological Aggressiveness

From the May 2022 John D. Sailer and Ray M. Sanchez "An Overt Political Litmus Test" *City Journal* article:

In May 2022, the Chancellor's Office of the California Community Colleges (CCC) system amended its proposed diversity, equity, inclusion, and accessibility (DEIA) competencies. Issued in March, 2022, the original proposal sought to establish "diversity" and "anti-racism" evaluations for every employee of the 116-college system—a political litmus test. The newly issued changes are merely cosmetic, indicating that, despite notable pushback to the proposal, it will likely become policy.

While DEI requirements are quickly becoming common, CCC's proposal stands out for its thoroughness and ideological aggressiveness. It defines "cultural competency" as "the practice of acquiring and utilizing knowledge of the intersectionality of social identities and the multiple axes of oppression that people from different racial, ethnic, and other minoritized groups face."

It calls for all community college districts to "include DEIA competencies and criteria as a minimum standard for evaluating the performance of all employees" and "place significant emphasis on DEIA competencies in employee evaluation and tenure review processes to support employee growth, development, and career advancement."

The Chancellor's Office also provides a list of competencies. Some of them: "Includes a DEI and race-conscious pedagogy," "Contributes to DEI and anti-racism research and scholarship," and "Engages in self-assessment of one's own commitment to DEI and internal biases, and seeks opportunities for growth to acknowledge and address the harm caused by internal biases and behavior."

Requiring faculty to embrace the politically-charged concepts of "intersectionality" and "multiple axes of oppression" clearly violates academic freedom—but the CCC system seems unperturbed by that prospect.

In 2021, a workgroup for the system's curriculum committee created guidelines called "DEI in Curriculum: Model Principles and Practices," which explain what "DEI and race-conscious" pedagogy looks like in practice. One of the document's recommended "culturally responsive classroom practices" reads: "Protect the cultural integrity of an academic discipline to support equity by no longer weaponizing 'academic integrity' and 'academic freedom' that impedes equity and inflicts curricular trauma on our students, especially historically marginalized students."

Perhaps unsurprisingly, the proposal has gained significant pushback.

The Foundation for Individual Rights in Education referred to the policy as "unacceptable and unconstitutional." The Pacific Legal Foundation condemned it in equally strong terms: "The proposed regulation will entrench a political orthodoxy, reduce intellectual diversity on college campuses, threaten First Amendment freedoms, and impair the education of students who deserve exposure to a rich and robust range of viewpoints on the critical issues facing our country."

Even Brian Leiter, law professor at University of Chicago and certainly no conservative, agreed with the Pacific Legal Foundation's First Amendment argument, noting on his blog that the "letter gets it right on the constitutional infirmities."

California often functions as a testing ground for the rest of the nation. What happens in California rarely stays in California—especially if it's an "innovation" in progressive politics. We should hope that this overt political litmus test will be unequivocally rejected. Unfortunately, that does not look likely.

It's Time to Roll Back Campus DEI Bureaucracies

Per the Jay P. Greene and Frederick M. Hess "It's Time to Roll Back Campus DEI Bureaucracies" *National Review* article in September 2022:

Diversity, equity, and inclusion are admirable things. We're quite fond of diversity and inclusion, in principle, and equity sounds a lot like equality, which we rather like. Unfortunately, in higher education, "Diversity, Equity, and Inclusion (DEI)" has taken on an Orwellian aspect—becoming a tool of "groupthink, censorship, and exclusion." At too many colleges and universities, DEI administrative units now pose a profound threat to free inquiry and academic integrity.

More than a few reputable observers have suggested that we've reached "peak woke" and that the stifling threat to free thought is no longer ascendant. But the status quo is not acceptable. Unless the DEI infrastructure is rolled back, it will continue to quietly distort higher education.

Given the relatively recent provenance of campus DEI bureaucracies, many readers may be unfamiliar with just what they do. After all, they are not academic units (like gender- or ethnic-studies departments). Nor are they legal-compliance staff charged with overseeing civil-rights laws (as with Title IX officials). In fact, because DEI staff are not charged with conducting research, teaching classes, or avoiding lawsuits, they enjoy an amorphous charge and remarkable leeway.

Universities have expanded the ranks of this DEI political commissariat at an extraordinary rate. A review of 65 universities in the Power Five athletic conferences found that the typical institution has 45 diversity-staff members on its payroll. That is more than four times as many employees as are devoted to supporting students with special needs (even though accommodations for disabilities, unlike DEI, is something institutions are legally required to provide). In fact, the typical university has roughly one DEI staffer for every 30 tenured or tenure-track professors.

Again, this sentiment is admirable in theory

In practice, there are big problems. For starters, there's little credible evidence for the claim that DEI staff strengthen identity and belonging in a way that promotes better outcomes. In fact, surveys of all students (as well as of minority students) which ask about how welcome they feel on campus tend to show worse results at universities with larger DEI staffs. What's going on? It's not complicated. A bigger, more aggressive DEI staff is better able to operate as an ideological commissariat, sowing division and distrust as it enforces campus orthodoxy.

This is exactly what Ryan Mills and Isaac Schorr found when they took a deep dive into DEI at the University of Michigan (U-M). As U-M more than quadrupled its DEI staff over two decades, from 40 in 2002 to 167 in 2021, the campus climate deteriorated: "Rather than make U-M a more tolerant place, there's evidence that its DEI push has instead created a more culturally rigid campus, the kind of place where woke students and staff are forever on the lookout for offenses against the politically correct orthodoxy." By signaling what views were "problematic" while helping to organize and amplify the voices of campus radicals, DEI staff stifled free inquiry and robust scholarly discussion among students and faculty.

At many campuses, the DEI bureaucracy started out as a humble "multicultural center," one which was later joined by a host of organizations focused on racial, ethnic, gender, and sexual identity. Over time, universities created centralized diversity offices to support all these entities and now have increasingly replicated these infrastructures across multiple academic units.

This has fueled bureaucratic bloat and rising costs. For example, Northwestern University's Office of Institutional Diversity and Inclusion boasts an "Assistant Provost of Diversity and Inclusion," a "Manager of Diversity and Inclusion," and a "Vice President & Associate Provost for Diversity and Inclusion & Chief Diversity Officer."

There is also an Assistant Director of Campus Inclusion & Community, an Associate Director of Multicultural Student Affairs, an Assistant Director of Native American and Indigenous Initiatives, and an Associate Director of the Women's Center. . . . Well, you get the idea. Similar positions are then replicated in the medical school, business school, and so forth.

Pioneering ACTA Analysis Confirms That Higher Education Tuition Is Linked To Spending

From the "Pioneering ACTA Analysis Confirms That Higher Education Tuition Is Linked To Spending, With Minimal Effect On Graduation Rates" ACTA report in August 2021:

The American Council of Trustees and Alumni (ACTA) released its groundbreaking report The Cost of Excess: Why Colleges Must Control Runaway Spending, a comprehensive analysis of college spending trends and the impact spending has on tuition and student success.

ACTA analyzed data from more than 1,500 four-year public and private, nonprofit colleges and universities. The data reveal that institutional spending has continued to surge alongside tuition but has contributed little to improve four-year graduation rates.

"A proper understanding of an institution's spending habits can provide valuable insights for governing boards seeking to allocate scarce resources efficiently toward what most benefits students," said Michael B. Poliakoff, Ph.D., president of ACTA. "This report illustrates the implications for students—both financially and academically—of the steady growth in spending since the Great Recession. It is our hope that public awareness of this trend's impact on student finances and student outcomes will encourage more prudent choices."

Some Key Findings:

- Spending at higher education institutions continued to climb both during and after the Great Recession.

- The report confirms that economic crises did little to restrain college spending. Since the Great Recession, higher education spending is noticeably decoupled from market forces and has instead relied heavily on tuition hikes to fuel its spending habits.

- Blame for tuition hikes is often laid at the door of legislatures that reduce state appropriations. However, increases in per-student spending on instruction, administration, and student services were each correlated with an increase in tuition for the next academic year, even after controlling for levels of appropriations.

- The average package of in-state tuition and fees at a four-year public college or university has nearly tripled over the past 30 years, a 178% increase since 1990.

- Sixty-five percent of all students borrow money to fund their education, and debt for the average borrower has reached $39,351.Student loan debt is the second largest source of debt behind home mortgages—rising to over $1.7 billion in 2021.

- Spending on student services had no correlation with graduation rates at public institutions, despite the fact that it is growing considerably faster than spending on instruction.

- From 2012 to 2018, colleges and universities prioritized hiring less expensive and often less-credentialed instructional staff and more expensive administrative staff.

The report's findings support a growing realization that colleges and universities have prioritized needless spending on ancillary activities instead of access and affordability and that this unnecessary spending relies largely on tuition hikes.

Statement by the American Council of Trustees and Alumni (ACTA) on President Biden's Loan Forgiveness Plan

From the "Statement by the American Council of Trustees and Alumni (ACTA) on President Biden's Loan Forgiveness Plan" ACTA report in August 2022:

A federal judge struck down President Biden's student loan forgiveness program in November 2022, declaring it unlawful. Biden's debt relief program would forgive up to $10,000 in student loans for borrowers who make under $125,000 and up to $20,000 for those who received Pell Grants.

District Judge Mark Pittman, a Trump appointee, ruled that the program, which would have provided borrowers with up to $20,000 in student loan relief, was "an unconstitutional exercise of Congress's legislative power."

A federal appeals court temporarily put the program on hold in late October 2022, following a challenge from six GOP-led states. However, the appeals court ruling only blocked the program while the states' appeal played out and did not strike down the program outright.

President Biden's action to forgive up to $20,000 in federal student loan debt is like fighting a wildfire with a garden hose, or perhaps more tragically, pouring kerosene on the fire. While for many graduates a reduction in what they owe for their college education is welcome, this action does not address the real problem.

The nation faces a $1.7 trillion student debt crisis. That is bigger than the gross domestic product of Canada, the world's 10th largest economy. This sword of Damocles hangs over millions of young Americans who are postponing marriage, buying a home, and starting a family as they confront an average student loan debt of $40,000. This is not only a heavy burden for those in debt, but also a serious drag on the nation's economy.

Since 1990, the average in-state tuition and fees at a four-year institution nearly tripled on an inflation-adjusted basis—snowballing faster than the cost of health care. That results in the sticker price at four-year institutions increasing by 178% since 1990.

How to Fix the Student Debt Crisis

So, why is college so expensive? Per the Steve Cohen "How to Fix the Student Debt Crisis: Stop Loaning Money to Students; Loan it to Colleges Instead" article in the *City Journal* in November 2015, there are three main reasons:

- First, because colleges, with enthusiastic support from politicians of all stripes, have convinced Americans that higher education is the ticket to success. While a college degree is no longer a badge of the upper class, it is still viewed as a luxury good and is priced accordingly.

- Second, colleges have joyfully suffered from what Andy Rosen, CEO of the testing and online-education company Kaplan, has called "an edifice complex." Colleges, including lots of state schools, continue to build luxury dorms, gourmet dining rooms, and lavish athletic centers to attract students—almost as if academics were an afterthought. Staffs have become bloated, too, not with more professors, but with administrators.

- Third, colleges have been playing with other people's money. Washington has pumped trillions into financial aid programs. Low-income families get outright grants; everyone else qualifies for easy-to-obtain loans.

Congress has also fueled the soaring cost of college through the irrational and unrealistic "Expected Family Contribution" (EFC) calculation, a formula that (supposedly) takes into consideration a family's size, income, and assets, and then spits out what it thinks the family should contribute to a child's college education. The EFC must have been created by proponents of legalized marijuana: the formula generates fantastical, almost delusional figures that few middle-income families can afford. For example, the EFC for a family of four earning $100,000, with $50,000 in assets and one child about to go off to college, is $17,375—every year.

What that means for colleges is that they don't have to dip into their own financial-aid reserves until the family comes up with their EFC portion. Families, faced with the choice of depleting their savings—not many families can tighten their belts by the 21 percent that the EFC requires—are forced to borrow more easy money from the government. No wonder some call this predatory lending.

Thus, candidates who promise free college get enthusiastic receptions. Never mind how the government will pay for all this. Even Bernie Sanders can only tax Wall Street so many times. Is there a way out of this death spiral of college costs and mounting student debt? Maybe:

- First, Congress would have to scrap the EFC. It's an artificial price support that serves no purpose other than to give colleges cover for not providing more financial aid.

- Second, the president and Congress would have to agree to change how financial aid flows. Instead of lending money to students and their families, Congress should lend money to colleges and universities. In turn, the schools would lend it to students and parents, with repayment going back to the school. In this way, colleges would have an incentive to limit tuition hikes—and thus how much students needed to borrow. Colleges might think twice before increasing tuition with this debt overhang and its credit-rating implications.

Today, the most popular loan programs have repayment plans pegged to a percentage of what graduates earn. Recent initiatives cap the repayment at 10 percent of a graduate's paycheck, which is reducing defaults. Lending money to the colleges themselves will foster a host of creative repayment options. Just as students need to have skin in the game in order to take college seriously, colleges must have something at stake to get costs under control.

10 – School Choices: Charter, Private, Religious, Homeschooling & Vocational Schools

Credit: InTech Center, Chaffey College.

From the Alexandra DeSanctis Nearly Three-Quarters of Americans Support School Choice *National Review* March 2022 report:

According to a new poll from RealClear Opinion Research, nearly three-quarters of Americans now say they support school choice, a marked increase from two years ago. Seventy-two percent of registered voters said they back school choice, while only 18 percent said they don't. The poll was conducted between February 5 and February 9 in 2022 and surveyed 2,000 registered voters.

That support for school choice held across the ideological spectrum: Eighty-two percent of Republicans, 68 percent of Democrats, and 67 percent of Independents said they like the idea of funding students instead of the public-school system.

Perhaps most interesting, support for school choice remained strong across all the demographic groups surveyed. Hispanic Americans were most supportive of school choice (77 percent), followed closely by white respondents (72 percent), black respondents (70 percent), and Asian respondents (66 percent). School choice is, in other words, a significant wedge issue for the Democratic Party.

This support for school choice has risen steeply across all these demographics since the start of the pandemic. As of April 2020, 64 percent of Americans supported school choice, along with 75 percent of republicans, 59 percent of Democrats, and 60 percent of Independents. Evidently, one major result of the Covid-19 pandemic has been to focus Americans' attention on education, and many parents appear not to like what they see.

School Choices Rising

Per the Steven Malanga "School Choice Rising" *City Journal* article in the Summer of 2022:

Economist Milton Friedman originally proposed the idea of school choice in a 1955 paper, arguing that the current model for government-financed and administered public education concentrated too much power in the public sector, leading inevitably to an ineffective monopoly. He suggested a dramatic way to stave off decline: give money to parents and let them choose where to send their children to school.

Over the years, as the performance of public schools, especially in urban districts serving low-income kids, declined, Friedman's criticism intensified. In a 1995 *Washington Post* essay, he decried a system that produced "dismal results: some relatively good government schools in high-income suburbs and communities; very poor government schools in our inner cities." Mounting support for school choice, he observed, suggested a tide that only the educational bureaucracy was holding back.

The pandemic proved a school-choice accelerant. When Covid hit, schools were among the institutions that officials shut down first, largely because we knew so little about the virus, how it spread, and who was most vulnerable. Fairly quickly, however, it became clear that children were among the least affected and that spread was not common in schools. In Europe, many school systems reopened in late spring 2020, just months after the virus struck. In America, openings were slower to happen.

A late 2021 UNESCO survey estimated that France had closed its schools for only 12 weeks over the previous two years. In Spain, the number was 15 weeks; in the U.K., schools shut down for 27 weeks, and in Germany for 38. American schools had closed for 71 weeks on average.

Union Power and School Closures

As time wore on, many American parents also got a lesson in the power of teachers' unions to dictate policy. School closures varied considerably by district and by state; one audit found that states with some of the least amount of in-person instruction during the pandemic included California, Oregon, Washington, Illinois, New Jersey, and Massachusetts—all with strong teachers' unions. In Chicago, the teachers' union made national headlines by shutting down schools several times, including during the spread of the Omicron variant. Meantime, two states where unions enjoyed far less bargaining power—Texas and Florida—boasted the most in-person instruction.

Pervasive discontent with public schools manifested itself in unprecedented enrollment declines. In the school year starting in September 2020, enrollment fell 3 percent, according to the National Center for Education Statistics—a trend that seems to have continued for a second year, according to a National Public Radio survey of major American school districts.

Early reporting in California, for example, suggests that enrollment fell by 1.8 percent in the 2021–22 school year, on top of a 2.6 percent drop the previous year. Bigger transformations may be coming. Los Angeles school officials recently warned that the district faces an unprecedented 30 percent enrollment drop in the next decade, driven by demographic factors and a shift toward alternative schools.

By contrast, a Cato survey of K–12 private schools estimated that recent enrollment gains may have been as high as 7 percent. The National Alliance for Charter Schools reported a similar rise among schools that it surveyed. These numbers are no mystery. In a 2022 poll, 18 percent of parents said that they had switched schools for one of their children recently, and more than half were considering changes. More than one-third reported that the main reason they were looking elsewhere was their current school's pandemic policies.

"School curriculum has taken on new importance—above all, with the rise of critical race theory."

Parental discontent with public education has sparked new momentum for alternatives

What followed Covid lockdowns and curriculum fights was a burst of education legislation, marking another milestone in the choice movement. Eighteen states launched new choice programs or added to existing ones in 2021.

The earlier emphasis had been on alternative schools like charters; but in 2021, legislation focused more on providing parents—including those in middle- and upper-income groups—with additional education options so that they could select those that suited them best.

Florida again took a leading role. In May 2021, Governor Ron DeSantis traveled to a Catholic high school in Hialeah to sign a bill that committed about $200 million to increased scholarships for low-income students, covering 100 percent of tuition at the school of their choice, while also raising the income cap on the program so that families making up to $100,000 a year could qualify. The state estimated that the expansion, which also exempts children of military personnel from scholarship waiting lists, would make it possible for 60,000 more kids to take advantage of the initiative.

The 2021 successes may be a prelude to further gains. For one thing, government schools are flush with cash after the 2021 Biden stimulus provided K–12 education with an unprecedented $128 billion in federal money. That has helped mute criticisms that school-choice programs take money away from traditional public schools, leaving them cash-starved. In addition, polls suggest that Republican candidates are poised to make substantial gains in November elections—not just in Washington but in state and local races, too. That could supercharge school-choice initiatives in places where Democrats or moderate Republicans have been blocking programs.

The last two school years may turn out to be the launching point of a transformational era in American education. School closures and other Covid-related measures, along with the outsize power that teachers' unions wielded over classrooms, have drawn far more parents into the school- reform fold than ever before. No longer is public school choice an issue largely confined to poor parents in failing districts.

More important, polls and interviews illustrate that many parents are upset enough to change how they vote in order to get reform. "Interviews with New Jersey voters revealed that some Democrats' breaks from their party last fall were neither flippant nor fleeting," the *Wall Street Journal* recently observed. "Many [voters] described personal struggles to stress what they viewed as the needs of their family or community over partisanship." The next six months will tell us just how deep those new priorities are.

The Pandemic Set Off a Homeschooling Boom

From the Eric Boehm "The Pandemic Set Off a Homeschooling Boom. Don't Be So Sure That a Bust Is Coming" Reason article in January 2022:

The COVID-19 pandemic disrupted schools and turned kitchens into classrooms. It also appears to have put a decisive end to a decade of stagnation in the growth of American homeschooling. In a new poll, more than two-thirds of parents say they have favorable views about homeschooling, and those numbers are on the rise.

Homeschooling, which is legal in all 50 states though the specific regulations vary widely from place to place, experienced a small boom during the late 1990s and early 2000s. By 2012, more than 3 percent of American school-aged children were being primarily educated at home.

Those numbers plateaued, then boomed again during the first full year of pandemic-era schooling: at the start of the 2020-21 school year, a whopping 11 percent of U.S. households with school-aged children were homeschooling, according to Census Bureau data. The biggest increase in homeschooling was reported by black families, who had historically been less likely to homeschool before the pandemic.

Much of the sudden increase was no doubt due to necessity—schools being closed or operating virtually—or due to parents' worries about the pandemic. And, unsurprisingly, those figures fell off a bit by Christmas 2020, though they remained well above pre-pandemic levels.

We won't have new census data about the number of families who homeschooled during the 2021-22 academic year for a few more months, but there are already indications that disruptions triggered by the pandemic might turn into a permanent shift. A poll released last month, for example, found that parents of school-aged children have favorable views of homeschooling by a margin of about 3-to-1, and that favorable views of homeschooling continue to grow as the pandemic drags on.

The poll, conducted by Morning Consult at the request of Ed Choice, a pro-school-choice nonprofit, surveyed 2,200 parents about various aspects of the K-12 education experience. The section asking about homeschooling found that 68 percent of parents have "favorable" views on the subject, with a recent uptick in those with strongly favorable opinions.

"December 2021 was one of the highest homeschooling favorability rates since we began asking this question," writes John Kristof, a research analyst at Ed Choice. "Those identifying themselves as 'much more favorable' toward homeschooling was at its highest point since October of 2020."

Homeschooling rates are on the rise in part because of the pandemic-era popularity of so-called "learning pods," small groups of children gathering together under adult supervision for homeschooling or virtual schooling. Organized on an ad hoc basis during the early phases of the pandemic, pods have quickly become a more mainstream part of American K-12 education.

The Morning Consult/Ed Choice poll found that 89 percent of families currently participating in learning pods use them to supplement regular schooling, while 11 percent of current podders are using them as a substitute for traditional school. But the ranks of the learning-pod homeschoolers might continue to grow, as 31 percent of parents who said they were interested in joining a learning pod were considering it as a substitution for school.

For some parents who started homeschooling during the pandemic, there's no going back to the old days, reports Laura Newberry, author of The *Los Angeles Times'* education-focused newsletter. After talking to 10 families that began homeschooling during the pandemic and plan to continue doing it, Newberry writes that "their rationales are diverse and the families span the socioeconomic and political spectrums: schools requiring too many COVID-19 safety protocols, or too few; the polarizing conversation around critical race theory; neurodivergent kids struggling with virtual instruction; and an overall waning faith in the public school system."

And, as the census data from last school year suggests, the rise in homeschooling is not merely a consequence of white, Christian families—the dominant demographic in homeschooling during recent times—exercising greater control over their children's educational path (or becoming disenchanted with the politicization of public schools). It's now black and Hispanic families who are exercising that choice.

"I can say that most of the parents I spoke with are thinking deeply about how to give their kids the most well-rounded education possible, as well as a variety of social opportunities. They see this choice as a reprioritization of values, an opportunity to really get to know their kids and nourish their natural curiosities," writes Newberry (though she repeats the inaccurate claim that "homeschooling is also largely unregulated in many states.")

Those ideas about how to best educate your own child might be flourishing now because of a pandemic and the ill-conceived public policy response to it. But the census data, polling, and reporting all indicate that parents choosing to homeschool during COVID are motivated by reasons that might transcend the current chaos.

School Choice Advances in States

From the Laurie Todd-Smith, Ph.D. "School Choice Advances in States" America First Policy Institute (AFPI) article in November 2021:

If ever there were a time to drive a big expansion of parental school choice in states, the time is right now. In 2020, school closures kept millions of children out of the classroom and caused parents to desperately seek help to educate their children during the pandemic. COVID-induced virtual education was an inferior substitute for in-person teaching, but it did provide a useful service to parents by giving them a firsthand window into what was happening in their children's schools.

In many cases, parents realized there was cause for concern. These circumstances also awakened governors, state legislators and local leaders to the fact that parents needed more options and flexibility when schools do not meet the needs of their children.

So far, 18 states have enacted new education choice programs or expanded existing ones. The movement for educational opportunity has gained serious momentum as elected officials across the country push for legislation that prioritizes parents and students.

The timing of this increase in new legislation expanding access to academic choice for families is an outcome of the COVID-19 pandemic. Governors across the country leveraged funds they received as a part of COVID-19 aid packages to empower parents through measures increasing school choice.

Governor Ron DeSantis of Florida recently signed a school choice bill that further increases "life-changing educational opportunities that support and cater to the unique needs of more students than ever before." The bill increases the number of students and families eligible to receive vouchers to use at the school of their choice.

In addition, this legislation eliminated several barriers to academic freedom like the requirement that students be in a public school prior to applying for a scholarship. This bill also expands the use of the funds to include additional educational expenses imposed on families, such as supplemental school fees, transportation, and other costs incurred by families with special needs students.

Polling data also indicates that Americans are in favor of parental school choice measures and in favor of education financing that funds students instead of systems. A recent poll conducted by RealClear Opinion Research found that 74 percent of registered voters support school choice (in April 2020, that number was only 64 percent). This enthusiasm is bipartisan, with 83 percent of Republicans, 70 percent of Democrats (previously only 59 percent), and 69 percent of Independents saying they support parental school choice efforts.

There is also consistent support for school choice across all ethnic backgrounds, with White voters supporting it at a rate of 76 percent, Black voters at 73 percent, Asian voters at 70 percent, and Hispanic voters at 69 percent. The failure of public schools to educate children during the pandemic has been devasting, especially for low-income minority children.

Educational freedom is a tool that has a proven record of putting American families and students first. America First Policy Institute's Center for Education Opportunity believes that every parent should be empowered to choose a high-quality education for their children, which is the gateway to fulfilling the American dream. Now is the time to ensure that school systems are responsive to the needs of students, and that parents are given the power to choose the best educational opportunity for their children.

How the Other Half Learns

Per the Oren Cass "How the Other Half Learns" *City Journal* article in the Winter of 2019: Vocational education is the better option for a substantial portion of students who will never earn bachelor's degrees. It's time to rethink our priorities.

2021 DATA DIGEST
CHARTER SCHOOLS OVERVIEW

CHARTER SCHOOL COVERAGE

44 STATES
have Charter School Laws
plus D.C., Puerto Rico, and Guam

7.2%
of all public school students
attend a charter school

+30 YEARS
have passed since the first charter law
was established.

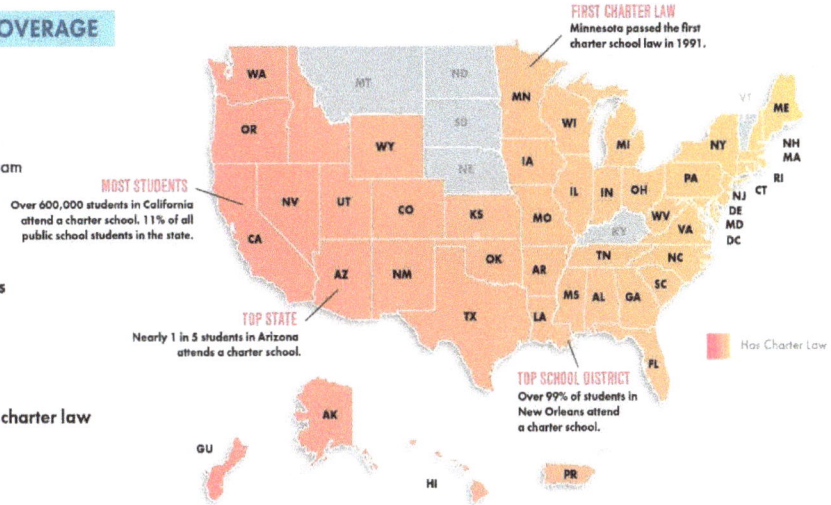

FIRST CHARTER LAW
Minnesota passed the first
charter school law in 1991.

MOST STUDENTS
Over 600,000 students in California
attend a charter school. 11% of all
public school students in the state.

TOP STATE
Nearly 1 in 5 students in Arizona
attends a charter school.

TOP SCHOOL DISTRICT
Over 99% of students in
New Orleans attend
a charter school.

Has Charter Law

CHARTER SCHOOLS & STUDENTS

Since the 2005-06 school year, the number of charter schools and campuses has more than DOUBLED, while charter school enrollment has more than TRIPLED.

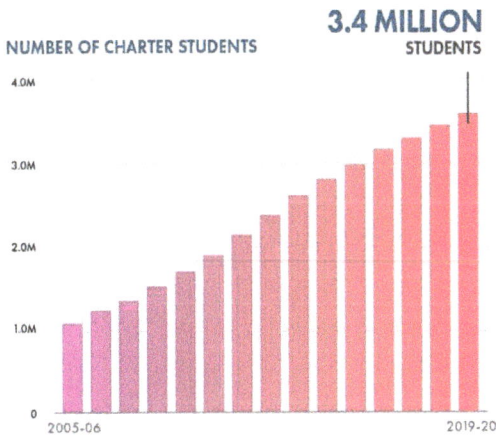

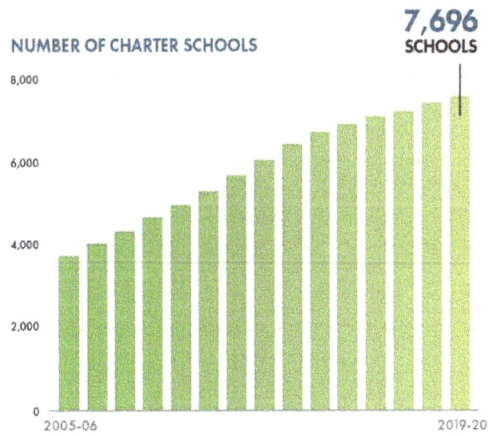

NUMBER OF CHARTER STUDENTS — **3.4 MILLION** STUDENTS

NUMBER OF CHARTER SCHOOLS — **7,696** SCHOOLS

Some proponents of vocational education note that American high schools offer a cornucopia of vocational or career technical education (CTE) opportunities. A CTE pathway is a sequence of two or more CTE courses within a student's area of career interest. Pathways are designed to connect high school classes to college, industry certifications, and/or a career.

Nearly all public high school students (95 percent of ninth-grade students in 2009) attended a school that offered CTE instruction," trumpets the U.S. Department of Education in its National Assessment of CTE. "In 2009, 85 percent of public high school graduates had completed one or more occupational CTE courses, 76 percent had earned at least one full credit in occupational

CTE, and 19 percent were CTE concentrators who had earned at least three credits in the same CTE field."

The problem: CTE courses don't guarantee that a credible non-college pathway exists. A CTE "concentrator," for instance, is any student earning three credits in a CTE field—hardly the basis for a genuine vocation.

Most CTE concentrators enroll in postsecondary education after finishing high school, and only 10 percent pursue the same field in which their CTE credits were concentrated; in total, that pathway accommodates fewer than 2 percent of students. At most, 6 percent of high school graduates go from CTE concentration to the workforce, and they earn little more than similarly situated non-concentrators; whatever preparation they gain appears to have minimal value in the labor market.

Following the money leads to the same conclusion. From 1985 to 2014, federal funding for both K–12 and postsecondary education more than doubled in real terms. Support for CTE declined. States spend $70 billion annually on their university systems and offer another $10 billion in grants to cover remaining tuition obligations that otherwise fall to students.

The federal government chips in $28 billion in Pell grants, plus $26 billion in tax breaks and $19 billion in loan subsidies. None of those funds or programs is available to students if they choose a vocational track. Congress's 2017 appropriation for CTE was $1.2 billion. A lower share of students earned CTE credits or became CTE concentrators in 2009 than in 1990.

Against this backdrop, college is less choice than ultimatum

Orienting the American educational system toward college ensures that the majority who would achieve greater success on an alternative pathway are poorly served—indeed, they're obstructed from reaching it. The approach also entails an enormous waste of public resources and student time, unleashing a vicious cycle in which, since everyone is encouraged to try college, all resources are focused on college-going—and so, of course, everyone tries college.

Enrolling in a program that you're unprepared for and unlikely to complete actually makes sense if society will throw gobs of money at you for doing it, and if the alternative is, well, nothing. This is doubly true if your high school emphasized only college preparation, so you've already sunk years of time into pursuing this path.

Even without an alternative pathway that supports the non-college-bound, the economic data belie the notion that pursuing college is always, or even usually, worthwhile.

Most people compare the earnings of the median high school and college graduates, find an enormous difference, and attribute to college the power to produce such a boost. But those two salaries are best understood not as two possible outcomes for one person but as outcomes for two very different people, with different academic trajectories and earning potentials. If placed among the population of high school graduates, the median college earner would presumably be far above average in academic performance and earning potential. Conversely, among college graduates, the median high school earner would likely land near the distribution's bottom.

Compare, instead, the earnings distributions for high school–only graduates with above-median earnings for their group and college graduates below their cohort's median earnings. Presumably, the marginal student who may or may not belong in college is an above-average performer among the high school–only cohort and a below-average one among the college grads. So those ranges roughly approximate the earnings distributions that he is headed toward, depending on how far his education progresses.

According to the U.S. Bureau of Labor Statistics, the median full-time salary for high school graduates in May 2016 was $34,000 per year; for college graduates, it was $58,000. But for the below-average college graduates—those in the 10th to 50th percentile—the wage range was $28,000 to $58,000. For the above-average high school graduates—the 50th to 90th percentile—it was $34,000 to $70,000. And that's without a strong pathway to prepare those graduates for the workforce.

Economic data belie the notion that pursuing college is always, or even usually, worthwhile

Those well-paying jobs for high school graduates include the quintessential plumber and welder—average earnings among more than 1 million plumbers and electricians and 1 million industrial-machinery mechanics and production supervisors exceed $50,000—but they go far beyond those fields, spanning the economy. In the health-care sector, half a million clinical laboratory and radiologic technicians have comparable prospects. Among hundreds of thousands of first-line supervisors for housekeeping and landscaping workers, average earnings are between $40,000 and $50,000. The same goes for 700,000 practical and vocational nurses.

Even in the technology sector, as the Brookings Institution has shown, fields assumed to require bachelor's degrees often do not. Less educated workers occupy two-fifths of nearly 1 million jobs in what researchers call "mid-tech": computer systems analysts, computer network-support specialists, and computer network architects. Less educated workers may earn relatively lower pay within those fields, but annual earnings even at the 10th percentile of the respective wage distributions are $54,000, $37,000, and $58,000.

What makes the education system's misallocation of resources not only wrongheaded but also galling is its fundamental regressivity. Funds flow freely to those on a path toward high lifetime earnings but remain inaccessible to those more likely to struggle. Firms hiring college graduates can tap a labor pool that has gone through four extra years of costly preparation at someone else's expense. Firms seeking to hire high school graduates, by contrast, find a potential workforce with little relevant training but get excoriated for offering those graduates low wages and not funding intensive training themselves.

Supposedly, the extensive public subsidies offered for college enrollment promote the social goods of economic opportunity and an educated population. But that's not quite right, because that argument treats as equal all time spent by all people on a college campus. College attendance by students equipped to succeed in college has social value, true, but attendance by those who'll probably fail frequently has social cost. And who better than the individual and his family to know into which camp he falls?

The education system's designers and funders should instead pursue a different goal: to balance the relative attractiveness of college and non-college pathways so that students who'll probably succeed in college choose to attend, while those unlikely to succeed pursue more promising alternatives. Vocational programs will be for everyone's kids, not just someone else's, once these programs become a smart economic choice.

The typical student from a low- to middle-income household, attempting to pursue college, can expect that society will spend roughly $15,000 on his education for each year of high school. If he then goes to a four-year public university, his state might fund $6,000 per year of education costs, and a Pell grant might cover another $5,000. If the student graduates on time, in other words, he will do so thanks to more than $100,000 of taxpayer investment.

What if the student would prefer—and benefit more from—pursuing a vocation? Today, if he's lucky, he might get a standard ninth- and tenth-grade education, as much as $10,000 of extra investment across 11th and 12th grade—and then nothing. In other words, the college-bound student receives 50 percent more public investment, along with higher long-term earnings.

A real vocational option would merge high-quality CTE in 11th and 12th grades with the start of subsidized employment and further training, offered in partnership between the state and an employer. For the same amount that taxpayers are prepared to spend on his behalf in pursuit of a bachelor's degree, the student could attend two years of traditional high school, spend a third year in a more technical classroom, and then work three years in a job for which the employer would receive an annual public subsidy of $5,000.

For the first two of those working years, the student might spend half his time on the job and the other half in more focused training, which would also get public support. All this would still cost less than the college track, so he could reach age 20 with job experience, an industry-recognized credential, and an additional $25,000 from the government in a savings account, perhaps for further training in the years ahead—in addition to what his employer might pay him.

A student pursuing a vocation deserves at least the same level of public support as one pursuing college. This vocational pathway might not be more attractive than a bachelor's degree—for those who'll earn a bachelor's, that is. For most of the students who won't earn such a degree, though, this would be a far superior option.

How Hybrid Schools Are Reshaping Education

As per the Kerry McDonald "How Hybrid Schools Are Reshaping Education" Foundation for Economic Education (FEE) story in April 2022:

The growing interest in and supply of hybrid schooling across the country reflect a larger educational trend away from traditional schooling and toward innovative, decentralized solutions.

They're not exactly schools, but they're not homeschools either. They have elements of structured curriculum and institutional learning, while offering maximum educational freedom and flexibility. They provide a consistent, off-site community of teachers and learners, and prioritize abundant time at home with family. They are not cheap but they are also not exorbitant, with annual tuition costs typically half that of traditional private schools.

Hybrid schools are, in the words of Kennesaw State University Professor Eric Wearne, the "best of both worlds," drawing out the top elements of both schooling and homeschooling while not being tied too tightly to either learning model.

Hybrid schools are as diverse as the people who launch them and the communities they serve. Some of these schools think of themselves as a group of homeschoolers that comes together in a physical building for formal learning several times a week, while other hybrid schools think of themselves as formal private schools that meet on a part-time basis.

In his earlier research, including his 2020 book on the topic, Wearne found that hybrid schools satisfy a rising demand by families for smaller, more personalized, more family-centered learning models rather than larger, more standardized conventional schooling. In fact, Wearne found that most of the hybrid school students in his sample had attended public schools prior to enrolling in a hybrid school, and most said they'd prefer full-time homeschooling, rather than full-time private schooling, if they could. Parents also indicated that they were much more satisfied with their children's hybrid school than with their previous schools.

The growing interest in and supply of hybrid schools across the country reflect a larger educational trend away from traditional schooling and toward innovative, decentralized solutions. Keeping government regulation and intrusion at bay will help hybrid schools and similar models expand and evolve to meet the distinct preferences and needs of local learning communities, and will introduce a greater variety of interesting and affordable educational options for families.

Microschools Have a Big Future

Per the J.D. Tuccille "Microschools Have a Big Future" *Reason* article in January 2022:

Based in Phoenix, Arizona, the Black Mothers Forum launched a network of microschools to "tear down barriers to academic excellence due to low expectations, and break the cycle of the school to prison pipeline" as the group's mission statement reads.

Originally partnered with Prenda, an Arizona-based company that specializes in getting microschools launched and operating, Black Mothers Forum has since converted its outlets to charter schools, which subjects them to greater regulation, but also comes with funding so that they don't have to charge tuition. The organization's efforts won the attention of Arizona Gov. Doug Ducey (R), who granted it $3.5 million to expand the network of microschools from seven to 50. Their success is reflected in similar efforts across the country.

"Micro schools are the latest schooling alternative to take off as more teachers and parents are becoming fed up with schools keeping their classrooms closed and students falling behind," Fox Business observed earlier this month.

If the term "microschools" confounds you, that may be because it came to the public's attention only recently, along with "learning pods," as families scramble to educate their children amid

COVID-19-fueled disruption. The dividing line between the two is more than a bit fuzzy, and they overlap with other categories of learning, such as homeschooling co-ops and even one-room schoolhouses.

Small-is-beautiful education avoids conflicts that plague larger one-size-fits-few institutions

"As their name suggests, microschools, which serve K-12 students, are very small schools that typically serve 10 to 15 students, but sometimes as many as 150," Barnett Berry, a research professor of education at the University of South Carolina, specified in a September 2021 article. "They can have very different purposes but tend to share common characteristics, such as more personalized and project-based learning. They also tend to have closer adult-child relationships in which teachers serve as facilitators of student-led learning, not just deliverers of content."

Meridian Learning, a microschool advocacy group, insists that learning pods are "temporary alternatives" for stranded families while microschools are "professional, long-standing" approaches rooted in homeschooling. But rather than get hung up on terminology, it's better to emphasize that these are all ways of describing flexible alternatives to rigid institutions that struggle in good times, founder at a hint of crisis, and become battlegrounds for disagreements about what should be taught. What matters is that children learn, not the details of the settings in which they absorb lessons.

"Grassroots microschools serve a variety of children and families, including those in underserved areas and those whose needs are not being met by the current system," Meridian adds.

Because the emphasis is on teaching kids through whatever approach works in different situations, guidance for starting up a microschool/learning pod/homeschooling co-op, etc. tends to be on the vague side. "Some microschools are run out of homes. Others build their own facilities. Shared space can often be rented from churches—which tend to remain vacant during the week—at a very low rate," advises Microschool Revolution, which connects school founders with funding.

Advocacy groups like Meridian Learning and companies such as Prenda offer guidance, structure, and teaching materials. Other microschools evolve out of homeschooling networks in which families share expertise to teach each other's kids. The results might be organized as private schools, charter schools, schools-within-public-schools, or homeschooling co-ops. That means the rules to which they're subject vary, although many fly under the radar as ad-hoc arrangements. Again, the emphasis is on small, flexible environments that address the needs of specific students.

If that sounds confusing, it's no more so than any other freedom to make your own arrangements. It also can't be any more confusing than what *The Wall Street Journal* describes as "low-grade chaos" prevailing at public schools struggling to adapt to lingering health challenges and labor shortages, and often failing to satisfy anybody in the process.

"Some are saying the guidelines are too strict, some are saying the guidelines are too lenient. It's almost a Catch-22. You do one thing for one, then you get heat from the other," one high school principal told the newspaper.

By serving students assembled from like-minded families, microschools and similar small-is-beautiful approaches avoid conflicts over policy as well as other disagreements that plague larger one-size-fits-few institutions. The one thing they have in common is their mission to educate students in a focused setting. The future of education may well be small, in a very big way.

Online Learning Finds Its Moment

Per the Andrew Sidamon-Eristoff "Online Learning Finds Its Moment" *City Journal* article in April 2020:

With the exception of junior or community colleges, as well as some urban schools, the traditional paradigm of American higher education has been a four-year residential college experience featuring life on campus, with lectures, seminars, labs, dorms, social and cultural activities, institutionalized sports, and—of course—lengthy recesses. This traditional campus experience can be personally, socially, and intellectually transformative.

Yet it all comes at an increasingly unsustainable price: the average cost this academic year of tuition, fees, room and board, books, and supplies at four-year public and private institutions was $21,950 and $49,879, respectively. Elite universities can cost much more—Harvard, despite its $40 billion endowment, charges $69,607. Costs continue to escalate. Over the past three decades, the average price tag to attend a public four-year institution has more than tripled; it has more than doubled at private four-year schools. Outstanding student loan debt reached an all-time high of $1.41 trillion in 2019.

Broad access to quality higher education is critical to American global economic competitiveness and is a linchpin of our democratic society. Maintaining or enhancing that access means controlling costs, enhancing productivity, or increasing public and private subsidies. Moving instruction online offers a unique opportunity to reinvent the traditional residential campus model.

Online education has been around for at least a quarter-century. It is effective, flexible, and inexpensive, a proven tool for adult education and professional continuing education. Up to now, though, the elite educational establishment has kept it at arms-length. Administrative matters, academic scheduling, curricula, assignments, and even some assessments have moved online, but most students are still expected to attend lectures, labs, and seminars.

This is one reason that, despite the proliferation of personal computing devices, the higher-education sector in general has not seen major technology-enabled productivity increases.

Covid-19 could force an overdue revolution in higher education

The coronavirus may change that. When the dust settles, millions of students will realize that they received some valuable education this spring, even though they were not on campus. Online education is not a perfect or easy substitute for the on-campus experience—but why not explore ways to combine the two delivery models?

Schools can leverage the impact and reach of the best (and most expensive) faculty by recording their popular large-class lectures and making them and related syllabi available online to students at any institution that pays an appropriate license fee, which would surely be less than full salary for celebrity faculty. There is no fundamental difference between this approach and using textbooks written by the same professors.

The ongoing experiment in distance learning will also challenge the traditional one-tuition-fits-all paradigm, which makes little or no distinction between the cost of teaching subjects that require expensive physical facilities—such as science labs or arts studios—and those that do not. Because online platforms are better suited to deliver a political-science survey course than a science lab or a studio in the performing or visual arts, large-scale online learning will inevitably accentuate the cost differential and thus the degree of de facto cross subsidization between academic disciplines.

There is no reason why a college education has to be paced along the traditional four years. For economic or other reasons, only 41 percent of first-time full-time college students earn a bachelor's degree in four years, anyway. Others choose an accelerated schedule by taking classes during the summer. Why not collaborate with employers to offer a lighter load of online courses designed to support and enhance summer internships?

Alternatively, students could spend two or three years on campus and then have the option to earn their final credits online, while working. Or they could complete their basic distribution requirements online and arrive at campus ready to focus on higher-level or specialized learning.

Whether one believes that the purpose of higher education today is to develop a capable workforce or to inculcate youth with a particular set of cultural values, there is no question that the traditional campus model has become too expensive and inefficient. That reality, and the unplanned, large-scale experiment in off-campus instruction necessitated by the coronavirus, make it all but certain that online learning is poised for explosive future growth.

11 – Student Outcomes vs. Family Backgrounds, Behavior, Income, Schools & Policies

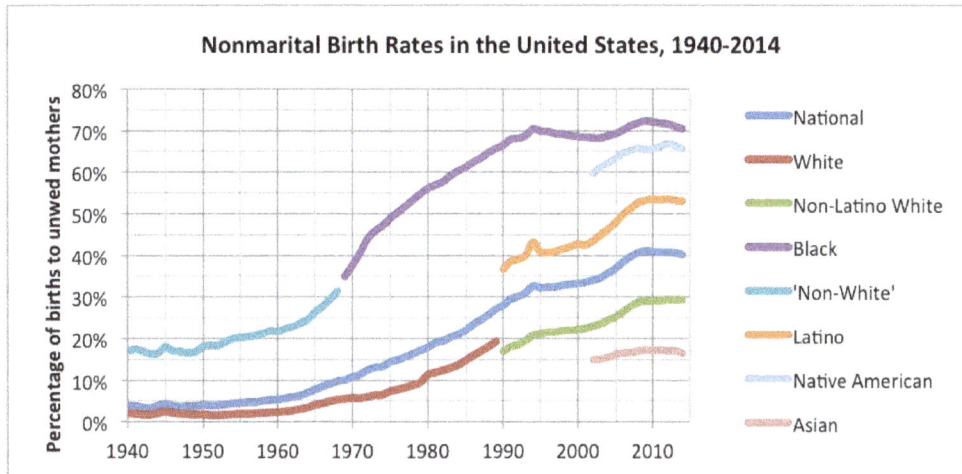

Credit: The Moynihan Report.

From the Anna J. Egalite "How Family Background Influences Student Achievement" report in Vol. 16, No. 2 of Education Next:

On the weekend before the Fourth of July 1966, the U.S. Office of Education quietly released a 737-page report that summarized one of the most comprehensive studies of American education ever conducted. Encompassing some 3,000 schools, nearly 600,000 students, and thousands of teachers, and produced by a team led by Johns Hopkins University sociologist James S. Coleman, "Equality of Educational Opportunity" was met with a palpable silence. Indeed, the timing of the release relied on one of the oldest tricks in the public relations playbook—announcing unfavorable results on a major holiday, when neither the American public nor the news media are paying much attention.

To the dismay of federal officials, the Coleman Report had concluded that "schools are remarkably similar in the effect they have on the achievement of their pupils when the socio-economic background of the students is taken into account." Or, as one sociologist supposedly put it to the scholar-politician Daniel Patrick Moynihan, "Have you heard what Coleman is finding? It's all family."

The Coleman Report's conclusions (similar but more conclusive than the 1965 Moynihan Report titled The Negro Family: The Case For National Action concerning the influences of home and family were at odds with the paradigm of the day.

The politically inconvenient conclusion that family background explained more about a child's achievement than did school resources ran contrary to contemporary priorities, which were focused on improving educational inputs such as school expenditure levels, class size, and teacher quality. Indeed, less than a year before the Coleman Report's release, President Lyndon Johnson had signed the Elementary and Secondary Education Act into law, dedicating federal funds to disadvantaged students through a Title 1 program that still remains the single largest investment in K–12 education, currently reaching approximately 21 million students at an annual cost of about $14.4 billion.

So what exactly had Coleman uncovered? Differences among schools in their facilities and staffing "are so little related to achievement levels of students that, with few exceptions, their effect fails to appear even in a survey of this magnitude," the authors concluded.

How Family Background Influences Student Achievement

Coleman's advisory panel refused to sign off on the report, citing "methodological concerns" that continue to reverberate. Subsequent research has corroborated the finding that family background is strongly correlated with student performance in school. A correlation between family background and educational and economic success, however, does not tell us whether the relationship between the two is independent of any school impacts.

The associations between home life and school performance that Coleman documented may actually be driven by disparities in school or neighborhood quality rather than family influences. Often, families choose their children's schools by selecting their community or neighborhood, and children whose parents select good schools may benefit as a consequence.

In the elusive quest to uncover the determinants of students' academic success, therefore, it is important to rely on experimental or quasi-experimental research that identifies effects of family background that operate separately and apart from any school effects.

In this essay I look at four family variables that may influence student achievement: family education, family income, parents' criminal activity, and family structure. I then consider the ways in which schools can offset the effects of these factors.

Parental Education

Better-educated parents are more likely to consider the quality of the local schools when selecting a neighborhood in which to live. Once their children enter a school, educated parents are also more likely to pay attention to the quality of their children's teachers and may attempt to ensure that their children are adequately served. By participating in parent-teacher conferences and volunteering at school, they may encourage staff to attend to their children's individual needs.

In addition, highly educated parents are more likely than their less-educated counterparts to read to their children. Educated parents enhance their children's development and human capital by drawing on their own advanced language skills in communicating with their children. They are more likely to pose questions instead of directives and employ a broader and more complex vocabulary.

Estimates suggest that, by age 3, children whose parents receive public assistance hear less than a third of the words encountered by their higher-income peers. As a result, the children of highly educated parents are capable of more complex speech and have more extensive vocabularies before they even start school.

Highly educated parents can also use their social capital to promote their children's development. A cohesive social network of well-educated individuals socializes children to expect that they too will attain high levels of academic success. It can also transmit cultural capital by teaching children the specific behaviors, patterns of speech, and cultural references that are valued by the educational and professional elite.

In most studies, parental education has been identified as the single strongest correlate of children's success in school, the number of years they attend school, and their success later in life. Because parental education influences children's learning both directly and through the choice of a school, we do not know how much of the correlation can be attributed to direct impact and how much to school-related factors.

Teasing out the distinct causal impact of parental education is tricky, but given the strong association between parental education and student achievement in every industrialized society, the direct impact is undoubtedly substantial. Furthermore, quasi-experimental strategies have found positive effects of parental education on children's outcomes. For instance, one study of Korean children adopted into American families shows that the adoptive mother's education level is significantly associated with the child's educational attainment.

Even small differences in access to the activities and experiences that are known to promote brain development can accumulate.

Family Income

As with parental education, family income may have a direct impact on a child's academic outcomes, or variations in achievement could simply be a function of the school the child attends: parents with greater financial resources can identify communities with higher-quality schools and choose more-expensive neighborhoods—the very places where good schools are likely to be. More-affluent parents can also use their resources to ensure that their children have access to a full range of extracurricular activities at school and in the community.

But it's not hard to imagine direct effects of income on student achievement. Parents who are struggling economically simply don't have the time or the wherewithal to check homework, drive children to summer camp, organize museum trips, or help their kids plan for college. Working multiple jobs or inconvenient shifts makes it hard to dedicate time for family dinners, enforce a consistent bedtime, read to infants and toddlers, or invest in music lessons or sports clubs. Even small differences in access to the activities and experiences that are known to promote brain development can accumulate, resulting in a sizable gap between two groups of children defined by family circumstances.

It is challenging to find rigorous experimental or quasi-experimental evidence to disentangle the direct effects of home life from the effects of the school a family selects. While Coleman claimed that family and peers had an effect on student achievement that was distinct from the influence of schools or neighborhoods, his research design was inadequate to support this conclusion. All he was able to show was that family characteristics had a strong correlation with student achievement.

Separating out the independent effects of family education and family income is also difficult. We do not know if low income and financial instability alone can adversely affect children's behavior, emotional stability, and educational outcomes. Evidence from the negative-income-tax experiments carried out by the federal government between 1968 and 1982 showed only mixed effects of income on children's outcomes, and subsequent work by the University of Chicago's Susan Mayer cast doubt on any causal relationship between parental income and child well-being.

However, a recent study by Gordon Dahl and Lance Lochner, exploiting quasi-experimental variation in the Earned Income Tax Credit, provides convincing evidence that increases in family income can lift the achievement levels of students raised in low-income working families, even holding other factors constant.

Parental Incarceration. The Bureau of Justice Statistics reports that 2.3 percent of U.S. children have a parent in federal or state prison. Black children are 7.5 times more likely and Hispanic children 2.5 times more likely than white children to have an incarcerated parent. Incarceration removes a wage earner from the home, lowering household income. One estimate suggests that two-thirds of incarcerated fathers had provided the primary source of family income before their imprisonment.

As a result, children with a parent in prison are at greater risk of homelessness, which in turn can have grave consequences: the receipt of social and medical services and assignment to a traditional public school all require a stable home address. The emotional strain of a parent's incarceration can also take its toll on a child's achievement in school.

Quantifying the causal effects of parental incarceration has proven challenging, however. While correlational research finds that the odds of finishing high school are 50 percent lower for children with an incarcerated parent, parents who are in prison may have less education, lower income, more limited access to quality schools, and other attributes that adversely affect their children's success in school.

A recent review of 22 studies of the effect of parental incarceration on child well-being concludes that, to date, no research in this area has been able to leverage a natural experiment to produce quasi-experimental estimates. Just how large a causal impact parental incarceration has on children remains an important but largely uncharted topic for future research.

Family Structure

While most American children still live with both of their biological or adoptive parents, family structures have become more diverse in recent years, and living arrangements have grown increasingly complex. In particular, the two-parent family is vanishing among the poor.

Approximately two-fifths of U.S. children experience dissolution in their parents' union by age 15, and two-thirds of this group will see their mother form a new union within six years. Many parents today choose cohabitation over marriage, but the instability of such partnerships is even higher.

In the case of nonmarital births, estimates say that 56 percent of fathers will be living away from their child by his or her third birthday. These patterns can have serious implications for a child's well-being and school success. Single parents have less time for the enriching activities that Robert Putnam, Harvard professor of public policy, has called "Goodnight Moon" time, after the celebrated bedtime storybook by Margaret Wise Brown.

The U.S. Census Bureau reports that 1- to 2-year-olds who live with two married parents are read to, on average, 8.5 times per week. The corresponding statistic for their peers living with a single parent is 5.7 times. And it's likely that dual-parent families in general have many other attributes that affect their children's educational attainment, mental health, labor market performance, and family formation.

More-rigorous quasi-experimental evidence also documents significant negative effects of a father's absence on children's educational attainment and social and emotional development, leading to increases in antisocial behavior. These effects are largest for boys.

Recent research by MIT economist David Autor and colleagues generates quasi-experimental estimates of family background by simultaneously accounting for the impact of neighborhood environment and school quality to investigate why boys fare worse than girls in disadvantaged families.

Comparing boys to their sisters in a data set that includes more than 1 million children born in Florida between 1992 and 2002, the authors demonstrate a persistent gender gap in graduation and truancy rates, incidence of behavioral and cognitive disabilities, and standardized test scores.

Policies to Counter Family Disadvantage

Policymakers who are weighing competing approaches to countering the influence of family disadvantage face a tough choice: Should they try to improve schools (to overcome the effects of family background) or directly address the effects of family background?

The question is critical. If family background is decisive regardless of the quality of the school, then the road to equal opportunity will be long and hard. Increasing the level of parental education is a multigenerational challenge, while reducing the rising disparities in family income would require massive changes in public policy, and reversing the growth in the prevalence of single-parent families would also prove challenging.

And, while efforts to reduce incarceration rates are afoot, U.S. crime rates remain among the highest in the world. Given these obstacles, if schools themselves can offset differences in family background, the chances of achieving a more egalitarian society greatly improve.

For these reasons, scholars need to continue to tackle the causality question raised by Coleman's pathbreaking study. Although the obstacles to causal inference are steep, education researchers should focus on quasi-experimental approaches relying on sibling comparisons, changes in state laws over time, or policy quirks—such as policy implementation timelines that vary across municipalities—that facilitate research opportunities.

Given what is currently known, a holistic approach that simultaneously attempts to strengthen both home and school influences in disadvantaged communities is worthy of further exploration. A number of contemporary and past initiatives point to the potential of this comprehensive approach.

Implications for Policy

Determining the causal relationships between family background and child well-being has posed a daunting challenge. Family characteristics are often tightly correlated with features of the neighborhood environment, making it difficult to determine the independent influences of each. But getting a solid understanding of causality is critical to the debate over whether to intervene inside or outside of school.

The results of quasi-experimental research, as well as common sense, tell us that children who grow up in stable, well-resourced families have significant advantages over their peers who do not—including access to better schools and other educational services. Policies that place schools at center stage have the potential to disrupt the cycle of economic disadvantage to ensure that children born into poverty aren't excluded from the American dream.

In opening our eyes to the role of family background in the creation of inequality, Coleman wasn't suggesting that we shrug our shoulders and learn to live with it. But in attacking the achievement gap, as his research would imply, we need to mobilize not only our schools but also other institutions.

Promise Neighborhoods offer cradle-to-career supports to help children successfully navigate the challenges of growing up. Early childhood programs provide intervention at a critical time, when children's brains take huge leaps in development. Finally, small schools of choice can help to build a strong sense of community, which could particularly benefit inner-city neighborhoods where traditional institutions have been disintegrating.

Back to Discipline

Per the Heather Mac Donald "Back to Discipline" *City Journal* article in December 2018:

A federal commission on school safety has repudiated the use of disparate-impact analysis in evaluating whether school discipline is racially biased. The Trump administration should go further, and extirpate such analysis from the entirety of the federal code of regulations, as well as from informal government practice.

Disparate-impact analysis holds that if a facially-neutral policy negatively affects blacks and Hispanics at a higher rate than whites and Asians, it is discriminatory. Noticing the behavioral differences that lead to those disparate effects is forbidden. In the area of school discipline, disparate-impact analysis results in the conclusion that racially neutral rules must nevertheless contain bias, since black students nationally are suspended at nearly three times the rate of white students.

In 2014, the Obama administration relied on this methodology to announce that schools that suspended or expelled black students at higher rates than white students were violating anti-discrimination laws.

To understand how counterfactual such an analysis is, consider Duval County, Florida, which has Florida's highest juvenile homicide rate. Seventy-three children, some as young as 11, have been arrested for murder and manslaughter over the last decade, according to the Florida *Times-Union*.

Black juveniles made up 87.6 percent of those arrests and whites 8 percent. The black population in Duval County—which includes Jacksonville—was 28.9 percent in 2010 and the white population 56.6 percent, making black youngsters 21.6 times more likely to be arrested for homicide than white youngsters. Nationally, black males between the ages of 14 and 17 commit homicide at ten times the rate of white and Hispanic male teens combined; if Hispanics were removed from the equation, the black-white disparity would be much greater.

Beneath Those Homicide Numbers is a Larger Juvenile Crime Wave

"The reason so many kids commit murder in Jacksonville is not because they are murderers, but because they are everything else: drug dealers, robbers, thieves, rapists and a bunch of other types of criminals whose crimes of choice has a great likelihood of leading to a murder," a teen murder convict, Aaron Wright, told the Florida Times-Union.

Fifty-nine percent of juvenile murder convicts from Duval County who responded to the paper's inmate survey reported that they were committing another crime such as robbery or burglary when they or their co-defendant killed their victim. Wright himself was robbing a woman when his fellow robber shot and killed her, making Wright guilty of felony murder.

The same family dysfunction and lack of socialization that create this juvenile crime wave inevitably affects classroom behavior.

Duval County Public Schools also have the highest number of violent campus incidents of any Florida school district. Nationwide, schools with the highest minority populations report the highest number of disciplinary infractions. Schools that are 50 percent minority or more experience weekly gang activity at nearly ten times the rate of schools where minorities constituted 5 percent to 20 percent of the population, according to the 2018 "Indicators of School Crime and Safety" report produced by the U.S. Justice and Education Departments.

Gang violence in schools with less than 5 percent minority populations was too low to be usable statistically. Widespread weekly disorder in classrooms was reported in schools with at least 50 percent minority populations at more than five times the rate as in schools with 5 percent to 20 percent minorities.

Disparate Impact Reflects Disparate Reality

More than four times as many high-minority schools reported weekly verbal abuse of teachers compared with schools with a minority student body less than 20 percent. Widespread disorder and teacher abuse at schools with less than 5 percent minority populations was again too low to be statistically reliable.

The "School Crime and Safety" reports produced during the Obama years contained identical disparities. And yet the Obama administration held that the only possible reason why blacks are disciplined in school more than whites is teacher and administrator bias. Never mind that teaching is the most "woke" profession in the country after social work, with education schools frantically indoctrinating their students in white privilege and critical race theory.

A substitute teacher who worked in Los Angeles's inner-city schools documents similar insubordination in his recent book, *Sit Down and Shut Up: How Discipline Can Set Students Free*. One student, recounts author Cinque Henderson, shoved a pregnant teacher in order to grab her laptop and watch a video. The dean then interrogated the teacher about why the student was not "jibing with her." An instructor from Miami-Dade County told Henderson: "It is virtually impossible to discipline a student. I know we are losing a generation of kids of color as a result of allowing them to run wild."

The *Times-Union* analysis identifies the biggest factor in juvenile violence: absent fathers. Eighty-four percent of the juvenile murderers who responded to the paper's survey had what the paper discreetly calls "divorced or separated parents"—the reality more likely being that their parents never married in the first place. "I believe that my life may have took a different turn . . . had my father been a man and raised me," a 61-year-old teen murderer and career criminal told the paper.

Excusing insubordination and aggression in the name of racial equity is not a civil rights accomplishment. The third-party victims of such behavior are themselves disproportionately minority—whether fellow classmates who cannot learn, or law-abiding residents of high-crime neighborhoods who have to worry about taking their children safely to school without being carjacked or caught in a drive-by shooting.

But the alleged beneficiary of a racial double standard in conduct is also a victim. Schools are usually the last chance to civilize children if their family has failed to do so. They accomplish that civilizing mission through the application of a color-blind behavioral code, neutrally enforced, that communicates to students that their behavioral choices have consequences.

A student who perceives that his race is an excuse for bad conduct will be handicapped for life. Pace the race advocates, it is this disparate-impact-induced state of affairs—not the supposed implicit racism of teachers and principals—that constitutes an actual school-to-prison pipeline.

No Thug Left Behind

Per the Katherine Kersten "No Thug Left Behind" *City Journal* report tin the Winter of 2017:

In the Obama years, America's public education system embarked on a vast social experiment that threatened to turn schools into educational free-fire zones. The campaign—carried out in the name of "racial equity"—sought to reduce dramatically the suspension rate of black students, who get referred for discipline at much higher rates than other students. From the top down, the U.S. Department of Education drove the effort; from the bottom up, local educational bureaucrats have supported and implemented it.

"Racial equity" has become the all-purpose justification for dubious educational policies. Equity proponents view "disparate impact"—when the same policies yield different outcomes among demographic groups—as conclusive proof of discrimination. On the education front, "equity" does not seek equal treatment for all students. Instead, it demands statistical equivalence in discipline referrals and suspensions for students of every racial group, regardless of those students' actual conduct.

Equity advocates' central premise is that teachers, not students, are to blame for the racial-equity discipline gap. They claim that teachers' biases, cultural ignorance, or insensitivity are the gap's primary causes. The key to eliminating disparities, they maintain, is to change not students' but adults' behavior. Equity supporters justify their agenda on grounds that the racial-equity discipline gap severely hampers black students' chances of success in life. Kids who get suspended generally fail to graduate on time and are more likely to get caught up in the juvenile-justice system, they say.

President Obama's Department of Education made racial equity in school discipline one of its top priorities. "The undeniable truth is that every day educational experience for many students of color violates the principle of equity at the heart of the American promise," according to Arne Duncan, who served as education secretary until early 2016. "It is adult behavior that must change," Duncan stated repeatedly. "The school-to-prison pipeline must be challenged every day."

Valeria Silva, who became superintendent of the St. Paul Public Schools in December 2009, was an early and impassioned proponent of racial-equity ideology. In 2011, she made the equity agenda a centerpiece of her Strong Schools, Strong Communities initiative. The district's website lauded the program as "the most revolutionary change in achievement, alignment, and sustainability within SPPS in the last 40 years."

Demographically, the St. Paul schools are about 32 percent Asian, 30 percent black, 22 percent white, 14 percent Hispanic, and 2 percent Native American. In 2009–10, 15 percent of the district's black students were suspended at least once—five times more than white students and about 15 times more than Asian students. In Silva's view, equity required that the black student population be excluded from school at no more than twice the rate of Asian-Americans, the group with the lowest rate of suspensions.

Silva attacked the racial-equity discipline gap at its alleged root: "white privilege." Teachers unfairly punish minority students for "largely subjective" behaviors, such as "defiance, disrespect and disruption," she told the *Minneapolis Star Tribune* in 2012. To overcome their biases, teachers must learn "a true appreciation" of their students' cultural "differences" and how these can "impact interactions in the classroom," she said.

Obsessed with "racial equity," St. Paul schools abandoned discipline—and unleashed mayhem

We have a segment of kids who consider themselves untouchable," said one veteran teacher as the 2015–16 school year began. At the city's high schools, teachers stood by helplessly as rowdy packs of kids—who came to school for free breakfast, lunch, and Wi-Fi—rampaged through the hallways.

"Classroom invasions" by students settling private quarrels or taking revenge for drug deals gone bad became routine. "Students who tire of lectures simply stand up and leave," reported *City Pages*. "They hammer into rooms where they don't belong, inflicting mischief and malice on their peers." The first few months of the school year witnessed riots or brawls at Como Park, Central, Humboldt, and Harding High Schools—including six fights in three days at Como Park. Police had to use chemical irritants to disperse battling students.

To cut black discipline referrals, Silva lowered behavior expectations and dropped serious penalties for misconduct.

Meanwhile, at many elementary schools, anarchy reigned. Students routinely spewed obscenities, pummeled classmates, and raced screaming through the halls, Benner wrote in his 2015 *Pioneer Press* article. Elementary school teachers, like their high school counterparts, risked physical danger. Teacher Donna Wu was caught in a fight between two fifth-grade girls and knocked to the ground with a concussion. "I've been punched and kicked and spit on" and called "every cuss word you could possibly think of," fourth-grade aide Sean Kelly told *City Pages*.

David McGill, a science teacher at Capitol Hill Gifted and Talented Magnet School, told the St. Paul school board that a black fourth-grade bully had "significantly compromised an entire year of science instruction" for his fellow students.

December 4, 2015, marked a turning point. That day, at Central High School, a 16-year-old student body-slammed and choked a teacher, John Ekblad, who was attempting to defuse a cafeteria fight. Ekblad was hospitalized with a traumatic brain injury. In the same fracas, an assistant principal was punched repeatedly in the chest and left with a grapefruit-size bruise on his neck. At a press conference the next day, Ramsey County Attorney John Choi branded rising student-on-staff violence "a public health crisis."

Assaults on St. Paul school staff reported to his office tripled in 2015, compared with 2014, and were up 36 percent over the previous four-year average. Attacks on teachers continued unabated in the months that followed. In March, for example, a Como Park High teacher was assaulted during a classroom invasion over a drug deal, suffered a concussion, and required staples to close a head wound.

"There are those that believe that by suspending kids we are building a pipeline to prison," said Harding High's Becky McQueen. "I think that by not [suspending], we are. I think we're telling these kids, you don't have to be on time for anything, we're just going to talk to you. You can assault somebody, and we're gonna let you come back here." District leaders, however, adamantly denied the charge that escalating violence and disorder were connected with recent disciplinary changes. The district took steps to mask the extent of the mayhem and to intimidate and silence teachers who criticized Silva's policies.

Social-media comments can also endanger teachers' jobs. On March 9, 2017, special-education teacher Theo Olson was placed on paid administrative leave after he, in two Facebook posts, criticized the administration's lack of support for teachers. Olson made no mention of race. Nevertheless, Silva put him on leave after Black Lives Matter St. Paul threatened to "shut down" Como Park High School unless Olson was fired.

As 2015 drew to a close, violence and anarchy had increased so dramatically that suspensions—though a last resort—finally began to rise

In December, Silva announced that first-quarter suspensions were the highest in five years. Seventy-seven percent involved black students, who make up 30 percent of the district's student population. As public outrage mounted, families of all races began flooding out of the St. Paul district to charters and suburban schools.

Many families are saying that "their children . . . don't feel safe even going to the bathroom," Joe Nathan of the St. Paul–based Center for School Change told the *Star Tribune* in 2016. Parents were also troubled by district students' declining reading and math scores. The district lost thousands of students, adding up to millions of dollars in lost state aid.

Asians, the St. Paul district's largest minority, especially resented the new discipline regime. These students—primarily of Hmong and other Southeast Asian backgrounds—tend to be well-behaved and respectful of authority, though many struggle academically. Harding High School teacher Koua Yang said that he had lost about 20 Hmong students to the exodus. "All we hear is the academic disparity between the whites and the blacks," he complained. "This racial equity policy, it's not equitable to all races . . . . Why do we have to leave?"

In November 2015, St. Paul voters vented their frustration with Silva's policies in a dramatic way. They overwhelmingly elected a new school board with a strong anti-Silva majority. Caucus for Change, a teachers'-union-organized group, engineered the victory.

But St. Paul citizens' confidence in Silva had evaporated. Teachers launched a petition demanding her resignation, and black, white, and Asian community leaders echoed that call in an op-ed in the *Pioneer Press*. At last, on June 21, 2016, the school board announced Silva's departure after buying out her contract at a cost of almost $800,000.

In its new contract, the union also won funding for 30 new school counselors, nurses, social workers, and psychologists. But unless district leaders resolve to adopt and enforce high standards of student conduct, a significant long-term improvement in school safety appears unlikely.

St. Paul's experience makes clear that discipline policies rooted in racial-equity ideology lead to disaster

This shouldn't be surprising, considering that the ideology's two major premises are seriously flawed. The first premise holds that disparities in school-discipline rates are a product of teachers' racial bias; the second maintains that teachers' unjustified and discriminatory targeting of black students gives rise to the school-to-prison pipeline.

In 2014, a groundbreaking study in the *Journal of Criminal Justice* by J. P. Wright and others discredited both these claims. The study utilized the largest sample of school-aged children in the nation. Unlike almost all previous studies, it controlled for individual differences in student behavior over time. Using this rigorous methodology, the authors concluded that teacher bias plays no role in the racial-equity suspension gap, which, they determined, is "completely accounted for by a measure of the prior problem behavior of the student."

Racial differentials in suspension rates, they found, appeared to be "a function of differences in problem behaviors that emerge early in life, that remain relatively stable over time, and that materialize in the classroom."

The deepest source of the racial-equity discipline gap is profound differences in family structure. Young people who grow up without fathers are far more likely than their peers to engage in antisocial behavior, according to voluminous social-science research. Disordered family life often promotes the lack of impulse control and socialization that can lead to school misconduct.

The City of St. Paul does not make out-of-wedlock birth data public. However, Intellectual Takeout, a Minnesota-based public-policy institution, has determined through a FOIA request to the Minnesota Department of Health that 87 percent of births to black, U.S.-born mothers in St. Paul occur out of wedlock, compared with 30 percent of white births. Tragically, the problem we confront is not so much a school-to-prison pipeline as a home-to-prison pipeline.

If those households are like the struggling single-parent homes studied by social scientists, then the children are experiencing radically different domestic lives than their middle-class black and white classmates—with few routines, disappearing fathers and stepfathers, and little adult interest in homework, teachers, and discipline. Researchers have repeatedly found that boys growing up in single-mother households are especially prone to "externalizing" behavior like fighting, impulsiveness, rudeness—in other words, precisely the sort of behavior that the community meeting was demanding the administration do something about.

Who pays the greatest price for misguided racial-equity discipline policies? The many poor and minority students who show up at school ready to learn. The breakdown of order that such policies promote is destined to make these children's already-uphill struggle for a decent education even more daunting.

A Nation Still at Risk

From the Chester E. Finn Jr. "A Nation Still at Risk" *Hoover Digest* article in the Winter of 2022:

No. 1 Much as happened after *A Nation at Risk* was released in 1983, the United States finds itself facing a bleak education fate, even as many deny the problem. Back then, however, the denials came mostly from the education establishment, while governors, business leaders, and even US presidents seized the problem and launched the modern era of achievement-driven, results-based education reform.

There was a big divide between what educators wanted to think about their schools—all's well, but send more money—and what community, state, and national leaders were prepared to do to rectify their failings. Importantly, those reform-minded leaders were joined by much of the civil rights community and other equity hawks, mindful that the gravest education problems of all were those faced by poor and black and brown youngsters.

Today, by contrast, we're surrounded by denial on all sides, including today's version of equity hawks, and we see little or nothing by way of reform zeal or political leadership, save for a handful of reddish states where school choice initiatives continue to flourish. We certainly see nothing akin to the bipartisan commitment to better school outcomes, higher standards, reduced achievement gaps, and results-based accountability that characterized much of the previous forty years.

Yet today's core education problem is much the same as what the National Commission on Excellence in Education called attention to way back then:

The educational foundations of our society are presently being eroded by a rising tide of mediocrity that threatens our very future as a nation and a people. What was unimaginable a generation ago has begun to occur—others are matching and surpassing our educational attainments. Our society and its educational institutions seem to have lost sight of the basic purposes of schooling, and of the high expectations and disciplined effort needed to attain them.

That was 1983. Today we find continued signs of weak achievement, arguably more menacing because during the intervening decades so many other countries, friend and foe alike, have advanced much farther in education, while the United States, with a few happy exceptions, has either run in place or slacked off. If you don't believe me, check any recent round of results from the Trends in International Mathematics and Science Study (TIMSS) or the Program for International Student Assessment (PISA).

In American Schools, the "Rising Tide of Mediocrity" Keeps Rising

As other countries' children surpass ours in core skills and knowledge, we face ominous long-term consequences for our national well-being, including both our economy and our security. But what's even more worrying than the achievement problem is the loss of will to do much about it and the creative ways we're finding to conceal from ourselves that it's even a problem—and doing that without necessarily even being aware of the concealment. These strategies take five main forms.

First, we change the subject. Instead of focusing on achievement failings, academic standards, and measurable outcomes, we've been redirecting our attention and energy to other aspects of education and schooling, such as social-emotional learning, and to beefing up inputs and services, such as universal pre-K and community college.

Second, we've been denouncing and canceling the metrics by which achievement (and its shortfalls and gaps) have long been monitored, declaring that tests are racist, barring their use for admission to selective schools and colleges, and curbing their use as outcome measures (e.g., states scrapping end-of-course exams) without substituting any other indicators of achievement. I understand the ESSA testing "holiday" as COVID-19 raged and schools closed in spring 2020.

But why did the College Board abruptly terminate the "SAT II" tests that for many college applicants served as a great way to demonstrate their mastery of particular subjects? Combine what was already a teacher-inspired (and parent-encouraged) "war on test-ing" with the allegation that tests worsen inequity and you have a grand example of shooting the messenger.

Third, we've been tinkering with the measures themselves, usually in the name of making them "fairer" and broadening access to them. Policy makers have built innumerable workarounds for kids who struggle with high school graduation tests. The College Board has twice "renormed" the SATs to bring the median back up to 500, and that practice has been joined by other score boosters, such as the invitation to mix and match one's top scores from the verbal and math sections on different test dates rather than simply adding the scores that one earns on a given day.

Fourth, we're inflating grades and scores to make things look better than they are. Grade inflation in high schools and colleges is widespread and well documented, now exacerbated by "no zero" grading policies and suchlike at the elementary- and middle-school levels. Standardized tests, too, can subtly be made to show higher scores—as many states did by setting their proficiency cut-points low—and even the National Assessment will gradually raise all boats as it supplies more "universal design" assists to test takers. (It may also artificially reduce learning gaps.)

Fifth and finally, we're scrapping consequences. In a no-fault, free-pass world that scoffs at both metrics and merit and practices the equivalent of social promotion and open admission for students, teachers, and schools alike, results-based accountability goes out the window. Out with it goes the central action-forcing element of standards-based education reform. Which is, in a sense, the ultimate erasure of achievement-related education problems and their replacement by an all's-well-and-don't-bother-telling-me-otherwise-much-less-doing-anything-about-it attitude. Which, let me say again, is pretty much what we faced from the education establishment after A Nation at Risk. The difference is that now it's coming from the political system, the culture, and many onetime reformers, too, and we don't appear to have any leaders pushing back against it. Instead, they're fussing about how many trillions more to pump into the schools.

12 – Carranza's Anti-White Racism & Asian Quotas vs. Racial Achievement Gaps

Average SAT Math Test Scores by Ethnicity, 1996 to 2016

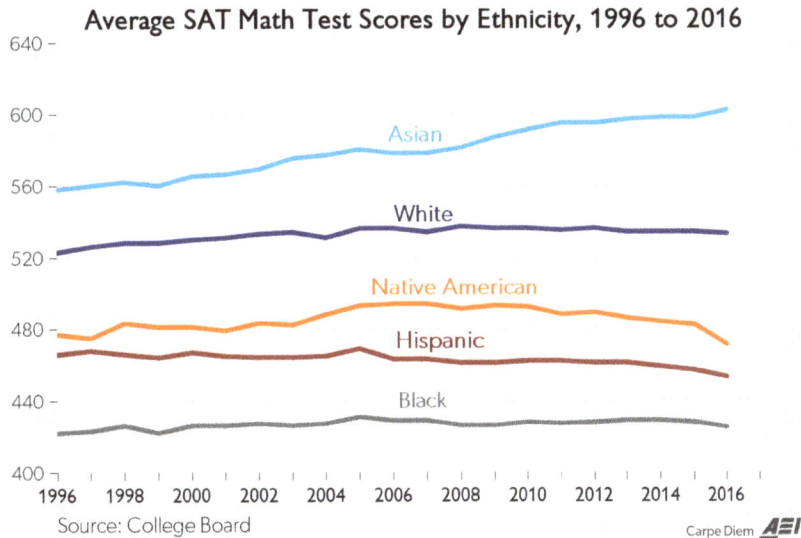

Source: College Board

Carpe Diem AEI

Per the Coleman Hughes "What the New Integrationists Fail to See" *City Journal* article in July 2018:

A liberal consensus has settled on the view that American schools must be more thoroughly integrated before black and Hispanic students can perform at the level of their white peers. The *New York Times* editorial board, for instance, recently described the city's elite high schools as "profoundly segregated," a state of affairs that calls to mind "the spirit of Jim Crow

If this statement was true, then we wouldn't see all-black schools that perform at the level of all-white or racially mixed schools. But such schools have existed for decades. Dunbar High, an all-black public school in Washington, D.C., outscored two out of three white academic high schools in the city as early as 1899. Neither destitute nor affluent, Dunbar students exceeded the national average on IQ tests, despite the school's paltry segregation-era funding. As Thomas Sowell quipped, "Dunbar was located within walking distance of the Supreme Court that essentially declared its existence impossible."

More recently, Success Academy in New York City, a chain of public charter schools that overwhelmingly serves poor black and Latino students, outperformed state averages on standardized tests in 2016. In 2018, Success middle-schoolers, though enrolled by lottery, were more than twice as likely as black and Latino students citywide to gain acceptance to New York's elite high schools.

The existence of schools like Dunbar and Success may surprise neo-integrationists, but it does not surprise those of us who reject the idea that black kids must sit near white kids in order to learn algebra.

A familiar neo-integrationist argument asserts that poor students do better in wealthy schools than they do in poor schools. Blacks are more likely to be poor than whites; therefore, we must integrate schools so that black kids can reap the benefits of going to school with kids from wealthier families. But this argument only works in a world where "black" is a synonym for "poor."

To the contrary, most black Americans aren't poor and most poor Americans aren't black. The same is true of Hispanics. If poverty is the real issue, then why not talk about it directly, instead of using race as a proxy?

According to the *Times*, "generations of poverty and racism" render modern-day blacks and Hispanics distinct from Asian-Americans—and thus not usefully compared— even though Asian-Americans have also experienced plenty of racism and poverty. But there is no reason to believe that racism and poverty cause academic apathy to begin with.

New York's Toxic Schools Chancellor and His Illiberal Policies

"What if the racism explanation for ongoing disparities is wrong as well?" asks Heather Mac Donald in her "Conformity to a Lie" *City Journal* article in the Summer of 2020:

What if racial economic and incarceration gaps cannot close without addressing personal responsibility and family culture—without a sea change in the attitudes that many inner-city black children bring with them to school regarding studying, paying attention in class, and respecting teachers, for example? What if the breakdown of the family is producing children with too little capacity to control their impulses and defer gratification?

With the university now explicitly committed to the racism explanation for all self-defeating choices, there will be little chance of changing course and addressing the behaviors that lie behind many racial disparities. The persistence of inequality will then produce a new round of quotas and self-incrimination—as well as more violence and anger. And the graduates of these ideologically monolithic universities will proceed further to dismantle our civilization in conformity to a lie.

Appointed by Mayor Bill de Blasio in May 2018 as New York City Department of Education and Schools Chancellor, Richard Carranza set to work accusing everyone around him of racism, degrading parents who dared speak up for their children. He focused primarily on destroying New York's best schools while doing absolutely nothing for the worst ones. His departure in February 2021 came too late for many kids across the city who have suffered under his leadership.

Obsessed with race and integration, and conforming to the lie, former New York City Department of Education and Schools Chancellor Richard Carranza has foisted an empirically baseless and socially destructive program on city schools. Three former high-ranking administrators have sued Carranza, claiming that they were demoted because they're white. It's an explosive charge, and one that must be proved—but the allegations reflect, at minimum, the intensifying racial tensions since Carranza took charge of the nation's largest, most complex public school system.

From the Bob McManus "New York's Toxic Schools Chancellor" *City Journal* article in June 2019:

The chancellor threw down the race gauntlet virtually on Day One. He picked fights with white parents on the Upper West Side and in Brooklyn's Park Slope, promised to achieve racial balance in the city's famous selective-admissions high schools by essentially "reforming" them out of existence, and commissioned a $23 million "implicit-bias" social-conditioning regimen that lies at the heart of the former administrators' $80 million lawsuit.

The program, first reported by the *New York Post*, assumes that New York City's majority-minority public school students struggle because the system's white-majority teachers and staff, consciously or otherwise, bring racist attitudes to work with them—and that this, rather than substandard teaching, administrative inertia, and non-classroom-related social issues, is the primary cause of classroom underperformance.

Carranza's reeducation program is the purported remedy, complete with racialist rhetoric, threats, and—if the suit is to be believed—race-based transfers and demotions. Eventually, all of the DoE's 130,000-plus teachers and administrators will be subjected to such social conditioning.

Yet the DoE, despite repeated requests, can produce no empirical evidence that implicit bias exists in New York City's schools. (This is likely because implicit bias itself is a dubious concept.) Rather than providing evidence of prejudice, the DoE justifies its program by pointing to a study prepared by an advocacy group, the Perception Institute, which itself makes no explicit case for racial bias in New York schools—or anywhere else, for that matter.

Instead, the institute asserts that inequality of public school outcomes across ethnic groups is all the evidence needed for racial bias. Its report, The Impact of Implicit Bias, Racial Anxiety, and Stereotype Threat on Student Outcomes, is an ambitious exercise in rhetorical gymnastics, but it makes no credible case for Carranza's race-driven social-conditioning policies.

"Racism [is] any act that even unwittingly tolerates, accepts or reinforces racially unequal opportunities or outcomes for children to learn and thrive," writes Glenn Singleton, another DoE consultant, paid $750,000 for his insights. This is nonsense. Unequal educational outcomes have many causes, ranging from social dislocation and inequitable resource distribution to uneven student ability and effort—and, of course, to differences in teaching competence. Without proper context for understanding them, disparate outcomes generally tell us little.

But one outcome dramatically undercuts Carranza's implicit-bias sophistry. The stunning success of most of the city's charter schools has rebuked conventional teaching practices since these schools first appeared two decades ago, and that goes double for Carranza's racial fixations.

Teacher ethnicity is essentially identical in charter and district schools—42 percent minority in charters versus 38 percent in traditional public schools. It's all but certain that a black or Hispanic charter school child will have a white teacher, since charter school kids are virtually all black or Hispanic. So whatever harm is done by implicit prejudices should be magnified in charter schools—yet charters for the most part prosper, while most district schools do not.

The chancellor appears oblivious to this.

Richard Carranza's Deflections

Per the Bob McManus "Richard Carranza's Deflections" *City Journal* article in July 2019:

Speaking at a recent middle school graduation, New York City Schools Chancellor Richard Carranza said, "We're going to move the agenda to serve our students, and people that have been very comfortable for a very long time doing absolutely nothing for the children that they're supposed to serve are going to feel uncomfortable."

Talk like this is cheap, and Carranza's approach—mandatory anti-bias training and charges that the opposition is racist—is deflection. He's covering up his lack of a programmatic approach to school improvement and the mayor's abandonment of any meaningful school accountability.

Quality is distributed inequitably within New York's school system, but not because of deep-seated racial bias among employees. Rather, it is the outcome of specific policies and programs that could be changed if the political will existed to do so.

For 40 years, each of Carranza's predecessors pursued policies that they believed would improve educational outcomes for the city's low-income minority children. Some were successful, others less so, but all were dedicated to educational equity. Carranza speaks constantly of his experience as a minority, as though he were the first to hold the chancellor's job in New York—but two-thirds of his predecessors dating back to 1978 were minorities, too.

Carranza does differ from them in one significant way: he has yet to articulate an approach to identifying the policies and people that stand in the way of meaningful school improvement. A generation ago, then-mayor Ed Koch's first chancellor, Frank Macchiarola, centered his efforts around affirmations that "all children can learn," and that "it is the responsibility of the public-school system to promote learning and equality for all children."

These statements, made in 1978, stood in direct conflict with the consensus among policymakers and social scientists that schools have little effect on student outcomes, relative to a student's family background.

Carranza's Classrooms of the Absurd

From the Bob McManus "Classrooms of the Absurd" *City Journal* article in July 2019:

The purveyors of higher-education theory have ginned up one more meritless rationalization for the subpar performance of traditional—read: heavily unionized—public schools in American cities. It's called "math equity," an emerging doctrine holding that schools can't teach city kids to count without first exorcising racism—or, as the National Council of Teachers of Mathematics declares, without forcing teachers to "reflect on their own identity, positions, and beliefs in regards to racist and sorting-based mechanisms."

According to The College Fix, an education-reform blog, math equity "refers to the growing insistence among educators that teaching math in the classroom comes with some inherently biased methodology that must be addressed. Proponents of 'math equity' also stress the importance of social justice issues such as race, diversity and gender in math education."

It's complete nonsense, as is so much of the effluvia now leaking from America's graduate schools of education, such as "implicit classroom bias"—the notion that white teachers can't instruct black students without first having subconscious racism washed from their brains. In New York City, the hustle has taken deep root in public schools, where it seems inevitable that "math equity" will emerge soon. That social-justice pedagogy is fatuous is demonstrated by the enduring success of Gotham's 216 charter schools, with their heavily minority student bodies, which have outperformed traditional public schools since the first one opened 20 years ago.

The reasons for charter schools' success are many and varied, but their triumph vaporizes the principle underlying the implicit-bias and math-equity evasions—that white teachers aren't equipped to teach minority kids without first adjusting their sensibilities. Meantime, New York City Schools Chancellor Richard Carranza pulls no punches on implicit bias—he calls it "white-supremacy culture"—and he's peeled $23 million off the Department of Education's budget to bring teachers up to speed on racial consciousness.

No significant difference in racial makeup exists between New York's traditional public school faculty—62 percent white, 38 percent minority—and its charter school faculty—58 percent white, 42 percent minority. Charter schools outperform traditional public schools regularly enough to discredit the idea that unconscious biases among white teachers seriously impede learning among minority kids. Official manipulation of performance metrics, both in Albany and at the DoE, sometimes makes direct comparisons a challenge, but the results are demonstrable: charters do it better.

New York's schools chancellor foregoes educational progress for cheap talk about bias

It's unclear why Carranza insists that implicit bias is such an obstacle in district schools, when it is clearly not a problem in the city's demographically indistinguishable charter schools. Repeated efforts over the last few weeks to get an answer to that question from the DoE yielded nothing. But it is clear that racialization is the only tool that Carranza brought to New York when Mayor Bill de Blasio hired him 15 months ago.

Whether it was his insistence that desegregation be a priority in a school system with an 86 percent minority student population, his threatening attitude toward the city's world-class selective high schools, his demotion of white DoE executives in favor of minority candidates, or his "implicit-bias" obsessions, it was evident from the start that Carranza did not come to New York to teach reading, writing, and arithmetic.

Reforming urban education means angering America's politically powerful teachers' unions, and nowhere is that truer than in New York City, where the United Federation of Teachers is the tail that wags the dog. Carranza is not about to challenge that arrangement—and even if he were, de Blasio and UFT president Michael Mulgrew wouldn't let him.

So the alternatives are racialized deflections, absurd educational theories, and intimidation. How much better it would be to accept the lessons being taught by charter schools and apply them to demographically similar traditional public schools. At least from the children's perspective, that would make more sense than pretending that "implicit bias" and "math equity" have something to tell us about urban public education.

Credit: New York Post – "Good riddance to Richard Carranza —
the worst schools chancellor in NYC history."

Re-Sinking CUNY

Per the Bob McManus "Re-Sinking CUNY" *City Journal* article in August 2019:

The City University of New York (CUNY) has announced plans to eliminate objective testing intended to determine which of its incoming students can do college-level work and which require remediation. Politico reports that CUNY chancellor Félix Matos Rodríguez plans to move the university "away from high-stakes testing" while "reducing its reliance on placement tests students must take to determine whether they need remedial interventions."

The City University of New York moves to eliminate objective testing—reversing the very reforms that had pulled it out of a long decline.

CUNY has been here once before—and the results nearly killed the university. Adjusted for euphemism, the decision points toward a reversal of 1990s-era reforms that pulled the university out of a long period of stagnation and decline.

Abandoning testing would represent an effective return to so-called open-admissions policies from the 1960s and 1970s. Those allowed virtually anybody who could stumble through CUNY's front door to enroll. Eventually, the university's classrooms filled up with unqualified students, severely degraded the quality of education, and reduced the once-great university to a national laughingstock.

CUNY's rescue, a joint venture of then-governor George Pataki, then-mayor Rudy Giuliani, and others, was not easily achieved—and it will doubtless take some time for the university's new admissions policy to start showing damaging effects. But that's just a matter of time.

The new policy is a huge win for teachers' unions and unaccountable bureaucrats because it greatly relieves pressure on New York City's public schools to do better. It was achieved with the silent acquiescence of Governor Andrew Cuomo, the only politician in the state who could have stopped it. Back in 2012, Cuomo declared himself the chief lobbyist for New York's public school students, and for a while, he really was—promoting and protecting charter schools, strengthening accountability for teachers and school administrators, and—critically—supporting student-performance benchmarks.

Cuomo was silent

Prior to his 2021 resignation amidst numerous allegations of sexual misconduct, Cuomo was silent, standing aside as the Albany legislature refused to allow New York City's astonishingly effective charter school movement to expand; as hard-won teacher-accountability reforms were peeled away and discarded; and as the state Board of Regents moved to abandon its 150-year-old practice of proficiency testing of high school students statewide. And now CUNY is following suit, embracing a new open-admissions era.

Perhaps most tragically, neither the governor nor any other political leader has had a word of remonstrance for Mayor Bill de Blasio or Schools Chancellor Richard Carranza as they cloak public school underperformance in a shroud of racialized rhetoric. If there is any common cause in public education in New York today, it is the top-to-bottom effort to bury evidence of failure.

Where success is encountered, it is all too often demonized or denied—as the state's hostility to charter schools shows, with the legislature refusing to authorize additional schools. The 50,000 families now on charter waiting lists are a standing embarrassment both to the city Department of Education and the United Federation of Teachers (UFT).

Objective evidence of classroom failure—high dropout and low graduation rates and embarrassingly dismal standardized test results—is camouflaged by grade inflation, increasingly inventive manipulation of performance standards, and the outright elimination of objective testing. CUNY's move to eliminate its test-driven remediation program fits this pattern, as does the Regents' pending decision to jettison its performance exams—itself the culmination of a two-decade process that saw the tests decline in quality from stringent to nearly pointless.

Part of the anti-testing momentum is cultural, driven by a national refusal to make adverse judgments of any sort. Part of it is ideological: public education is heavily populated with employees who insist that equality of outcome must trump equality of opportunity. When that doesn't happen, they blame a racially biased system—never mind that the enduring success of charter schools refutes that theory.

Let's face it: if more people were aware of how badly the school system performs, there's no telling what might happen. So the three R's must be replaced by the three D's—distraction, deflection, and deceit. The integrity of the City University of New York is just the latest casualty in New York' ongoing education tragedy.

Diversity—Unless You're Asian

From the Kenny Xu "Diversity—Unless You're Asian" *City Journal* article in June 2021:

The Supreme Court will soon consider whether to take up the long-awaited *Students for Fair Admissions v. Harvard* case, which pits Harvard's race-conscious admissions process against a group of Asian-American applicants who don't fit into Harvard's idea of "favored minorities." The central idea behind the case is whether Harvard's use of race to create what it sees as a "diverse" class runs afoul of the Fourteenth Amendment and Title VI of the Civil Rights Act.

If there is one area in which the American elite seems to be moving in lockstep, it is increasing racial diversity. Many Fortune 500 businesses now operate Diversity and Inclusion offices. Every selective college is quick to tout its "diverse student body." These initiatives sound good in theory, but the movement for racial diversity too often comes at the expense of hiring or admitting the most qualified candidate. Increasingly, the qualified candidate who gets denied is Asian-American—member of a minority group still considered, for diversity purposes, not in need of rescuing.

The reason why Harvard admissions officers don't consider Asian-Americans a "minority" for assistance purposes is because in their eyes, Asian-Americans are too successful to be helped. As a group, Asian-Americans are socioeconomically on par with whites; educationally, they outpace whites (though there is nationwide variation, just as there is among any racial group). Yet, Asian-Americans did not gain their status in this country because of inherited "privilege"—as many on the left allege whites have done—but through a relentless focus on academic preparation and self-sufficiency.

As I write in my book *An Inconvenient Minority: The Attack on Asian American Excellence and the Fight for Meritocracy,* "Asian American students compete hard for their educational opportunities . . . Poor and rich Asians alike study an average of thirteen hours per week, more than twice as much as the typical non-Hispanic white student who studies a mere 5.5 hours per week at home." Harvard prefers to ignore the reality of Asian-American students' hard work and preparation—that is, their merit—and instead treat them in the admissions process as if they were a privileged group.

The consequence of considering Asian-Americans unfavored minorities is clear: less qualified individuals from other social groups get their shot before Asian-Americans with higher qualifications do. According to Students for Fair Admissions' analysis, a black applicant to Harvard in the 40th academic percentile of all applicants has a higher chance of admission than an Asian-American in the 90th academic percentile. Asians in the 90th academic percentile are unfavored compared with Hispanics in the 60th percentile and whites in the 80th percentile as well.

This phenomenon extends to medical schools and other graduate schools. A 2017 American Enterprise Institute (AEI) study revealed that a black American with a 3.2–3.39 GPA and a 24–26 MCAT (under an older MCAT scoring system, since replaced) had a ten times higher chance of admission than an Asian-American with the same scores, and a higher chance than even an Asian-American with a 3.6–3.79 GPA and a 30–32 MCAT.

College admissions data reveal that Asians have been kept between 15 percent and 20 percent of admissions to Harvard. The same data reveal similar effective quotas for other top colleges, including Yale, MIT, and Stanford. As more Asians enter universities and perform well, universities resort to increasingly harsh racial balancing procedures against them.

Racial discrimination should not be tolerated at any professional level. Yet a vast network of racial discrimination exists at the university level against Asian-American students simply because they don't fit into a category of favored minority that other races and ethnicities enjoy. This is a form of racial engineering that excludes one minority in favor of another. It should end—and the Harvard case is an opportunity to end it.

Top High Schools Scrap Merit-Based Admission

Per the Larry Elder "Top High Schools Scrap Merit-Based Admission" Front Page Magazine story in March 2021:

San Francisco's Lowell High School is one of the top public high schools in California. Beginning with its 2021 freshman class, Lowell plans to switch from a merit-based admission system to that of a lottery. How good is Lowell? It ranked 68th nationwide by *U.S. News* in 2020.

About the school's reputation for academic excellence, the San Francisco Unified School District website says: "(Lowell) has been recognized 4 times as a National Blue Ribbon School, 8 times as a California Distinguished School, and one time as a Gold Ribbon School. Lowell has been consistently ranked #1 in the Western Region for the number of Advanced Placement Exams given."

How did students get admitted to Lowell? The SFUSD website still says: "Admission to Lowell is competitive and merit-based, serving students from throughout the city who demonstrate academic excellence and are motivated to pursue a rigorous college preparatory program."

About 60% of the student body is Asian, 18% white and1.8% Black. This is apparently a problem and explains why the SFUSD recently unanimously voted to admit students via this lottery system. According to *The Wall Street Journal*, the "problem" is Asian American excellence: "One school board commissioner, Alison Collins, has called merit-based admissions 'racist.' The real problem progressives have with Lowell is that too many Asian-Americans are passing the entrance exam."

This brings us to Thomas Jefferson High School of Science and Technology in Fairfax, Virginia, often the top-rated public high school in the country. TJ also plans to drop their admissions test and are debating on how to replace it.

The problem? Over 70% of the student body is Asian American.

Fairfax County Public School Board Superintendent Scott Brabrand proposed a "merit-based" lottery for 400 of the 500 spots in the school's classes. About that alternative, *The Washington Post* said: "The lottery proposal spurred controversy from the moment Brabrand introduced it on Sept. 15, 2020. He promised it would cause TJ's student body—which is more than 70% Asian and about 20% white, with single-digit percentages of Black and Hispanic students—to more closely resemble the demographics of Fairfax County."

So much for merit. So much for a colorblind society.

Let's assume that Lowell and TJ's competitive merit-based admissions policy resulted in a student-body population that is predominately Black, as is the case with the National Basketball Association. In 2020, the league that prides itself on its racial "wokeness" consisted of 81% Black players and 18% white players. In the NFL, in 2019, approximately 59% of players were Black. As to Major League Baseball, UPI, in 2019, wrote: "By 2017, 27.4 percent of MLB players were Latinos, according to the date compiled by the Society of American Baseball Research." This is roughly 50% more than percentage of the population of Latinos in America.

To correct for these "racial imbalances " and the "underrepresentation" of some groups, suppose professional sports organizations decided, like Lowell High, to use a lottery system? The new rules would prevent the Black player-heavy NBA, the Black player-heavy NFL and the Latino-heavy MLB from drafting the best college players, provided, of course, they had the misfortune of being born Black or Latino.

In 2012, Pew Research Center polled Asian Americans and asked their reaction to the statement, "Most people who want to get ahead can make it if they're willing to work hard." Sixty-nine percent of Asian Americans agreed, as opposed to 58% of the general population. Pew explained: "Compared with the general public, Asian Americans stand out for their success in education and career. Most also believe that the U.S. offers more opportunities and freedoms than their countries of origin. A large majority of Asian Americans believe that hard work pays off and most place a strong emphasis on higher education, career and family."

Why punish the best college players because "too many" Blacks excel in sports? Why punish Asian American students for the crime of working hard and outperforming others academically?

Grievance Proxies

From the Heather Mac Donald "Grievance Proxies" *City Journal* article in May 2019:

For decades, the College Board defended the SAT, which it writes and administers, against charges that the test gives an unfair advantage to middle-class white students. No longer. Under relentless pressure from the racial-preferences lobby, the Board has now caved to the anti-meritocratic ideology of "diversity."

The Board will calculate for each SAT-taker an "adversity score" that purports to measure a student's socioeconomic position, according to the *Wall Street Journal*. Colleges can use this adversity index to boost the admissions ranking of allegedly disadvantaged students who otherwise would score too poorly to be considered for admission.

The College Board plans to introduce a new "adversity score" as a backdoor to racial quotas in college admissions. Advocates of this change claim that it is not about race. That is a fiction.

In fact, the SAT adversity score is simply the latest response on the part of mainstream institutions to the seeming intractability of the racial academic-achievement gap. If that gap did not exist, the entire discourse about "diversity" would evaporate overnight.

The average white score on the SAT (1,123 out of a possible 1,600) is 177 points higher than the average black score (946), approximately a standard deviation of difference. This gap has persisted for decades. It is not explained by socioeconomic disparities.

The Journal of Blacks in Higher Education reported in 1998 that white students from households with incomes of $10,000 or less score better on the SAT than black students from households with incomes of $80,000 to $100,000. In 2015, students with family incomes of $20,000 or less (a category that includes all racial groups) scored higher on average on the math SAT than the average math score of black students from all income levels. The University of California has calculated that race predicts SAT scores better than class.

Those who rail against "white privilege" as a determinant of academic achievement have a nagging problem: Asians. Asian students outscore white students on the SAT by 100 points; they outscore blacks by 277 points.

Asian elementary school students vastly outperform every other racial and ethnic group

It is not Asian families' economic capital that vaults them to the top of the academic totem pole; it is their emphasis on scholarly effort and self-discipline. Every year in New York City, Asian elementary school students vastly outperform every other racial and ethnic group on the admissions test for the city's competitive public high schools, even though a disproportionate number of them come from poor immigrant families.

Colleges pay lip service to socioeconomic diversity, but that concept is inevitably a surrogate for race. Colleges have repeatedly rejected admissions schemes that purport to substitute socioeconomic preferences for racial preferences, on the ground that those socioeconomic schemes do not yield enough "underrepresented minorities."

Harvard admits richer black students with a lower academic ranking over poorer but more qualified white and Asian applicants; it admits more than two times as many middle-class blacks as "disadvantaged" blacks and confers no admissions preference to disadvantaged blacks compared with their non-disadvantaged racial peers.

The SAT's critics notwithstanding, no alternative measure of student capacity exists that better predicts student success. "Leadership," "character," "persistence"—all these earlier attempts to come up with a more politically palatable proxy for racial preferences are far less valid as a measure of academic capacity than the SAT. The College Board's "adversity score" will be no different. And it will subject its alleged beneficiaries to the same problem as overt racial preferences—academic mismatch.

Students admitted to a selective college with significantly weaker academic credentials than the school norm will, on average, struggle to keep up in their classes. Many will switch out of demanding majors like the STEM fields; a significant portion will drop out of college entirely.

Had those artificially preferred students enrolled in a college for which they were academically prepared, like their non-preferred peers, they would have a much higher chance of graduating in their chosen field of study. There is no shame or handicap in graduating from a non-elite college.

The proponents of racial preferences, like all "woke" advocates, claim to be against privilege. Yet those anti-privilege warriors adopt a blatantly elitist view of college, holding, in essence, that attending a name-brand college is the only route to life success.

The College Board's adversity score will give students a boost for coming from a high-crime, high-poverty school and neighborhood, according to the *Wall Street Journal*. Being raised by a single parent will also be a plus factor. Such a scheme penalizes the bourgeois values that make for individual and community success.

The solution to the academic achievement gap lies in cultural change, not in yet another attack on a meritocratic standard

Black parents need to focus as relentlessly as Asian parents on their children's school attendance and performance. They need to monitor homework completion and grades. Academic achievement must no longer be stigmatized as "acting white." And a far greater percentage of black children must be raised by both their mother and their father, to ensure the socialization that prevents classrooms from turning into scenes of chaos and violence.

At present, thanks to racial preferences, many black high school students know that they don't need to put in as much scholarly effort as non-"students of color" to be admitted to highly competitive colleges. The adversity score will only reinforce that knowledge. That is not a reality conducive to life achievement.

The only guaranteed beneficiaries of this new scheme are the campus diversity bureaucrats. They have been given another assurance of academically handicapped students who can be leveraged into grievance, more diversity sinecures, and lowered academic standards.

An Affirmative Action Endgame?

Per the Joel Zinberg "An Affirmative Action Endgame?" *City Journal* article in January 2022:

The Supreme Court has agreed to hear two cases challenging racial preferences in university admissions. It's an important move that could pave the way toward restoring the equality principles that our Constitution and laws afford. The Court granted petitions for writs of certiorari in lawsuits brought by the nonprofit Students for Fair Admissions against Harvard University and the University of North Carolina and consolidated the cases into one.

Lower courts had rejected both challenges, citing Supreme Court decisions that allow colleges and universities to consider race in a narrowly tailored way to promote diversity. The Trump administration had backed the Harvard plaintiffs and initiated a case alleging discrimination against Asian and white students at Yale. The Biden administration dropped the Yale lawsuit and filed a brief urging the Supreme Court not to take the Harvard case.

The Harvard case alleged that the school discriminated against Asian-Americans by accepting them at lower rates than any other racial group, while giving preference to black and Hispanic students with lower grades. Though Harvard is a private rather than state institution, it is barred from discriminating on the basis of race by Title VI of the Civil Rights Act of 1964 (42 U.S.C. 2000d), which prohibits discrimination by "any program or activity receiving Federal financial assistance."

Harvard admissions officers consistently gave Asian-American applicants the lowest marks on a subjective "personal rating." Nonetheless, the First Circuit Court of Appeals held that "Harvard's limited use of race in its admissions process in order to achieve diversity . . . is consistent with the requirements of Supreme Court precedent."

The North Carolina case claimed that the state-run university gave preferences to minority students to the detriment of Asian and white applicants. Three months ago, a federal District Court held that the school's program was a legitimate attempt to produce a diverse student body. The plaintiffs appealed directly to the Supreme Court, hoping that the justices would hear the North Carolina case with the Harvard case.

The consolidated cases present an opportunity to reverse more than 40 years of state-sanctioned racial discrimination in higher education

The Supreme Court will have to narrow or reverse a long line of judicial precedents allowing universities to favor selected racial and ethnic groups over others in admissions policies by claiming that they are promoting diversity.

The precedents date back to the 1978 Supreme Court case of *Regents of the University of California v. Bakke*, in which an applicant to medical school claimed he was unfairly denied admission due to the medical school's practice of reserving 16 of 100 seats for minority students, some of whom had lesser academic credentials than he did. The Court held that institutions could use race as a factor in admissions in pursuit of the purported educational benefits of having a diverse student body, but also that they could not employ a quota system.

Since then, universities have dropped affirmative-action programs with overt quota systems but continued programs that grant racial preferences. Several Supreme Court decisions have upheld such programs: Gratz v. Bollinger(2003), Fisher v. University of Texas (2013), and Fisher v. University of Texas, or "Fisher II" (2016) dealt with undergraduate programs; Grutter v. Bollinger (2003) looked at law school admissions.

The court decided the most recent case, Fisher II, by a 4-3 vote (Justice Elena Kagan was recused and Justice Antonin Scalia had recently died). Only two of the four-justice majority—Stephen Breyer and Sonia Sotomayor—remain on the Court. We can expect Justice Kagan to join them in upholding affirmative action. But the three dissenting justices in Fisher II—Samuel Alito and Clarence Thomas, along with Chief Justice John Roberts—joined by newer Justices Neil Gorsuch, Brett Kavanaugh, and Amy Coney Barrett, comprise a majority that may cast a skeptical eye on racial preferences.

The time for a change in direction is long overdue. Both Justice Sandra Day O'Connor, writing for the majority in Grutter, and Justice Ruth Bader Ginsburg, writing in concurrence, respectively expressed a hope that affirmative action could end within 25 years or a generation. Grutter was decided 19 years ago. Since then, conscious, institutional bias against minorities has been largely eliminated, and most institutions are committed, perhaps excessively so, to eliminating even unconscious bias.

State-sponsored discrimination against any group in the name of diversity has become a less compelling interest than it was in the time of Grutter. We should reassert the precepts of the Equal Protection Clause to shield all races and ethnicities from unfairness. As Chief Justice Roberts wrote in 2007 in reviewing a Seattle school system affirmative-action plan, "The way to stop discrimination on the basis of race is to stop discriminating on the basis of race."

13 – Parental Rights & Alumni Activists For School Choices & Free Speech Alliances

Credit: Shelley Slebrch and other angry parents at Loudoun County School Board meeting – REUTERS/Evelyn Hockstein.

From the Jay Greene, Ph.D. and James Paul "Time for the School Choice Movement to Embrace the Culture War" The Heritage Foundation article in February 2022:

Conventional wisdom holds that the culture war is bad for school choice advocates. But, as a nationally representative survey shows, it could be extremely helpful for promoting education scholarship accounts, tax credit scholarships, and school vouchers. Whether education reform organizations embrace cultural debates or not, the culture war is here to stay. School choice advocates are armed with an obvious solution. They should not squander the opportunity to use it.

Critical race theory (CRT) and the high-profile projects pushing the radical ideology's discriminatory ideas, such as *The New York Times* Magazine's 1619 Project, are trying to divide Americans by skin color and pit them against each other.

The cultural fissures are manifesting in education, with heated arguments about curricula and classroom activism. Some observers expected that tensions would subside with the election of President Joe Biden, but debates—about CRT, restrictive coronavirus measures, and the general culture—appear more heated with each passing month. Prolonged school closures, mask mandates, pornographic books in school libraries, the FBI designating parents as "domestic terrorists," and racial essentialism for third graders have elevated education policy to the forefront of America's culture war.

Rather than seeing these cultural divides as an opportunity to highlight a problem that expanded school choice might help to solve, education reform organizations have responded by either endorsing social justice ideology or ignoring the controversies. Many foundations are comfortable declaring that "Black Lives Matter" and drafting canned press releases about diversity, equity, and inclusion (DEI).

Very few education reform advocacy groups have been willing to emphasize the ever-increasing cultural division in public schools as part of a strategy for advancing school choice.

The inclination of the education reform movement to embrace woke perspectives, or simply to avoid cultural controversy, is counterproductive.

Time for the School Choice Movement to Embrace the Culture War

The time is now for the school choice movement to embrace the culture war. Education reform organizations have traditionally preferred to stay above the cultural fray, which is partly driven by the fear that engaging in cultural debates would inflame tensions and make school choice seem less appealing to potential allies.

Such concerns are overblown. To the contrary, school choice offers a sensible resolution to cultural debates. School choice gives parents what they want, regardless of which side they are on—more control over their children's education. And, it acknowledges that parents have pluralistic views about which values to instill in their children. Of course, nearly all parents tend to share some essential beliefs—for example, that schools should teach the "success sequence."

Advocacy groups would be foolish not to promote choice as a solution that can connect large majorities of parents with schools that align with their values—especially when public schools are not meeting their needs.

Moreover, it is hard to imagine how espousing a positive vision of education freedom can be decoupled from cultural issues. The culture wars are not going away. The forces driving these conflicts will continue even if education reform organizations continue to put their heads in the sand and pretend those issues do not exist.

Rather than embracing the woke agenda or ignoring the subject, the best arrow in their quiver is one they have so far been unwilling to deploy: a ready-made policy solution that can bring peace to cultural conflicts, namely, parent choice in education, school choice.

Empowering Parents with School Choice Reduces Wokeism in Education

As per the Jay Greene, Ph.D. and Ian Kingsbury "Empowering Parents with School Choice Reduces Wokeism in Education" The Heritage Foundation report in November 2022:

American K–12 education is currently mired in an unmistakable radical leftward lurch. Whether changing the pronouns of students without informing their parents, eradicating academic standards in the name of "equity," infusing ahistorical curricula meant to engender contempt for the United States, or lobbying the Department of Justice to label anyone who opposes any of the former "domestic terrorists," progressive activists are increasingly able to use America's schools as a tool for advancing their woke agenda.

Those concerned about these trends have been in debate about how best to curb this "wokeism" in education. Some argue that empowering parents by expanding school choice is the best strategy for re-aligning schools' values and priorities with those of parents. As Inez Feltscher Stepman put it: "School choice is the only reform that finally connects parental discontent with the only thing the people running large, well-funded systems actually care about: a diminished paycheck."

Since parents, on average, demand far less wokeism than schools supply, shifting more power to parents will reverse this leftward lurch of the education system. Poll results confirm that most Americans hold negative views of woke classroom endeavors, such as the 1619 Project and critical race theory, and indeed opposition to race essentialism, gender theory, and other progressive projects helped to fuel the rapid expansion of school choice programs across the country over the past two years.

However, the degree to which school choice programs are designed to satisfy parental rather than elite preferences might make a critical difference. Indeed, some conservative skeptics of school choice are raising alarm that choice could exacerbate wokeism in American schools if choice programs succumb to regulatory capture by the radical Left.

These skeptics tend to favor direct political action, such as banning the teaching of critical race theory in schools, over expanding school choice as the preferred tactic for combatting wokeism

Of course, there is no reason why people could not pursue both strategies, empowering parents through the expansion of school choice and advancing policies that directly limit political indoctrination. But movements must make choices about which arguments to emphasize and how best to allocate political resources, so the debate over strategy remains important.

The Great Parent Revolt

From the Katharine Cornell Gorka "The Great Parent Revolt" The Heritage Foundation report in August 12, 2021: As overreach in classrooms by progressive school administrators, nonprofits and the federal government has reached new heights, and parents are stepping up to fight back.

Moms for Liberty, Informed Parents of California, EdFirstNC, NJ Parental Rights, No Left Turn in Education and Parents Against Critical Theory are just a few of the hundreds of new parent groups that have emerged across the country in recent months (see the Appendix for links to each of their websites). Many parents have become education activists because of schools' failure to bring children back into the classroom or their continued imposition of mask mandates.

Others are engaging because of the content being taught. Whether it's age-inappropriate sex education, critical race theory, or anti-American history, parents are seeing more of what their children are learning—thanks to COVID's virtual learning—and they don't like it. As a result, parents are organizing, speaking out, and pushing back, and they are having a noticeable impact.

Some of the most effective efforts have begun with individual parents who reached a boiling point and decided to speak out. Mom and investigative journalist A.P. Dillon helped expose critical race theory training in Wake County, N.C., public schools. Elana Fishbein was a lone parent in Lower Marion, Pa. who objected to content in her children's curriculum, which, in her words, "described 'whiteness' as an entitlement to steal land, garner riches, and get special treatment on equity and race." That letter reached a national audience when Tucker Carlson invited her onto his Fox News Channel show.

Critical Race Theory

Andrew Gutmann also made national news when he sent a letter to 650 families criticizing New York City's Brearley School, which his daughter attended, for its obsession with race and for "desecrating the legacy of Dr. Martin Luther King Jr."

Meanwhile, the 11-minute takedown of a Putnam County, N.Y., school board by Tatiana Ibrahim has well over 1 million views on YouTube.

Individual parents speaking out have helped to kick off what is proving to be a rapidly growing parent revolt. They have helped to galvanize others who were either unaware of the bad content or too afraid to speak out. After Elana Fishbein appeared on Carlson's show, hundreds of parents across the country reached out to her on social media. And today No Left Turn in Education has 35 chapters across the country and is growing.

When Tina Descovich and Tiffany Justice finished their terms as school board members in Florida, they decided to form Moms for Liberty to teach parents how to serve as watchdogs of their local schools boards. When they established the organization in January of 2021, they had intended it to serve as a statewide entity in Florida. But today, just over six months later, they have 65 plus chapters nationwide and have more applications for new chapters.

Wherever these parent groups have emerged, they are finding creative ways to challenge the attempted progressive takeover of K-12 education. Sloan Rachmuth, founder of EdFirstNC, has held webinars and in-person events to educate parents on how the North Carolina Department of Public Instruction rewrote the social studies standards for K-12 based on critical race theory. Patti Hidalgo Menders, a mother of five boys in Loudoun County, Va., read aloud to school board members obscene passages from Tiffany D. Jackson's "Monday's Not Coming" and Gretchen McNeil's "#Murder Trending."

Educating parents is a critical part of the work

As Hannah Smith, a newly elected board member in Texas explained, "There were a lot of people who had, by their own admission, just kind of fallen asleep. They just thought we've got these award-winning schools, we've got this awesome community, everything's going well. I don't need to show up at board meetings. I don't need to be worried about what's happening in the schools."

In addition to raising the alarm about what's happening in the schools, parent groups are challenging school boards through recalls—for example in Loudoun County and San Francisco—and by actively running candidates for school board, with some notable successes.

When the Carroll, Texas, Independent School District introduced a Cultural Competence Action Plan, which would require "social justice training" and establish a "diversity and inclusion" week, at the cost of $3 million over 10 years, local father Cameron Bryan decided to run for school board and won.

As Bob Lubke, from Civitas, has written, "Historically, conservatives have not been as vocal about down-ballot races. That's a mistake. Education is often the largest expenditure for state and local government. Local school board members not only make budget and policy decisions that impact the day-to-day operations of how our schools are financed and administered but also how our children are educated. Few local positions are as consequential."

With the growing anger over the indoctrination of their children, parents have become much more engaged in school board elections, and it is having an impact: In 2021, the number of board member recalls has more than doubled from previous years, according to Ballotpedia.

Parents are also initiating lawsuits as an important tool in their fight against overly progressive schools

According to John Murawski at RealClearInvestigations, about a dozen lawsuits and administrative complaints have been filed since 2018. A new wave of lawsuits is being driven by the recent surge of concern among parents over critical race theory and its implementation in schools.

The first lawsuit against CRT was filed on Dec. 22, 2020, in Nevada. Gabrielle Clark and her son William brought the suit on the grounds that the school violated William's free speech and due process rights. According to the No Left Turn in Education website: "the Sociology of Change teaching in his civic classes required him to publicly reveal his race, gender, religious, and sexual identities, and then attach derogatory labels such as 'privileged' or 'oppressor' to those identities. Students were then asked to 'undo' and 'unlearn' their 'beliefs, attitudes, and behaviors that stem from oppression.' William and his mother objected, and he was punished with a failing grade and his graduation was at risk."

The lawsuit was brought by a coalition of organizations, led by The Discovery Institute's Center on Wealth and Poverty, with support from the Southeastern Legal Foundation, Upper Midwest Law Center, Schoolhouserights.org, and others. According to CRT expert Chris Rufo, several more lawsuits are in preparation.

In June 2021, Patti Hidalgo Menders, Scott Mineo and several others, represented by the Liberty Justice Center, filed a lawsuit against the Loudoun County School Board (*Menders v. Loudoun County School Board*). On June 23, 2020, LCPS published its Action Plan to Combat Systemic Racism. The plan included the creation of a Student Ambassador Equity Program, which was only open to "students of color" and those with "a passion for social justice." The lawsuit also states, "The 'Share, Speak-up, Speak-out' meetings in which Student Equity Ambassadors are entitled to take part are not an everyday opportunity for student/faculty engagement. Rather they are part of an explicit initiative to stifle speech under the guise of eliminating 'bias'."

Parents Are a Vital Part of Kids' Civic Education

While 26 states have introduced or passed bills to reject the teaching of critical race theory, it will likely be the courts that ultimately decide whether it fundamentally violates American principles, and even in that process, the role of parents will be pivotal.

As John Yoo, a law professor at the University of California, Berkeley, recently said, "I think that what's going to happen is that there have to be more parents, more communities involved, challenging these kinds of efforts to use race explicitly in the schools or in their local governments, and those will generate the cases that get to the Supreme Court. And the Supreme Court can make clear, as I think it should, that race is just never to be used in the government and in state and local at all, for whatever reason, whether it's allegedly benign or it's for malign reasons."

The bottom line is that education in America will likely never be the same, thanks to the Great Parent Revolt of 2021, and that's good news.

For decades, many parents have outsourced the raising of their children to the schools, trusting that administrators, school board members, and teachers would share their values. We blindly believed that schools would care about our children as much as we do. We believed that if the teaching went astray, if the books were inappropriate, or if the civics and history were a little un-American, what we did at home would serve as a gentle correction and all would be well. The past two years have taught us how wrong we were.

Thankfully, parents are reengaging in their children's education and reasserting their rightful place in decisions about curriculum and content. The question will be whether their efforts are strong enough and sufficiently sustained to win the battle against the radical tide of educators, nonprofits and federal education bureaucrats who are working to rewrite American history.

Education Freedom Report Card: State Rankings for Parents

From the "Education Freedom Report Card: State Rankings for Parents" The Heritage Foundation report in September 2022:

Education is a top priority to millions of American families, and parents should be empowered to choose a safe and effective education for their children. To serve that goal, The Heritage Foundation has published the Education Freedom Report Card, to serve as a guide for assessing education freedom in each state.

There are 76 private school choice programs in the U.S. Our report card measures four broad categories (School Choice, Transparency, Regulatory Freedom, and Spending) that encompass more than two dozen discrete factors.

In this inaugural 2022 edition of the Education Freedom Report Card, Florida is the top-ranked state across the board. Families looking for a state that embraces education freedom, respects parents' rights, and provides a decent ROI for taxpayers should look no further than The Sunshine State.

In second place overall inn 2022 in our report card is Arizona, a state that will certainly give Florida a run for its money next year in light of its recently expanded, now-universal ESA program. Idaho takes third place overall, thanks in large part to a strong ROI for taxpayer dollars and high levels of transparency to parents.

At the other end of the spectrum, New Jersey, New York, and the District of Columbia came in 49th, 50th, and 51st, respectively, doing little to provide transparency, accountability, and choice to families. This report card sets a high bar for achieving and maintaining education freedom in the states. Our goal is that this annual ranking of states will not only inform parents and policymakers of what their states do well and where they need improvement, but that it will spur necessary and lasting reform.

For a list of state rankings please follow the All State Scores – The Heritage Foundation link in the Appendix.

A Necessary Intervention

Progressive critics insist that the campus free speech crisis is a right-wing fabrication, but the data show otherwise. Why, and how, the government should step in to reform universities reflects these uncomfortable facts as noted by the Eric Kaufmann "A Necessary Intervention" *City Journal* article in March 2021:

This is an urgent problem for policymakers. The intolerance and censorship that began on campus are now spilling out into the wider world of elite institutions, from tech firms and major news organizations to corporations and government agencies. Universities are a crucial site of struggle that will help set the tone for the wider culture of elite institutions. Policymakers at the state and federal level should push back against the tide of progressive authoritarianism and political discrimination on campus.

Two main groups, which I term "libertarian" and "interventionist," advocate different approaches to the issue. Libertarians place their faith in cultural change, working to convince progressives and administrators that free speech is an important value that has protected the Left in the past and continues to do so on select issues, such as the study of the Middle East and Israel.

Heterodox Academy, founded in 2015, is at the forefront of this intellectual project. Many liberal writers are also on board, such as those who signed a much-publicized letter in defense of free expression that ran in *Harper's Magazine*. Commentators such as Helen Pluckrose and Yascha Mounk believe that a liberal Left can be mobilized to resist the illiberal Left within elite institutions.

Some libertarian-leaning thinkers, such as Foundation for Individual Rights in Education (FIRE) president Greg Lukianoff, believe that when universities are publicly ranked on free speech, these signals can shape consumer behavior and provide incentives for change.

Good ideas, practices, and universities can drive out the bad without the need for government intervention, they argue, giving rise to a new academic culture that respects free speech. FIRE helps the accused with legal advice and assists in legal cases to help some of those whose rights have been violated by universities. In Britain, the Free Speech Union has recently taken up a similar role and is now branching into the United States.

Though welcoming libertarian efforts, interventionists believe that only government policy can alter the incentive structure that currently permits both hard and soft authoritarianism—overt silencing of dissenting views, and self-censorship amid an unwelcoming environment—in universities.

While many interventionists ultimately aspire to build what Lukianoff terms a "free speech culture" that makes intervention redundant, they believe that sacrificing young scholars (and potential scholars) while permitting today's campus biases to continue to distort scholarship, all in the hope that change may be forthcoming, is both unjust to the victims of this climate and a waste of society's resources. They note that progressive illiberalism, which began to be institutionalized in the 1980s with speech codes, is now nearly four decades old and shows no signs of disappearing.

The interventionists have the better argument

Unfortunately, universities seem unable to reform from within. Self-censorship has become far more likely as dissenters seek to avoid the university's disciplinary apparatus, leaving authoritarian structures and practices untouched. Governments should therefore act to protect the freedom of dissenting faculty and students on campus.

In any case, the role of government intervention should be to enforce the laws that today's universities break routinely. For instance, around nine in ten American universities currently maintain speech codes that violate the First Amendment.

An interventionist approach would require universities to adopt the Chicago Principles, or a set of academic freedom principles that is functionally equivalent, and to remove or amend all noncompliant speech codes and internal policies. Yet such a requirement would not itself be sufficient to ensure academic freedom, as universities can simply ignore such principles in practice when they collide with cherished progressive values around emotional safety.

To be effective, legislation must mandate regular audits of individual universities for academic freedom violations. Repeat violators would be fined. Rather than wait for aggrieved parties to go through a disciplinary process and take their university to court to get justice—with all the chilling effects this process entails for defendants and those witnessing their tribulations—regulators would actively ensure that state-funded universities obey the law. Legislation should also empower plaintiffs to circumvent university proceedings by appealing to an ombudsman in cases where their free speech was violated.

While lawmakers should keep regulations to a minimum, they must use them as much as is necessary to ensure the protection of legally guaranteed rights. Progressive activists possess a deep influence on university governance that can be checked only by proactive, vigilant, and persistent external intervention. Fines and negative publicity from audits would discourage repeated violations of academic freedom.

Pro-freedom political parties should appoint people to regulatory roles who believe in the mission of academic freedom and are willing to confront universities as needed. Regulators should apprise students and staff of their academic freedoms and rights each year to prevent universities from leaving the accused in the dark about the scope of their rights. And to prevent harassment and chilling effects, regulators should direct universities to impose time, place, and manner restrictions, enforced by security and appropriate punishments, on any protest directed against an individual member of staff that goes beyond the law to interfere with speech.

Universities should therefore be obliged to reject all claims that stand little chance of overriding free speech protections, and to desist from notifying the accused unless the complaint clears a threshold of likeliness to succeed.

Bias-response teams or equity complaints hotlines, where they exist, should act only in cases that pass legal thresholds for interdicting expressive freedom. Reports of how often complaints have been taken forward and accusers notified, as well as the complaints' success rates, would form part of the annual OFS audit of universities. The goal is to reduce false positives to zero, and to make free speech the starting presumption—with the burden of proof on those who would override it.

Though universities already submit to a range of government regulations, they would likely oppose these

Universities' political tenor, and the ideological power of progressive activists and administrators within them, makes them likely to implement eagerly and maximally progressive-leaning government regulations such as the Department of Education's 2011 "Dear Colleague" letter on sexual violence. But the same ideological forces are likely to resist free speech guidance

The Trump administration's Title IX reforms and implementation of a "free speech hotline" were steps in the right direction.

State governments in the U.S. have an important role to play here. Eleven states have passed laws against so-called "free speech zones" that protect speech only in a few designated areas.

The Goldwater Institute's 2017 proposals seek to audit colleges to ensure that they uphold their free speech obligations and penalize those who disrupt speech; four states have adopted them. Rolling out similar efforts across other states should be a higher legislative priority for state legislatures, as free speech debates increasingly have ramifications beyond academia.

The problem of progressive free speech restrictions, as Donald Downs notes, is entering its fourth decade. It cannot be compared with episodic periods of speech restriction in the recent past. After all, McCarthyism burned out relatively quickly. Today's universities break the law repeatedly, abridging the rights of political minorities in a way that we would not tolerate for discrimination against, say, Sikhs or critics of the police. And the problem extends beyond the campus, as illiberal practices migrate to other institutions. Now is the time to act.

The Civics Alliance: A Toolkit

From the "The Civics Alliance: A Toolkit" National Association of Scholars article in March 2021:

The National Association of Scholars is pleased to release a toolkit for citizens concerned about strengthening traditional civics education and defending the civics curriculum from being taken over by "New Civics," "action civics," or any similar radical initiative. This toolkit informs American citizens about the principles and the programs of the Civics Alliance's Open Letter and Curriculum Statement.

What is the Civics Alliance and why is it needed?

The Civics Alliance, which has been formed to educate citizens about the strengths of traditional civics and the deleterious effects of action civics, will unite education reformers, policymakers, and every citizen of the United States who wants to preserve civics education that teaches the founding principles and documents of the United States, the key events of American history, the structure of our self-governing federal republic, the functions of government at all levels, how our governing institutions work, and the spirit of liberty and tolerance that should animate our private interactions with our fellow citizens.

Such civics education should teach students to take pride in what they share as Americans—an exceptional heritage of freedom, a republic that has succeeded in making liberty a fundamental principle of our government, and the joyful accomplishments of their common national culture.

By the time students leave high school, they should comprehend the rule of law, the Bill of Rights, elections, elected office, checks and balances, trial by jury, grand juries, civil rights, military service, and many other points in the traditional American civics curriculum. College undergraduates, and especially graduates of education schools, should also learn how these civic fundamentals emerged from Western Civilization, including through developments in Western political theory and American history.

This conception of civics education should not be controversial. The Civics Alliance is necessary because American civics education is under sustained assault by radical activists. Their New Civics uses the pedagogy of service-learning to teach action civics, also known by names such as civic engagement, civic learning, community engagement, global civics, and project-based civics. The New Civics threatens to replace traditional civics education with Neo-Marxist "social justice" propaganda, vocational training for left-wing activism, and techniques adapted from Alinsky-style community organizing for use in the classroom.

What can be done?

Citizens can learn about three areas of concern to the Civics Alliance.

Federal engagement: Citizens can immediately contact their federal Senators and Members of Congress to express their opinion on the Civics Learning Act of 2021 and the Civics Secures Democracy Act, two federal bills which will channel enormous amounts of money to support action civics. The weblinks above connect to two articles by Stanley Kurtz, which summarize the likely effects of these bills.

State engagement: Citizens can immediately organize to express their opinion in each state of The Partisanship Out of Civics Act (POCA). POCA not only will disable much action civics on the state level but also will prevent state bureaucracies from taking federal money that supports action civics—a prohibition of great practical import, should either the Civics Learning Act of 2021 or the Civics Secures Democracy Act become law.

Gather information: Action civics advocates are working to pass bills that fund, require, or otherwise advance action civics in states throughout the union, and we simply do not know what all these efforts are. Citizens should search the list of proposed bills (via means such as LegiScan) to see which bills are supporting action civics. (Keyword searches for terms such as history, history education, civics, and civics education will probably be helpful.)

About the Free Speech Alliance

Per the "About the Free Speech Alliance Alumni" Free Speech Alliance report in June 2022:

On many campuses, students and faculty are attacked for exercising free speech. According to the FIRE survey, over 80 percent of students at the schools surveyed said they self-censor in the classroom, on campus, and online.

To preserve the purpose of their institutions, alumni must become involved to make the case for free speech and academic freedom and to provide support for faculty and students who speak up on their campuses.

The Free Speech Alliance provides a mechanism for the exchange of information among its members on substantive and organizational issues. A priority for the Alliance is to encourage the creation of alumni free speech groups for other colleges and universities, and the Alliance will create tools to help new alumni groups organize. We believe the number of alumni groups supporting free speech on their campuses will grow.

While members of the Alliance are alumni focused, other interested parties, such as faculty and students, may also be involved. Each of the members is different in terms of its organizational structure and activities but is committed to promoting free speech, academic freedom, and viewpoint diversity.

Listed below are the members of the Free Speech Alliance, with a click through to their websites:

- Bucknell: Open Discourse Coalition
- Cornell: Cornell Free Speech Alliance
- Davidson: Davidsonians for Freedom of Thought & Discourse
- Harvard: Harvard Alumni for Free Speech
- Lafayette: Alumni/Alumnae Coalition for Lafayette
- Massachusetts Institute of Technology: MIT Free Speech Alliance
- Princeton: Princetonians for Free Speech
- University of North Carolina: UNC Free Speech Alliance
- University of Virginia: The Jefferson Council
- Virginia Military Institute: The Spirit of VMI

- Washington & Lee: The Generals Redoubt
- Wofford: Alumni for the Wofford Way
- Yale: Fight for Yale's Future

Institutional Neutrality: Blueprint for Reform

Per the "Institutional Neutrality: Blueprint for Reform" The James G. Martin Center for Academic Renewal report card:

To perform its mission in the society, a university must sustain an extraordinary environment of freedom of inquiry and maintain an independence from political fashions, passions, and pressures. A university, if it is to be true to its faith in intellectual inquiry, must embrace, be hospitable to, and encourage the widest diversity of views within its own community. It is a community but only for the limited, albeit great, purposes of teaching and research. It is not a club, it is not a trade association, it is not a lobby.

Academia's primary mission is the discovery, preservation, and dissemination of knowledge in a free, neutral, and unbiased manner. The expression of dissenting opinions is crucial to this mission and to achieve a well-examined understanding of the world.

Thus, "Institutional Neutrality" is a guiding principle that states institutions of higher education "cannot take collective action on the issues of the day." To take such actions will endanger the university's mission, since it will inhibit the expression of dissenting opinions.

In general, the college or university must strive to keep its practices politically neutral in a wide range of activities, including hiring, curriculum formation, and campus life.

Institutional neutrality is especially important for public institutions. Public universities belong to all the residents of the state, not to those who are currently and temporarily employed there. This means that university officials cannot take a specific political stance on a contested issue when speaking in their official capacity. (They may, however, take a specific position when speaking as an individual scholar, not as a school official.) An example of this is the American College and University Presidents' Climate Commitment, in which presidents of academic institutions signed onto a controversial political statement about climate change in their official capacities—a clear violation of institutional neutrality.

Similarly, university boards and financial officers may not use the resources of the university for political reasons; this most commonly involves an investment strategy for the school's endowment. Those charged with investing a college or university endowment have a fiduciary duty to seek the highest returns. Recently, though, the University of North Carolina at Asheville divested part of its endowment from energy companies that produce fossil fuels and moved the money to more "socially responsible" investment funds. That, too, was a violation of institutional neutrality.

Institutional neutrality also means schools may not compel officers, employees, or students to express specific opinions on political, intellectual, or social issues. An example is so-called "diversity statements," which require faculty and staff to express commitment to a politicized agenda of "diversity, equity, and inclusion."

The principle of institutional neutrality is often unpopular within the academy, as many academics view it as an unnecessary and irrelevant barrier to their activist agenda. Yet, without it, academia's highest ideal—the spirit of free investigation—will be constrained and ignored by political agendas.

Recommendations

The Martin Center recommends that colleges, universities, and legislatures adopt policies that take the following steps in order to establish and maintain institutional neutrality:

Universities should:

Comply with the spirit of institutional neutrality laid down in the Kalven Report. These guidelines include:

- Forbidding mandatory expression of specific beliefs on contested issues.

- Forbidding mandatory compliance with specific beliefs on contested issues in classroom or workplace activities.

- Forbidding the use of institution resources for ideological purposes, particularly the investment of the institutional endowment for ideological purposes.

- Forbidding university officials from taking a specific political stance on a contested issue when speaking in their official capacity

Conduct periodic reviews to ensure compliance with principles of institutional neutrality of the following:

- The curriculum;

- Policy documents, handbooks, guidelines, handbooks, and bylaws;

- Institutional investing practices;

- The hiring of faculty employees.

End all mandatory courses, modules, trainings, and statements on ideological issues.

Accurately report to the state legislature concerning all possible infringements of institutional

Policymakers should:

Encode mandatory compliance with the principles of institutional neutrality outlined in the Kalven Report, including:

- Forbidding mandatory compliance with specific beliefs on contested issues in classroom or workplace activities.

- Forbidding mandatory expression of specific beliefs on contested issues.

- Forbidding the use of institution resources for ideological purposes, particularly the investment of the institutional endowment for ideological purposes.

- Forbidding university officials from taking a specific political stance on a contested issue when speaking in their official capacity

Withhold appropriated funds for schools that persist with activities in violation of institutional neutrality.

Mandate that public institutions and their governing bodies report annually about possible violations of institutional neutrality.

Penalize institutions that fail to accurately report on violations of institutional neutrality.

The Silent Serpent: Why China's Influence on U.S. Universities Has Gone Unnoticed

As warned in the Lee Edwards, Ph.D. "Confucius Institutes: China's Trojan Horse" the Heritage Foundation report in May 2021:

When the Left and the Right agree on something in these disputatious times, the wise man will want to know what it is. And what has brought these warring factions together, however briefly? The Confucius Institutes that dot American campuses.

The progressive *New Republic* magazine and the conservative National Association of Scholars (NAS) both warn that the Institutes are not the innocent cultural centers offering Chinese language instruction they pretend to be. They are, rather, a key stratagem of China's "soft war" against America, crafted, in the words of NAS senior researcher Rachelle Peterson, to "teach political lessons that unduly favor China."

Founded in 2004, the Confucius Institutes are a global phenomenon, enrolling more than nine million students at 525 institutes in 146 countries and regions. More than 100 institutes have opened in the United States, including at prestigious universities such as Columbia and Stanford. They are mostly staffed and funded by an agency of the Chinese government's Ministry of Education—the Office of Chinese Languages Council International, or Hanban. The Hanban also operates Confucius Classrooms in an estimated 500 primary and secondary schools in the United States.

A 243-page NAS report described in detail the many strings attached to the goodies offered by Confucius Institutes:

The Confucius Institutes pretend to be a Chinese version of cultural institutions like the Alliance Française or the Goethe Institute, but they are in reality a propaganda machine funded and directed by the Chinese government. Based on the findings of its 2017 report, the NAS recommends that "all universities close their Confucius Institutes."

14 – School Board & College Trustee Reformers Are Crucial For Education Reform

Credit: KATV.

Conservative candidates who ran for school boards saying they would change what students learn about race, sex and gender, or who opposed Covid protocols, saw mixed results in Tuesday's 2022 midterms election, according to supporters and a sampling of nationwide results.

Ballotpedia, a nonpartisan election site, analyzed 361 races and found that about 36% of candidates who opposed school Covid protocols, diversity initiatives or the use of gender-neutral learning materials, won their elections.

About 28% of winning candidates in the analysis supported those policies or efforts. That percentage is down from elections in April and November 2021, according to Ballotpedia. About a third of candidates in Tuesday's election analysis didn't take clear positions on these issues, according to the site.

Many candidates received financial support from political-action committees outside their local school communities or from advocacy groups, a relatively new feature in school board elections.

Per the Alia Wong "Did Republicans take over school boards? Key education takeaways from the 2022 midterms" *USA Today* article in November 2022:

"It really does feel like a mixed bag," Ballotpedia's Doug Kronaizl said. One reason so many of the candidates are now hard to categorize, he said, is because many campaigns began to distance themselves from the critical race theory rhetoric and similar messaging that were popular in 2021. "Candidates are out there choosing to hedge their language," he said.

Either way, observers say that, given all the money and attention conservatives pumped into these normally sleepy races, the results are underwhelming at best.

Of the more than 270 school board candidates nationally endorsed by Moms for Liberty, a network of parents' rights activists who have pushed for book restrictions and policies banning discussions about LGBTQ+ issues, 49% won, with roughly three dozen seats still outstanding.

"I know some people would say 'Oh that's not good.' We think it's fantastic," Justice said about the results. "For us, we're looking at first time candidates who never had their names on ballot, running against incumbents who have name recognition and are funded by teachers unions who are like the Goliath." The group did succeed in flipping the board in Charleston, South Carolina, among other wins.

Curriculum Is the Cure

From the Sol Stern "Curriculum Is the Cure" *City Journal* article in December 2016:

Our Millennials and Zillennials know not the Founding Fathers, nor the Civil War and World War II, nor anything, really, about the world we live in. And that's true whether these young people come from poor or middle-class families and regardless of the types of schools or colleges they might have attended. Surveys conducted by NAEP and other testing agencies reveal an astonishing lack of historical and civic knowledge.

Two-thirds of high school seniors were unable to identify the 50-year period during which the Civil War was fought; half didn't know in which half-century World War I took place. Over half couldn't name the three branches of government. A majority had no idea what the Gettysburg Address was all about. Fifty-two percent chose Germany, Japan, or Italy as "U.S. allies" in World War II. Such widespread ignorance is the result of adult malfeasance.

The next phase of education reform must include restoring knowledge to the classroom and fighting the ignorance it brings forth that also reminds us of a frightening premonition from Adolf Hitler, "Let me control the textbooks and I will control the state."

A solid body of scholarship has long been available showing that proven instructional practices were abandoned in the nation's schools beginning in the 1960s. Both sides of the school-reform debate ought to familiarize themselves with the education theories of E.D. Hirsch, Jr. Next year marks the 30th anniversary of the publication of Hirsch's seminal work, *Cultural Literacy*, which became an instant and surprise best seller.

Here's the essential discovery that Hirsch first made three decades ago, the missing link that explains why our schools spend more money than ever, yet produce increasingly worse academic results and increasingly ignorant Americans: starting in the 1960s, the nation's schools were subjected to a pedagogical upheaval fomented by self-styled "progressive" educators that succeeded in stripping away any semblance of a coherent grade-by-grade curriculum. The progressives resurrected romantic theories of child development dating back to Jean-Jacques Rousseau and then powerfully reinforced in the 1930s by the American philosopher John Dewey.

In the nation's education schools, future teachers were now instructed that children were capable of "constructing their own knowledge" and that the classroom teacher should be a "guide on the side" rather than a "sage on the stage." Most elementary schools concluded that it was more important for children to "learn how to learn" rather than to accumulate "mere facts" and useless knowledge.

New "child-centered" pedagogy turned classroom instruction upside down

In Hirsch's critique, this new "child-centered" pedagogy turned classroom instruction upside down, disrupting the transmission of civic values and traditions from one generation to the next. This was precisely a reversal of the Founding Fathers' insight that the nation's schools must follow a common curriculum in order to teach future generations the historical facts and general knowledge needed to sustain the Republic. But few teachers-in-training learn this civic wisdom. Instead, in their ed-school courses they are often urged to use the classroom to turn children into social-justice warriors.

Hirsch also showed how the new pedagogical doctrines harmed disadvantaged children and made it more difficult for schools to reduce racial-achievement gaps. The anti-equality effect of progressive education shows up in the early grades in the teaching of reading. Because of family and home influences, poor minority kids begin school lagging far behind middle-class children in vocabulary acquisition and background knowledge. The gap can be narrowed in the classroom, but only through explicit instruction, guided by a coherent, grade-by-grade, knowledge-based curriculum.

Relying on consensus findings in cognitive science and psycholinguistics, Hirsch showed that there was no such thing as "mere" facts—indeed, that factual knowledge was essential for students' ability to read and comprehend challenging texts. When, instead, progressive educators led schools into a curricular wasteland and decided that their students could create their "own knowledge," they effectively abandoned the very disadvantaged children they claimed to be championing.

Over the next several years, Hirsch published more books elaborating on the argument for explicitly teaching knowledge in the classroom. Meanwhile, progressive educators continued to dig in deeper. They also condemned the former English professor as an interloper and an elitist. Year after year, the progressives insisted that the schools didn't have to teach a "Eurocentric" curriculum, while promising that, with just enough funding for the public schools, their humane, child-friendly pedagogical methods would eventually prove effective in lifting up the children of the poor. Year after year, the results from national and international tests revealed something else.

Education researchers have concluded that the average reading score of high school seniors is among the most useful standards for evaluating a school system's effectiveness. Reading comprehension is the most accurate predictor of a high school senior's college preparedness and future economic prospects. Using this yardstick, American education has steadily stagnated since the progressives achieved hegemony in the classrooms.

Verbal scores on the SAT tanked in the 1960s and 1970s and have remained flat ever since

The most recent long-term NAEP assessment of the reading proficiency of American 17-year olds revealed a steep decline, confirming the bad news from the SAT tests. During the same period, American students' scores plummeted on various international assessments. In the 2015 Program for International Student Assessment (PISA) tests, the U.S. ranked 23rd in reading and 31st in math among the major industrial nations.

In his nineties, Hirsch has just published his fifth education book, *Why Knowledge Matters*. It offers a useful recapitulation of his critique of the failed ideas bringing down the nation's schools. Hirsch also cites new studies in cognitive science confirming that "the achievement gap is chiefly a knowledge gap and a vocabulary gap," as he puts it.

I see little chance that Hirsch's powerful new warning will provoke second thoughts among the stand-pat defenders of the public schools as they are, or the progressive education professors. After all, the progressives aren't unhappy with the qualities of mind of the young people that our knowledge-free schools are producing, including their political predilections and activism.

The millennial and Zillennials generations now vote overwhelmingly for the progressive Left; they have been taught all their lives that personal feelings are more important than facts. They don't know anything about the history of socialism and don't recognize the names of Eugene V. Debs or Vladimir Lenin, but they believe that socialism is a good thing because it feels like a good thing, just as their favorite political candidate repeatedly told them in 2016.

The only realistic hope of restoring a knowledge curriculum in the schools rests with the reformers. I don't question the motives of the many philanthropic-minded billionaires (yes, they really are billionaires) who have spent enormous sums of money in recent years promoting charters and vouchers. The problem is that the donors have so far paid too little attention—and spent little money—promoting the teaching of knowledge in the classroom.

Since the choice movement is predominantly conservative in its political leaning, this is a classic case of shooting oneself in the foot. The success of the conservative vision for the country depends on broadly educated citizens and requires exactly what Jefferson called for—graduates of our schools "whose memories may here be stored with the most useful facts from Grecian, Roman, European, and American history." Will conservatives at long last begin working to restore a knowledge-based curriculum? We can only hope. The survival of the American republic is at stake.

E. D. Hirsch's Curriculum For Democracy

From the Sol Stern "E. D. Hirsch's Curriculum for Democracy" *City Journal* report in Autumn of 2009: Though educational progressives deride teaching facts, research shows that cultural literacy is crucial to educational success.

Hirsch was at the pinnacle of the academic world, in his mid-fifties, when he was struck by an insight into how reading is taught that, he says, "changed my life." He was "feeling guilty" about the department's inadequate freshman writing course, he recalls. Though UVA's admissions standards were as competitive as the Ivies,' the reading and writing skills of many incoming students were poor, sure to handicap them in their future academic work.

In trying to figure out how to close this "literacy gap," Hirsch conducted an experiment on reading comprehension, using two groups of college students. Members of the first group possessed broad background knowledge in subjects like history, geography, civics, the arts, and basic science; members of the second, often from disadvantaged homes, lacked such knowledge.

The knowledgeable students, it turned out, could far more easily comprehend and analyze difficult college-level texts (both fiction and nonfiction) than their poorly informed brethren could. Hirsch had discovered "a way to measure the variations in reading skill attributable to variations in the relevant background knowledge of audiences."

This finding, first published in a psychology journal, was consistent with Hirsch's past scholarship, in which he had argued that the author takes for granted that his readers have crucial background knowledge. Hirsch was also convinced that the problem of inadequate background knowledge began in the early grades.

Elementary school teachers thus had to be more explicit about imparting such knowledge to students—indeed, this was even more important than teaching the "skills" of reading and writing, Hirsch believed. Hirsch's insight contravened the conventional wisdom in the nation's education schools: that teaching facts was unimportant, and that students instead should learn "how to" skills.

Hirsch gave a lecture on the implications of his study at a Modern Language Association conference and then expanded the argument in a 1983 article, titled "Cultural Literacy," in *The American Scholar*. The article caused a stir, not so much in the academy (and certainly not in the ed schools) as among public intellectuals. William Bennett, then chair of the National Endowment for the Humanities, encouraged Hirsch to pursue his theme. Education historian Diane Ravitch urged him to get a book out fast and to call it *Cultural Literacy* as well.

Hirsch heeded the advice, and in 1987, the book landed on the New York Times's bestseller list, where it stayed for 26 weeks, resulting in a dramatic career change for the author. He kept researching and writing about how to improve the "cultural literacy" of young Americans and launched the Core Knowledge Foundation, which sought to create a knowledge-based curriculum for the nation's elementary schools.

A Content-Rich Pedagogy Makes Better Citizens and Smarter Kids

A wide range of scholars assisted him in specifying the knowledge that children in grades K–8 needed to become proficient readers. For example, the Core Knowledge curriculum specifies that in English language arts, all second-graders read poems by Robert Louis Stevenson, Emily Dickinson, and Gwendolyn Brooks, as well as stories by Rudyard Kipling, E. B. White, and Hans

Christian Andersen. In history and geography, the children study the world's great rivers, ancient Rome, and the Constitution and the Declaration of Independence, among other subjects.

By the late 1980s, Hirsch had all but abandoned academic literary studies and become a full-time education reformer. His curriculum appeared at an opportune moment. Four years earlier, the U.S. government had released *A Nation at Risk*, a widely publicized report about falling SAT scores and the mediocre education that most American kids were getting. The report set off shock waves among parents, many of whom weren't thrilled, either, when they heard educators dismissing the report's implications. Parents saw Hirsch's call for a coherent grade-by-grade curriculum as an answer.

Like *A Nation at Risk*, *Cultural Literacy* came under fierce attack by education progressives, partly for its theory of reading comprehension but even more for its supposedly elitist presumption that a white male college professor should decide what American children learn. Critics derided Hirsch's lists of names, events, and dates as arbitrary, even racist.

Hirsch's next book, *The Schools We Need and Why We Don't Have Them* (1999), took the argument about core knowledge and educational equity to the next level by dismantling those faulty theories. Hirsch's early academic work on Wordsworth and the Romantics helped him in this project, since he could see how the progressives' education agenda was rooted in a deeply flawed understanding of child development that went back to Rousseau. "The Romantics were wonderful for poetry but wrong about life," Hirsch tells me, "and they were particularly wrong about education."

European Romanticism, he argued in the book, "has been a post-Enlightenment aberration, a mistake we need to correct."

Influenced by the Romantics, progressive-education doctrine held that children learn best "naturally" and that we should not drill "lifeless" facts into their developing minds. Such views, which became prevalent in American teacher training by the 1920s, Hirsch shows, represented a sharp break with the Founding Fathers, who believed that children needed to learn a coherent, shared body of knowledge for the new democracy to work. Thomas Jefferson even proposed a common curriculum, so that children's "memories may here be stored with the most useful facts from Grecian, Roman, European, and American history."

By the time Hirsch turned his attention to education reform in the mid-1980s, Romanticism's triumph was complete

Most public schools, for instance, taught reading through the "whole language" method, which encourages children to guess the meaning of words through context clues rather than to master the English phonetic code. In many schools, a teacher could no longer line up children's desks in rows facing him; indeed, he found himself banished entirely from the front of the classroom, becoming a "guide on the side" instead of a "sage on the stage."

More powerfully than any previous critic, Hirsch showed how destructive these instructional approaches were. The idea that schools could starve children of factual knowledge, yet somehow encourage them to be "critical thinkers" and teach them to "learn how to learn," defied common sense.

But Hirsch also summoned irrefutable evidence from the hard sciences to eviscerate progressive-ed doctrines. Hirsch had spent the better part of the decade since Cultural Literacy mastering the findings of neurobiology, cognitive psychology, and psycholinguistics on which teaching methods best promote student learning.

The scientific consensus showed that schools could not raise student achievement by letting students construct their own knowledge. The pedagogy that mainstream scientific research supported, Hirsch showed, was direct instruction by knowledgeable teachers who knew how to transmit their knowledge to students—the very opposite of what the progressives promoted.

The ed-school establishment has worked busily to discredit Hirsch. In 1997, the journal of the American Educational Research Association (AERA), the umbrella organization representing most education professors and researchers, launched an unprecedented 6,000-word dismissal of his work.

Hirsch shrugs off these slights and keeps working. In his nineties, he has written what may be his most important book, *The Making of Americans: Democracy and Our Schools*, which deepens his argument about the American Founders' support for core knowledge.

After Hirsch has memorialized early American education, you can almost hear his remorse as he surveys what passes for higher thinking today in the education schools and teachers' organizations. In *The Making of Americans*, Hirsch again shows how consensus science proves that "a higher-order academic skill such as reading comprehension requires prior knowledge of domain-specific content." But the ed schools' closed "thoughtworld" (Hirsch's term) has insulated itself from science.

For that matter, future classroom teachers must search far in ed-school syllabi to find a single reference to any of Hirsch's work—yet required readings by radical education thinkers such as Paulo Freire, Jonathan Kozol, and ex-Weatherman Bill Ayers are common.

From these texts, prospective teachers will learn that the purpose of schooling in America isn't to create knowledgeable, civic-minded citizens, loyal to the nation's democratic institutions, as Jefferson dreamed, but rather to undermine those institutions and turn children into champions of "social justice" as defined by today's America-hating far Left.

The Massachusetts miracle

The "Massachusetts miracle," in which Bay State students' soaring test scores broke records, was the direct consequence of the state legislature's passage of the 1993 Education Reform Act, which established knowledge-based standards for all grades and a rigorous testing system linked to the new standards. And those standards, Massachusetts reformers have acknowledged, are Hirsch's legacy. If the Obama administration truly wants to have a positive impact on American education, it should embrace Hirsch's ideas and urge other states to do the same.

In the new millennium, Massachusetts students have surged upward on the biennial National Assessment of Educational Progress (NAEP)—"the nation's report card," as education scholars call it. On the 2005 NAEP tests, Massachusetts ranked first in the nation in fourth- and eighth-grade reading and fourth- and eighth-grade math. It then repeated the feat in 2007. No state had ever scored first in both grades and both subjects in a single year—let alone for two consecutive test cycles.

On another reliable test, the Trends in International Math and Science Studies, the state's fourth-graders ranked second globally in science and third in math, while the eighth-graders tied for first in science and placed sixth in math. (States can volunteer, as Massachusetts did, to have their students compared with national averages.) The United States as a whole finished tenth.

It is hard to imagine in other states and school districts, that our students, in other states and thousands of school districts, particularly in grades 3–8, wouldn't have done much better if the schools had adopted the Hirsch solution of a content-rich, grade-by-grade curriculum and recognized that the way for students to achieve advanced reading comprehension is to master a broad range of background knowledge.

The most hopeful alternative to dead-end progressive education is still to be found in Charlottesville. The national headquarters of the Core Knowledge Foundation is located a block or two from the University of Virginia in a sprawling, two-story residential house with a wraparound porch. A staff of about 25 people is working on a new K–3 reading program and bringing the Core Knowledge K–8 curriculum up to date with the latest relevant subject matter. The staff also maintains contact with a network of about 1,000 Core Knowledge schools around the country (many of them charters).

Progressives Against Transparency

As per the Zaid Jilani "Progressives Against Transparency" *City Journal* article in January 2022:

In at least a dozen states, Republican lawmakers have introduced bills seeking to make instruction in public schools more transparent. Pennsylvania's bill, for example, would require public schools to post their curricula online. The ACLU joins Democratic politicians in opposition to making school curricula available to parents.

Democrats have largely opposed these bills, viewing them as the latest conservative salvo against critical race theory–inspired pedagogy. In vetoing the Pennsylvania legislation, Democratic governor Tom Wolf warned that the "legislation is a thinly veiled attempt to restrict truthful instruction and censor content reflecting various cultures, identities, and experiences."

Taken literally, Wolf's statement is false. Requiring schools to be transparent about what they're teaching does not inherently restrict instruction or censor content. But Wolf, like many progressives, is obviously concerned that if citizens knew what is being taught in schools, then they might demand a change in curriculum.

As debates over school curricula have raged for the past year, progressives have openly expressed anti-democratic views about how the education system should operate. Nikole Hannah-Jones, progenitor of the New York Times's 1619 Project, made her view clear during an NBC appearance. "I don't really understand this idea that parents should decide what's being taught," she said. "I'm not a professional educator. I don't have a degree in social studies or science. We send our children to school because we want them to be taught by people who have expertise in the subject area."

Meantime, Virginia Democratic gubernatorial candidate Terry McAuliffe arguably cost himself a second term in the governor's mansion by admitting that he didn't "think parents should be telling schools what they should teach."

Next Step for the Parents' Movement: Curriculum Transparency

Per the December 2021 James R. Copland, John Ketcham and Christopher F. Rufo "Next Step for the Parents' Movement: Curriculum Transparency" *City Journal* article:

In 2021, public school parents vaulted to the forefront of America's fractured political landscape. Around the country, parents objected both to Covid-related school closures and to racially divisive curricula. Parental frustration helped secure sweeping GOP wins last month in Virginia, highlighted by Glenn Youngkin's victory over former governor Terry McAuliffe. Youngkin has promised to rein in public-school radicalism and "ban critical race theory" on his first day in office.

Perhaps the central moment in the Virginia gubernatorial race was McAuliffe's comment during a debate: "I don't think parents should be telling schools what they should teach." Like most Virginia voters, we couldn't disagree more. Research shows that greater academic success follows when parents actively engage in their children's education.

To be sure, this doesn't mean that we should decide the finer points of curricular design by plebiscite; nor does it mean that a minority of objecting parents should dictate school pedagogy. But public schools are institutions created by "We the People" and should be responsive to the input of parents and the broader voting public at the state and local level.

At a minimum, parents should be able to know what's being taught to their children in the classroom. Transparency is a virtue for all of our public institutions, but especially for those with power over children. To that end, we have drafted a template—building on one of our earlier efforts at the Manhattan Institute and the work of Matt Beienburg at the Goldwater Institute— to inform state legislatures seeking to foster school transparency. The policy proposal is designed to provide public school parents with easy access—directly on school websites—to materials and activities used to train staff and teachers and to instruct children.

The last year and a half since 2020 has demonstrated the need for transparency measures. As many public schools migrated to "virtual only" learning in response to the pandemic, parents received a first-hand look at the divisive, racialist curricula being taught to their children. They learned that public schools were forcing third-graders to deconstruct their racial and sexual identities, showing kindergarteners dramatizations of dead black children and warning them about "racist police," and telling white teachers that they were guilty of "spirit murdering" minorities. These were not isolated incidents.

These revelations prompted parents to demand to know exactly what was being taught to their children. They felt that the public-school bureaucracies had been hiding controversial materials and exerting undue influence over their children, all in the service of fashionable left-wing ideologies.

Frustrated parents understandably pushed back

Frustrated parents understandably pushed back, protested at school board meetings, and, in some cases, forced the resignations of school superintendents who refused to listen to their concerns. School officials often responded to parents' concerns with resentment. Some were so agitated by the parental pushback that they sought federal intervention—including through a well-publicized (and since retracted) letter from the National School Boards Association comparing parents to "domestic terrorists."

Other school officials insisted that they, not parents and not voters, should be in charge of children's pedagogy. This is precisely backward. While government schools necessarily cannot meet every parent's demands, parents have a fundamental right, long recognized in law, to guide their children's education and moral conscience. To exercise those rights, parents need accurate information about the learning materials and activities their kids are encountering in government schools.

Our "A Model for Transparency in School Training and Curriculum" can be found in the Appendix.

It does not attempt to define specific concepts, methods, or ideologies. Nor does it seek to ban, restrict, or discourage any materials, activities, or pedagogies. Its aim is simply to provide parents with information about the curricula used in the classroom across all subjects—and to let families, teachers, and schools negotiate disagreements at the local level. If they cannot resolve their differences, parents have options: petition elected leaders or run for school board seats themselves, move to a different area, or remove their children from the public school system.

By focusing on transparency, our prescriptions sidestep arguments about "censorship" in public schools. (Realistically speaking, any school necessarily has to pick and choose what to teach among near-infinite options.

Openness will not necessarily engender trust. Parents will certainly disagree about pedagogy. There's no simple way to reconcile all competing perspectives. But the answer to these inevitable disagreements cannot be to hide from parents what's being taught to their own children. We believe that funding common schools in our democratic system requires information and engagement—and so we propose that public schools open their books and let parents see what's inside.

Educating Patriots

From the Robert Pondiscio "Educating Patriots" *City Journal* article in October 2020:

In his "farewell" book, E. D. Hirsch, our foremost thinker on American schooling, sets his sights on fixing America itself. *How to Educate a Citizen: The Power of Shared Knowledge to Unify a Nation*, by E. D. Hirsch, Jr.

Decades before "equity" became a buzzword in education, E. D. Hirsch, Jr. had his finger on what the word actually means: equal access for all children to the knowledge and verbal proficiency that makes full participation in American life possible. In a series of books and journal articles stretching back decades, Hirsch has argued that we will not have a just and prosperous society until our schools ensure that every child has access to the knowledge that the children of well-off families take for granted.

Hirsch's scholarship rests on the hypothesis, validated by volumes of evidence from cognitive science, that language comprehension—particularly the ability to read with understanding—is not a discrete, transferable "skill," like riding a bike, that can be learned, practiced, and mastered. Rather, it rests on a common base of knowledge, literary and cultural allusions, and idioms common to a nation's "speech community."

Hirsch's egalitarian vision is as empirically verifiable as it is out of step with current education fashions. Not surprisingly, his work has been mischaracterized as "banking" and canon-making, or even as an effort to impose "whiteness" on nonwhite students. In fact, it's an effort to catalogue the taken-for-granted knowledge of the broad American speech community so that it can be taught.

The most misunderstood education book of the last fifty years

This fundamental disconnect led University of Virginia professor of psychology Daniel Willingham to describe Hirsch's landmark 1987 book Cultural Literacy, which spent six months on the *New York Times* best-seller list, as "the most misunderstood education book of the last fifty years."

The years since the firestorm over Cultural Literacy have been kinder to Hirsch. The content-rich elementary education he champions has not overthrown the progressive, "child-centered" pedagogies he has criticized, but the education world that once reviled him as a reactionary trying to impose an archaic canon on children has increasingly accepted that he was right: there is no escaping the connection between broad general knowledge and broad general literacy.

Hirsch launched the Core Knowledge Foundation over 30 years ago to promote his ideas and produce a curriculum built on his insights. Today, many publishers promote and sell a "content-rich" English Language Arts curriculum.

Hirsch has refined his message and mustered fresh evidence in each of his subsequent books, but now, in his nineties, in what he says is his farewell book, his project has taken on fresh urgency. The aim of *How to Educate a Citizen* is not merely to save American education from demonstrably false ideas about teaching and learning, but to save America itself. This sounds grandiose, but it follows from Hirsch's core thesis. Education and nationhood are functionally the same idea. "Intellectual error has become a threat to the well-being of the nation," Hirsch warns. "A truly massive tragedy is building."

We are far more accustomed to thinking of schools as a means to promote the private ends of college or career. Hirsch reminds us that "nation-creating" was the explicit aim of American public education at its founding, "reinforced in primers and spelling books on a scale never before seen in human history." New York in particular, with its diversity of immigrants and religions, was "especially alert to the need to build up a shared public sphere where all these different groups could meet as equals on common ground," he writes. "How prescient the founders were in being worried about factions and lack of public spirit and even disloyalty to the republic," he laments. "We have, to our distress, acquired some of the evils they feared."

How to Educate a Citizen arrives at a moment when the dominant ideas in education are once again working against his unifying vision for common schools. On the right, advocates often put a higher priority on school choice; on the left, a strident social justice orthodoxy insists that all institutions, especially public schools, must be "anti-racist" and "decolonize" their curriculum.

Recall how Colin Kaepernick pressured Nike to discontinue a sneaker adorned with the 1776 flag, which he claimed was an offensive symbol from the era of slavery. A nation that cannot agree whether its flag is a symbol of pride or racial hatred is not ready to agree on what its children should be taught.

Hirsch is fond of invoking the words of Thomas Jefferson, chiseled over a doorway on the campus of the University of Virginia, where he taught for decades. "For here we are not afraid to follow truth wherever it may lead, nor to tolerate any error so long as reason is left free to combat it."

Guided by those words over his long, admirable, and prolific career, E. D. Hirsch, Jr. has worked patiently to correct the errors of the false prophets of progressive pedagogy and to restore the public purpose of American education and its founding ideals. It is up to the rest of us now to follow his lead.

Bolstering the Board: Trustees Are Academia's Best Hope for Reform

Per the Jay Schalin "Bolstering the Board: Trustees Are Academia's Best Hope for Reform" The James G. Martin Center for Academic Renewal report in July 2020:

Higher education is approaching an existential crisis. It is in danger of rejecting its most fundamental value, the search for truth, and replacing it with political dogma and opportunistic careerism. Other problems abound, but none so serious as this one.

Indeed, in many departments on many campuses—even on campuses that seem well-ordered—the spirit of free inquiry is under attack. Irrational theories, such as the belief that race and gender are mere social constructs, are proliferating. Political correctness and corporate and government money are distorting scientific exploration. Many departments are dominated by adherents of fundamentally flawed philosophies, such as French post-modernism or communism.

Disturbed or hostile individuals are routinely hired, while conservative scholars "need not apply" to many departments. On occasion, even political liberals who express moderate views in public are hounded out of their jobs; one widely publicized incident occurred in 2018 at Evergreen State University when a liberal biology professor, Bret Weinstein, was forced to resign because of harassment from students after he refused to leave campus on a specified "day of absence" for white people.

Certainly, much of academia is still functioning at high levels, in technological research and STEM (science, technology, engineering, and mathematics) education, for instance. But the continued success of some programs merely provides cover for the erosion of standards and quality elsewhere in the Ivory Tower. In much of the humanities and social sciences, political dogma has already replaced objective inquiry. In some schools of education, for example, science is considered dependent upon the background of the individual instead of having universal principles for all, with indigenous myths considered equal to rigorous research methods.

It is still possible to get an excellent education at many universities, even in the humanities. But it is not likely to happen by chance; either a student must be intensely focused on a career path in the financial or empirical fields, or he or she will need considerable guidance and awareness to make it through the maze of nonsense. And the maze is getting increasingly difficult to maneuver.

How can this be happening in plain sight, without spurring a massive campaign for reform?

In a well-run higher education system based on the honest pursuit of truth, the marketplace of ideas would permit critics to attack, refute, and even satirize such ideas. The worst theories would be prevented from gaining even a tiny foothold; the rest would be condemned to some musty little corner while more reasoned ideas displaced them. But that is not the case; the free market of ideas is broken, replaced by a one-sided, dogmatic consensus.

At the heart of the problem is higher education's tradition of sharing governance functions and authority among the board, the administration, and the faculty. Few observers are willing to criticize it; it is truly a "sacred cow."

The prescriptions of experts for fixing higher education's problems call for more of the same practices that led to the crisis in the first place. That is, most of the acclaimed writers call for heightening the shared components of higher education governance, not reducing them.

But that may be the worst thing institutions can do. If higher education's governance practices are working, why then is academia increasingly struggling to protect its most important goals? To increase the shared component of governance by empowering faculty and administrators is to essentially do more of the same thing that causes the current failure to correct the problems.

For shared governance, by definition, inhibits reform

It is based on developing a consensus among widely differing constituencies, and therefore tends to clog and tangle rather than attack problems directly. If you wish to maintain the status quo, instituting a system with multiple layers and involved processes is the way to go. Of course, to maintain the status quo in academia doesn't mean that no change will occur. It means that the system will continue to move in the same direction: toward more politicization.

If, on the other hand, you wish to address problems aggressively, it is best to instill a hierarchical form of governance with a clear chain of command. And with the trustees in charge. Only boards can represent all interests. And the American system of higher education was intended to function with boards in charge.

To preserve the best of higher education, something more fundamental—a "Copernican revolution," or "Kuhnian paradigm shift," if you prefer—is needed to turn academia back toward the spirit of open inquiry. Such a paradigm shift is called for when the existing framework is no longer sufficient to explain or solve existing puzzles; a new perspective is needed with greater explanatory power.

Such a shift in higher education would require reordering power relationships, elevating the power of governing boards, the public, and the alumni while reducing the power of faculty and administrators.

To many, such a recommendation may seem drastic, even alarming

Most commentary on higher education remains within fairly narrow boundaries; much of the best-known literature tends to be written by former college administrators, who have the seeming advantage of being "inside" the system, or else written by policy professionals from professional associations that have risen to prominence within the current system.

But their insider status also tends to blind them to the overall picture. They may decry the gridlock that an outside observer will perceive to be the natural result of shared governance, but they blame it on the governing boards, whom they would prefer to keep at a distance and forego their legal and natural authority. More faculty involvement, a more powerful administration, more shared governance is their solution.

But to support the current system is to permit antagonistic forces to incrementally dislodge the best of the Western intellectual heritage from the academy. This must not be allowed to happen!

15 – Reversing America's 'D -' Grade Education System to an Ascendant 'A +' Grade

Credit: The Family Foundation – Parents' Bill of Rights.

Per the Jay Schalin "The Pushback Against Classroom Indoctrination Begins" The James G. Martin Center for Academic Renewal article in July 2022:

America is finally waking up to the fact that poisonous, divisive ideas are proliferating in public education, from pre-K to graduate school. The question is how to push back against such ideas, and recognize the damage that is being done to young minds. We must never downplay how serious this issue is as we consider another frightening quote, this one from Vladimir Lenin: "Give me four years to teach the children and the seed I have sown will never be uprooted."

Solutions are easier in K-12; primary and secondary teachers do not have the same protections of academic freedom that college faculty have, and the K-12 curriculum is more tightly controlled by state agencies. The issue is more complex in academia, where academic freedom reigns and the curriculum is controlled by a decentralized faculty.

The situation is also more dire at the college level: Higher education is where the bad ideas originate, and, for a long time, academia has seen little opposition to radicalization of the public universities. While boards of trustees have the legal right to control curricula, they have almost universally relinquished that power to the faculty in practice.

In recent years, however, with the degradation of much of the academy reaching an advanced stage, state legislatures have begun to rise to the challenge and push back against radical encroachment on the public-college curriculum.

State legislatures have begun to push back against radical encroachment on the public-college curriculum.

The Pushback Against Classroom Indoctrination Begins

One such attempt is Florida's "Stop the Wrongs to Our Kids and Employees (WOKE) Act." This 2022 law statutorily prohibits discriminatory classroom teaching. It targets such divisive ideas as Critical Race Theory (CRT), which demands that members of a racial group must perpetually atone for injustices committed by members of their group centuries before, and that claims by aggrieved minorities against the offending groups should pass unchallenged.

It should be obvious that such a system of preferences and punishments along racial and ethnic lines will make a pluralistic society such as the United States unworkable without oppressive government control. Simply accepting the status quo of this biased indoctrination is no longer acceptable to the majority of Americans who, as taxpayers, provide many of the funds for public universities. Thus, the situation screams for reform.

But not everybody wants that reform, and the Stop Woke Act is a point of departure from many long-established academic practices. As can be expected, the law has received a hailstorm of criticism from faculty and civil-rights organizations that favor the status quo. A rapidly filed lawsuit intended to render the law unconstitutional was thrown out of a U.S. district court because the plaintiffs lacked the necessary "standing."

Much of the criticism depends on a fundamentally incorrect assumption about who "owns" the public universities and is therefore in charge of institutional policies such as who decides what and how to teach. Many academics and their supporters claim that higher education belongs to the faculty, deriving this notion of ownership from the formation of medieval universities in Northern Europe (especially England) as "guilds" of faculty.

Our public institutions of higher education were created by state legislatures explicitly for the benefit of the state and its residents

But this self-interested claim—obviously advantageous to those making it—is false with respect to public universities in the U.S. Our public institutions of higher education were created by state legislatures explicitly for the benefit of the state and its residents; the residents, citizens, and taxpayers of the state are the rightful owners and express their control through their elected representatives. As such, they are the ones who should hold the ultimate power over classroom content. This fact was expressed in Florida by the legislature and governor when they enacted the Stop Woke Act.

Another wrong assumption in the critics' reasoning is the claim that academic freedom is a First Amendment issue. It is not; it is a matter of employment, not a matter of legality. Nobody's rights as a citizen or resident to express themselves are infringed by the Florida law; nobody will face criminal charges or civil fines for speaking their minds.

But even as a matter of employment, the Florida law does not silence faculty members from expressing their opinions. It is only concerned with classroom teaching, not with research or extramural comments, and these vehicles for speech are still protected by traditional academic-freedom conventions.

Even the oft-cited 1967 decision *Keyishian v. Board of Regents of the State University of New York*, from which faculty and others derive their claim that academic freedom is a First Amendment right, would not apply in this case. It concerns "membership in a subversive organization," not classroom teaching. Furthermore, even Keyishian's declaration that academic freedom "is … a special concern of the First Amendment, which does not tolerate laws that cast a pall of orthodoxy over the classroom" does not apply here. The Florida law does not impose "orthodoxy" but attempts to remove from the classroom the imposition of orthodoxy in the form of one-sided discriminatory politics. It does so while protecting open discussion by encoding it within its text:

It is not the role of a professor to teach his or her opinion of racial preferences.

Legal Coalition Forming to Stop Critical Race Theory Training Around the Country

Per the Sam Dorman Fox News January 2021 legal brief "Legal Coalition Forming to Stop Critical Race Theory Training Around the Country":

A network of private attorneys and the conservative organizations are launching a "war" against critical race theory trainings across the country as President Biden rolls back the Trump administration's efforts on the issue. Why? Because federal diversity trainers weaponize critical race theory to systemically attack the unifying ideals of America.

Led by Discovery Institute researcher Chris Rufo, the network's stated goal is to bring a complaint before the U.S. Supreme Court and "effectively abolish critical race theory programs from American life."

It comes just after Biden repealed Trump's executive order banning critical race theory training from the federal government, a move by Trump that Rufo appeared to precipitate by releasing documents leaked from federal employees.

"Critical race theory is a grave threat to the American way of life," read Rufo's press release, which echoed Trump's previous condemnation of the training.

"It divides Americans by race and traffics in the pernicious concepts of race essentialism, racial stereotyping, and race-based segregation—all under a false pursuit of 'social justice.' Critical race theory training programs have become commonplace in academia, government, and corporate life, where they have sought to advance the ideology through cult-like indoctrination, intimidation, and harassment."

The Discovery Institute's Center on Wealth and Poverty is leading the effort with help from the Southeastern Legal Foundation, Upper Midwest Law Center, Jonathan O'Brien with Schoolhouserights.org, The Pivtorak Law Firm, Wally Zimolong of Zimolong, LLC, and Eric Early and Peter Scott of Early, Sullivan, Wright, Gizer, & McCrae.

Fox News previously reported on O'Brien's lawsuit, which involved a multiracial high school student's complaint over a Nevada charter school course directing him and others to choose oppressive aspects of their identity.

That particular lawsuit alleged discrimination "on the basis of race and color, in addition to sex, gender, and religion, in violation of Title VI and Title IX of the Education Amendments of 1972."

Critical race theory, or diversity training, appeared to grow in the aftermath of George Floyd's death, which prompted a wave of calls to dismantle alleged institutional racism. Governments and schools from around the country have adopted so-called anti-racist initiatives with training for employees and students.

Florida Parents Take Back the Classroom

Per the Zach Weissmueller "Florida Parents Take Back the Classroom" *Reason* article in January 2022:

"It is a fundamental right of parents to direct the upbringing, education, and care of their minor children." That's the opening line of Florida's Parents' Bill of Rights, signed into law in June 2021. Similar bills have been proposed in Missouri, Kentucky, Texas, and even at the federal level.

"Our children do not belong to the government," says Patti Sullivan, state coordinator for Parental Rights Florida, which has pushed for legislation of this sort since 2013. But parental rights laws and anti–critical race theory bills can't end the curriculum wars. Only school choice can. "We do not co-parent with the government. And these entities seem to think that they are entitled to our children, and they are not," says Sullivan.

State bans on the teaching of critical race theory (CRT), which have swept the nation, are a more aggressive attempt to limit the discretion that teachers and administrators have over what's taught in school. They've been especially popular with voters.

Republican Glenn Youngkin ousted the heavily favored Terry McAuliffe in the Virginia governor's race after he campaigned against CRT in schools, and on his first day in office, he banned it from classrooms via executive order. Four other states have also banned CRT, and several more are considering similar bills.

However, opponents of CRT bans and more modest bills to force schools to post their curricula online say that "curriculum transparency bills are just thinly veiled attempts at chilling teachers and students from learning and talking about race and gender in schools," as the American Civil Liberties Union recently tweeted.

Parents have never had the "right to shape their kids' school curriculum," authors of a recent *Washington Post* op-ed argued. If that's what parents want, it says, they should opt out and "send their children to private or religious schools."

But why should families who can afford private school be the only ones who have a say in how their children are taught?

"I'm pretty skeptical of the government deciding what should be taught in any type of school," says Corey DeAngelis, national director of research for the American Federation for Children and a senior fellow at Reason Foundation (the nonprofit that publishes this website). He says public school parents should also have the right to choose the most fitting academic setting for their kids. The solution is to "fund students, not systems," giving families the choice to spend education dollars on the schooling of their choosing instead of the one-size-fits-all approach offered by traditional public schools.

"[CRT] bills are just a form of whack-a-mole, where your CRT battles of today were the common core battles of yesterday, and it'll be something else going forward because the reality is parents disagree about what kind of education they want their kids to have…And the better solution is the bottom-up accountability in allowing families to vote with their feet," says DeAngelis.

This has become such a hot-button issue because the pandemic gave parents direct exposure to exactly what their children were and weren't being taught.

"Parents are awake now that they have seen the curriculum," says Tina Descovich, a former Brevard County, Florida, school board member and co-founder of Moms for Liberty. "They now understand school district policies, which they had never looked at before. They are understanding the structure, who holds authority, and what types of authority, within the education system. I think that's vital, and it's something that's been lacking for a long time."

Florida Parents' Bill of Rights

In contrast to CRT bans, the Florida Parents' Bill of Rights broadly affirms that parents have a right to know what schools are teaching and providing to their children.

One of the most controversial aspects of the bill is how it applies to medical and mental health services. It establishes that any medical services provided without parental consent can result in misdemeanor charges.

Sullivan says some parents are particularly concerned that schools are counseling their kids on their sexuality and gender identity without parental consent. The parents of one student in a Tallahassee public school sued after the staff held a meeting without their knowledge to discuss accommodating their 13-year-old's shift to a nonbinary gender identity. They also noted in a file that the student's "privacy when [staff are] speaking to parents" must be considered.

"The law states that they must share all information with the parent," says Sullivan. "I think that it's very important that we maintain the fact that these parents are entrusting their children to these [government] entities, and they are not qualified or equipped to make those decisions [regarding sexuality and gender]."

DeAngelis maintains that the clash of values is best addressed through increased school choice.

"We force families into a one-size-fits-all, government-run school system, and these bills try to prohibit or encourage certain types of policies in that one-size-fits-all system," says DeAngelis. "The only way to move forward with freedom rather than force is to allow the money to follow the child to wherever they want to get an education that aligns best with their parents' values."

The pandemic-related school closures have bolstered the school choice movement, with 22 states expanding, improving, or implementing new school choice programs in 2021.

Florida is already far ahead of most states in providing parents with school choice, but DeAngelis says it should go further by offering universal vouchers and education savings accounts, which would truly empower parents and children to opt for any school of their choosing.

"What better way to assert parental rights are important than to empower them directly by allowing the money to follow their child to wherever they get an education? Funding students directly truly empowers parents when it comes to their kid's education. That is the best way to assert those rights," says DeAngelis.

DeSantis Introduces 'Stop WOKE Act' to Ban Critical Race Theory in Schools

From the Bethany Blankley "DeSantis introduces 'Stop WOKE Act' to ban critical race theory in schools" Just the News story in December 2021:

Gov. Ron DeSantis announced another bill for the legislature to consider when it convenes next year: a law banning so-called critical race theory from being taught in K-12 schools.

But the law goes beyond other similar CRT bans passed in other states in that it also protects employees from CRT training in the workplace and allows workers and parents to sue those that violate the ban.

DeSantis' "Stop WOKE Act," or "Stop Wrongs Against Our Kids and Employees Act," would statutorily ban the teaching of CRT in all K-12 schools in Florida. It would also prohibit Florida school districts, colleges and universities from hiring CRT consultants—and allow employees and parents to sue if they did.

"In Florida we are taking a stand against the state-sanctioned racism that is critical race theory," DeSantis said. "We won't allow Florida tax dollars to be spent teaching kids to hate our country or to hate each other. We also have a responsibility to ensure that parents have the means to vindicate their rights when it comes to enforcing state standards. Finally, we must protect Florida workers against the hostile work environment that is created when large corporations force their employees to endure CRT-inspired 'training' and indoctrination."

Critical Race Theory is broadly defined as a set of concepts used for "examining the relationship between race and the laws and legal institutions," according to Merriam-Webster's dictionary.

Thomas Lindsay, a distinguished senior fellow of higher education and constitutional studies at the Texas Public Policy Foundation, explains that CRT programs are "being instituted down to the third grade, where they're telling third-grade children that because of the color of their skin, they are oppressors, meaning that because of the color of their skin, they're bad."

"That used to be called racism," he said. "And unfortunately, critical race theory is the new racism."

According to the UCLA School of Public Affairs, CRT "is an outgrowth of Critical Legal Studies, which was a leftist movement that challenged traditional legal scholarship. It recognizes that racism is engrained in the fabric and system of the American society. The individual racist need not exist to note that institutional racism is pervasive in the dominant culture. This is the analytical lens that CRT uses in examining existing power structures. CRT identifies that these power structures are based on white privilege and white supremacy, which perpetuates the marginalization of people of color."

The new Florida law codifies the CRT ban issued in June by the state Board of Education. Because not all schools are necessarily following the department's ban, DeSantis implied, the legislation will give "parents a private right of action to be able to enforce the prohibition on CRT and they get to cover attorney fees when they prevail."

Speaking Up

As per the Teresa R. Manning "Speaking Up" *City Journal* article in September 2021:

In 2021, North Carolina congressman Greg Murphy introduced the Campus Free Speech Restoration Act, designed to enhance free expression in American universities. Murphy's bill defines "expressive activities" to include peaceful assembly, speaking, and listening and protects them from "improperly restrictive" institutional incursions, such as speech codes, bias response teams, and "free speech zones."

That legislation of this kind might be necessary is a sad commentary on academia. But as observers of American higher education know, college is now a place where free inquiry, free speech, and intellectual growth are imperiled. Surveys show that many professors and students now self-censor for political reasons. A punitive progressivism has become dogma, and vague harassment policies, zealous students, and ideological administrators chill dissent. Laws such as Murphy's can help, but it's vital to get the details right.

Public universities, legally subject to the First Amendment, get away with unconstitutional practices when authorities fail to respect and enforce the law. This is because no constitutional provision is self-enforcing. To give it effect, an injured party must sue a school. But after filing suit, that party often endures years of "lawfare"—stonewalling, appeals, trials, re-trials, and remands—that public universities, with taxpayer funds and lawyers at their disposal, greet with a yawn. All too often, individual lawsuits against universities are simply pebbles thrown against the citadel.

Murphy's bill addresses this problem with two innovations. First, it authorizes the Department of Education to condition Title IV federal funding on First Amendment compliance at public schools. While the bill does not specify how this would be implemented, it could easily appear alongside longstanding requirements in each school's Program Participation Agreement, which requires that institutions refrain from discriminating based on race and sex.

The condition could also be the subject of an independent, annual certificate of compliance filed separately by the school with the Department of Education. The certification would force schools to document their efforts to protect free expression and to record where and when it was threatened—whether in "shout-downs," intimidation of speakers resulting in rescinded invitations or canceled lectures—and to list measures taken to prevent such events from recurring.

Second, the bill creates a new position in the Education Department to oversee the status of free speech on campus and to enforce the First Amendment there, independent of time-consuming and expensive litigation. This official would investigate credible complaints of First Amendment threats and would be authorized to impose penalties in the event of noncompliance.

Finally, the bill should require the Department of Education to notify a school's regents or trustees of any complaint, investigation, or injunction, as well as the associated costs. The board can then communicate with the general assembly to deduct such costs from the school's annual appropriations, which would, of course, be refunded or re-appropriated should a final judgment exonerate the school.

Taken together, these provisions would ensure that the institution bears the cost of likely constitutional violations—not the individual and not the taxpayers. More could be said about required elements for injunctive relief and about finding the right person to fill this new position. But with time and some tinkering, Murphy's legislation could be an important step toward rescuing American higher education.

Why the Fight Over Critical Race Theory Matters

CRT is not just an attack on the American inheritance of political institutions; it is an attack on the social function of public schools as noted by the Michael Brendan Dougherty "Why the Fight Over Critical Race Theory Matters" *National Review* article in June 2021:

Moms are rising up in counterrevolutionary revolt. I'll say it again, moms are rising up in counterrevolutionary revolt against critical race theory, "anti-racism," the introduction of the 1619 Project into high-school curricula, and the suddenly invasive demands of diversity, equity, and inclusion consultants who are being hired by their school districts. Although progressives wish, in vain, that this movement were an Astroturf operation run by shadowy right-wing donor networks, it has been springing up in school districts in reaction to initiatives led by administrators themselves.

Tatiana Ibrahim stood up in front of the Carmel school board in Putnam County, N.Y., and denounced what she termed the "communist values" that teachers and administrators in the district are promoting. "Stop indoctrinating our children. Stop teaching our children to hate the police. Stop teaching our children that if they don't agree with the LGBT community, they're homophobic," Ibrahim demanded. "You have no idea of each child's life," she said, before announcing, in an only-in-America moment, that she is a Christian and her daughter is a Muslim.

She's far from alone. "Telling my child or any child that they are in a permanent oppressed status in America because they are black is racist—and saying that white people are automatically above me, my children, or any child is racist as well," said Quisha King, a mother in Duval County, Fla. "This is not something that we can stand for in our country." Other revolts—as in Southlake, Texas, and Loudoun County, Va.—have been even more dramatic.

But there is something else at work that is drawing liberals and populists into the fight: Progressives have abandoned the dream of Martin Luther King Jr. and instead are dedicated to thoroughly re-racializing America's civic space. The mainstream of life in the United States is recoded from its national name, "American," to a racial one, "white."

This destabilizes the entire idea of a mainstream or a common civic inheritance. A refusal to recognize oneself as an oppressor is reframed as "white fragility." A simple allegiance to equality under the law, traditionally understood, is ridiculed as color blindness, a stubborn unwillingness to recognize how racial identity structures power. And perhaps strangest of all, an odor of religiosity permeates the proceedings. Microaggressions are repented of and confessed. Identity experiences are received as testimonials. Privilege is recognized, like original sin, as an inherited guilt.

Critical race theory is not just an attack on the American inheritance of political institutions, it is also an attack on the social function of public schools as described by the once-radical education theorist and pragmatist philosopher John Dewey (1859–1952), who was the primary influence on the development of America's public schools. The critical-pedagogy movement would overturn Dewey's vision in key respects, and the popular defense of the social function of public schools should be recognized as some popular allegiance to the Deweyite philosophy, however unconscious.

Parents' Guide to Children's Rights Aims to Save America's Public Schools From CRT

Per the Jack Fitzhenry The Heritage Foundation June 14, 2022 article "Parents' Guide to Children's Rights Aims to Save America's Public Schools From CRT":

The most important battleground in the fight to save our American republic is the public schools." So says Kimberly Hermann, general counsel at the Southeastern Legal Foundation, in the introduction to the foundation's guide for parents, "Your Child's Rights and What to Do About Them: A Parent's Guide to Saving America's Public Schools."

Hermann's outlook is increasingly common among anyone taking stock of the proliferation of lessons on critical race theory (a radical worldview that advocates for the primacy of racial identity) in public school curriculums. And her foundation, a national nonprofit law firm that has litigated numerous cases arising in public schools and universities, is ready to persuade anyone else who will listen.

Renewed interest in curricular content is not coming from conservative quarters alone—parents of various political stripes have been galvanized by their children's encounters with critical race theory-based lessons to oppose its dominance in classrooms. That's the audience the Southeastern Legal Foundation addresses in its guide—those who "have had enough."

Why should any parent feel they've had enough of critical race theory? To many parents, the theory's doctrines of "white supremacy" and black/brown victimhood are anathema to their civic or religious convictions on the nature of the person, his or her agency, and the sources of his or her goodness, guilt, and redemption.

To others, critical race theory is just a time- and resource-intensive distraction from their schools' persistent failure to bring students somewhere near a grade-level competence in reading and mathematics.

Fair-minded parents can and should be skeptical of the pedagogic value in a theory that dismisses "legal reasoning" and "rationalism" as mere instruments of white supremacy. After all, critical race theory-based impulses led the Smithsonian to opine that "objective, rational linear thinking" was only an "assumption of whiteness."

Yet for all the legitimate concern parents feel when they find this racialist thinking in their child's homework, there is often a gap between their desire to oppose critical race theory-based instruction and their ability to advocate effectively for that outcome. The foundation's guide is meant to bridge that gap with introductions to the core legal concepts in play when a public school introduces a critical race theory-based curriculum.

Gov. Youngkin Bans Critical Race Theory, But More Reform is Necessary

From the David Randall "Gov. Youngkin Bans Critical Race Theory, but More Reform is Necessary" National Association of Scholars article in January 2022:

The National Association of Scholars and the Civics Alliance are delighted that newly inaugurated Virginia Governor Glenn Youngkin has begun his term by declaring that he will make good on his campaign promises.

His Executive Order #1 directs the state administration to remove Critical Race Theory (CRT) from the public K-12 schools. His Executive Order #2 directs the state administration to remove the mask mandate from the public K-12 schools. We congratulate Governor Youngkin for moving so swiftly to redeem his promises—and to redeem Virginia's children from the authoritarian whims of the public school bureaucracy.

Yet the state of Virginia must do more, to institutionalize education reform in Virginia. Virginia's education bureaucracy, as education bureaucracies throughout the nation, remains deeply committed to CRT and other radical ideologies. We urge Governor Youngkin to address these priorities during his administration:

PARENTS' RIGHTS: Governor Youngkin rightly stated in his Executive Order #2 that "parents, not the government, have the fundamental right to make decisions concerning the care of their children." Virginia should pass laws that will give parents the power to enforce their rights to determine their children's education. These laws should include:

- An Academic Transparency Act, to require public schools to publicize transparently every category of document relating to schools' policies and procedures.

- A Financial Transparency Act, to require school districts to post immediately on a public website a transparent, detailed financial statement that itemizes all expenditures.

- A School Board Election Date Act, to shift school board election dates to the same day as the general election, and thereby improve education reformers' chances to win school board elections.

- A School Board Member Recall Act, to establish straightforward procedures by which to recall school board members.

Virginia's parents should not need to depend on Virginia's governor to find out what their schools are doing or to remove school board members devoted to indoctrination rather than education. These laws will give Virginia's parents real power to run their schools.

CRITICAL RACE THEORY AND ACTION CIVICS: Governor Youngkin's Executive Order #1 is good within its scope, but it should be expanded to be effective. Virginia should pass laws to remove CRT and action civics (which is used to provide vocational training in radical activism) entirely from the state's public K-12 schools. These laws should include:

- A Partisanship Out of Civics Act, to prevent teachers from giving credit to action civics or any other sort of public policy advocacy in history, government, civics, or social studies, and to bar civics classes from using the discriminatory ideology at the heart of Critical Race Theory.

- A Classroom Learning Act, to eliminate service-learning pedagogy from public K-12 schools.

- A Values Assessment Act, to prohibit public schools from assessing, rewarding, or punishing students, teachers, or administrators for their level of commitment to any value or attitude.

- A Contractor Nondiscrimination Act, to require contractors for school districts to prohibit the use of Critical Race Theory policies that require discrimination by race, sex, or other group identity.

REFORMED STATE STANDARDS: Radical education bureaucrats impose their ideology by distorting the state education standards as well as by explicit injection of CRT and action civics. Virginia should pass laws to restore proper education standards to its public K-12 schools. These laws should include:

- A Social Studies Curriculum Act, to mandate K-12 instruction in Economics, State History, United States History, Civics, and Western Civilization.

- A Civics Course Act, to mandate a year-long high school civics course, including requirements to study the primary documents of the American founding and bans on action civics and the components of Critical Race Theory.

- A United States History Act, to mandate a year-long high school United States History course, including requirements to study the primary documents of American history and bans on action civics and the components of Critical Race Theory.

- A Western Civilization Act, to mandate a year-long high school Western Civilization course, including requirements to study the primary documents of Western Civilization and bans on action civics and the components of Critical Race Theory.

- A Schools Nondiscrimination Act, to mandate that no one should be either included or excluded from our nation's content standards, curricula, trainings, textbooks, and other school materials on account of their race, sex, or other group identity.

- A Historical Documents Act, to mandate instruction in historical documents and the liberty to use historical documents.

- A Legislative Review Act, to require all existing academic standards, and all forthcoming revisions, to be submitted to the state legislature and the governor for review and possible veto.

HIGHER EDUCATION: Radical advocates have also seized control of universities, education schools, and teacher licensure. The campaign against CRT and action civics, if it is to succeed, must also include work to reform these institutions. Legislative priorities should include:

- A modified version of the Partisanship Out of Civics Act, to forbid administrative trainings and policies that inculcate CRT, but which incorporates recognition of the constitutionally established sphere of academic freedom in higher education.

- An American History Act, to add an American History and Government general education requirement to public universities.

- Dual-Course Credit. Virginia should make sure that the American History and Government course added to the public university General Education Requirements is also available as a dual credit course in public high schools. This dual credit course should possess rigorous standards, forbid action civics or activism, and have transparent syllabi.

- Reform Teaching Licensure. Education schools abuse their monopoly on teaching licensure to train teachers to teach social justice propaganda and action civics. States should establish teaching licensure pathways that allow teachers to avoid education schools and that establish a preference for subject-matter specialists over education majors. States should also require teachers in state public schools who teach English or Social Studies to pass six (6) survey courses in Western Heritage, American History, and American Government. These courses should include no action civics or activism.

We make these recommendations for a broad array of laws to institutionalize the prohibition of CRT, and to make sure it cannot return. We are aware, however, that education reformers do not yet possess a sure majority in Virginia's General Assembly. We urge Governor Youngkin and his administration to push for these laws both in hopes that they can secure immediate passage and to prepare the ground for legislation when a legislative majority can be secured.

We make these recommendations, and we make one further one of the utmost importance. Make sure the Virginia education bureaucracy enforces Executive Orders #1 and #2. Bureaucrats are past masters of the arts of noncompliance. We urge Governor Youngkin and his administration to make it a top priority that these Executive Orders actually go into effect, both in the state Education Department and in each public school district. We urge in particular that they take all necessary disciplinary measures to ensure that CRT advocates do not sabotage these reforms.

Governor Youngkin has begun his term very well. He will do even better by enforcing his Executive Orders. We urge him to ensure the long-term success of his agenda by passing a broad range of laws to institutionalize education reform.

The Greatest Education Battle of Our Lifetimes

Per the Stanley Kurtz "The Greatest Education Battle of Our Lifetimes" *National Review* article in March 2021:

With the 2021 introduction in Congress of the misleadingly named Civics Secures Democracy Act, we are headed toward an epic clash over the spread of extremely controversial pedagogies—Critical Race Theory and Action Civics—to America's classrooms

Because this new legislation is a backdoor effort to impose a de facto national curriculum in the politically charged subject areas of history and civics, the battle will rage in the states, at the federal level, and between the states and the federal government as well. The Biden administration's Education Department will almost certainly collaborate in this attempt to develop a set of national incentives, measures, and penalties that effectively force Critical Race Theory and Action Civics onto states and localities.

The likelihood of education controversies moving from third-tier to first-tier issues in federal elections has never been greater.

The Obama administration pushed the K–12 Common Core on states, but the founders of Common Core made a calculated decision to omit the controversial subjects of history and civics from that effort. They understood the dangers of mixing education policy with high-intensity culture war issues.

Now, however, in an attempt to complete the creation of a de facto national curriculum, the top supporters of Common Core (including, sad to say, a few conservatives) have formed an alliance with the top national advocates of Action Civics and Critical Race Theory. The result is what we see in the "Civics Secures Democracy Act"—and what we're likely to get very soon from the Biden administration—a de facto national curriculum in Action Civics and Critical Race Theory.

And all of this is happening as woke culture is spilling out of the campuses and into the wider society. Once the reality of this new push for education "reform" comes into the open, we will see the culture war merge with the details of federal education policy in unprecedented fashion.

Critical Race Theory, of course, is antithetical to the classically liberal principles upon which our constitutional republic rests. Teaching it is actually a form of anti-civics. Yet that is what hundreds of millions of dollars disbursed by the "Civics Secures Democracy Act" is going to be used for.

The Civics Secures Democracy Act of 2021 is very much part of an effort to use NAEP to force a revisionist history and civics curriculum down the throats of unsuspecting states and localities. The bill would increase and regularize NAEP assessments in history and civics, facilitate state-by-state comparisons, and condition grants on the willingness of a state to participate in the history and civics portions of the test on a regular basis. Grant renewals would also be conditioned on statewide performance on the reorganized NAEP.

In effect, we are looking at an effort to impose a new federal Common Core in the politically explosive subject areas of history and civics. Worse, the program in each of these areas does more than just lean a bit toward the left side of the political spectrum. Instead, it sharply breaks with fundamental assumptions in American education, first by promoting illiberal Critical Race Theory, and second by turning what should be a politically neutral classroom into a training ground for leftist advocacy and lobbying.

All around us, the culture war has broken the bounds of the university and spilled into our day-to-day lives. Conservatives and traditional liberals are rightly up in arms about the woke assault on our most fundamental freedoms, extending to inculcating guilt and shame in elementary-school students for the color of their skin.

The Democrats in Congress, in league with the Biden administration and the leftist Action Civics movement, are about to supercharge this culture war by injecting it into the heart of federal education policy. Whether sooner or later, this is destined to become the greatest education battle of our lifetimes.

Appendix

1965 Moynihan Report – The Negro Family: The Case For National Action:
https://www.blackpast.org/african-american-history/moynihan-report-1965/)

40 *MADNESS* Textbook Titles: https://www.fratirepublishing.com/madnessbooks

- *Fake News Madness*
- *Crime Rate Madness*
- *Voting Madness*
- *California Madness*
- *Free Speech Madness*
- *Democratic Party Madness*

American Council of Trustees and Alumni (ACTA): https://www.goacta.org/

A Model for Transparency in School Training and Curriculum – Manhattan Institute:
https://www.manhattan-institute.org/transparency-school-training-curriculum

EdFirstNC: https://www.edfirstnc.org/

Educating for American Democracy (EAD) - Pedagogy Companion to the EAD Roadmap:
https://www.educatingforamericandemocracy.org/wp-content/uploads/2021/02/Pedagogy-Companion-to-the-EAD-Roadmap.pdf

Education Freedom Report Card: State Rankings for Parents – The Heritage Foundation:
https://www.heritage.org/educationreportcard/pages/all-state-scores.html

Fighting Indoctrination In Public Schools - NC Family Policy Council: https://www.ncfamily.org/fighting-indoctrination-in-public-schools/

Free Speech Alliance – Media Research Center (MRC): https://www.mrc.org/freespeechalliance

Freedom Forum Institute: https://www.freedomforuminstitute.org/

Freedom to Read Foundation: https://www.ftrf.org/page/About

Foundation Against Intolerance and Racism (FAIR): https://www.fairforall.org/

Foundation for Individual Rights in Education (FIRE): https://www.thefire.org/

Glossary of CRT Related Terms – Center for Renewing America:
https://americarenewing.com/issues/glossary-of-crt-related-terms/

Goldwater Institute – Campus Free Speech: A Legislative Proposal:
https://goldwaterinstitute.org/article/campus-free-speech-a-legislative-proposal/

Informed Parents of California: https://www.californiafamily.org/tag/informed-parents-of-california/

Inside the Woke Indoctrination Machine: https://ricochet.com/1204723/inside-the-woke-indoctrination-machine/

Institute For Free Speech: https://www.ifs.org/cases/marshall-v-amuso/

Judicial Watch: https://www.judicialwatch.org/jwtv/

Minding The Campus: https://www.mindingthecampus.org/author/pwood/

Moms for Liberty: https://www.momsforliberty.org/

NJ Parental Rights: https://parentalrights.org/news/

No Left Turn in Education: https://www.noleftturn.us/

No U.S. History? How College History Departments Leave the United States out of the Major: https://www.goacta.org/wp-content/uploads/2021/11/No.-U.S.-History_2.pdf

Pacific Legal Foundation: https://pacificlegal.org/

Parents Against Critical Theory: https://www.facebook.com/photo/?fbid=1062960787883099&set=a.1062960794549765

Parents Defending Education: https://defendinged.org/

Pennsbury School Board Aggressive Censorship of CRT Debate: https://www.ifs.org/wp-content/uploads/2021/10/PennsburySchoolBoard.mp4

Pew Research Center: https://www.pewresearch.org/about/

Report Card on American Education: K-12 Performance, Progress and Reform https://www.alecreportcard.org/app/uploads/2018/01/2017-ALEC-Report-Card_Final_WEB.pdf

SAPIENT BEING PROGRAMS:

- **Sapient Conservative Textbooks (SCT) Program:** https://www.sapientbeing.org/programs

- **Conservative Campus Advisor (CCA) Program:** https://www.sapientbeing.org/programs

- **Make Free Speech Again On Campus (MFSAOC) Program:** https://www.sapientbeing.org/programs

- **SAPIENT Being program handbooks:** https://www.sapientbeing.org/resources

Student Press Law Center: https://splc.org/about/

The S.A.P.I.E.N.T. Being: https://www.fratirepublishing.com/books

Top School Listings by Category- public School Review: https://www.publicschoolreview.com/top-school-listings

Glossary

Affinity Group – Is meant to be safe spaces for educators or students who share an identity, such as a common race or heritage, to discuss mutual concerns.

Antiracism – An illiberal term by Ibram X Kendi who argues unsapiently that the opposite of racist is anti-racist rather than simply non-racist, and that there is no middle ground in the struggle against racism; one is either actively confronting racial inequality or allowing it to exist through action or inaction.

Colorblindness – Is a term that has been used by justices of the United States Supreme Court in several opinions relating to racial equality and social equity, particularly in public education.

Critical Legal Theory (CLT) – A progressive movement that challenges and seeks to overturn accepted norms and standards in legal theory and practice.

Critical Race Theory (CRT) – Programs, based on a neo-Marxist ideology that originated in law schools a generation ago, purport to expose and correct "unconscious racial bias" and "white privilege" among their employees. Critical race theory treats "whiteness" as a moral blight and maligns all members of that racial group as complicit in oppression.

Critical Theory (CT) – A Marxist-inspired movement in social and political philosophy originally associated with the work of the Frankfurt School.

Culturally Responsive Teaching – Is an educational pedagogy that uses students' customs, characteristics, experiences, and perspectives as tools for better classroom instruction.

Deconstruction – Doesn't actually mean "demolition;" instead it means "breaking down" or analyzing something (especially the words in a work of fiction or nonfiction) to discover its true significance, which is supposedly almost never exactly what the author intended.

DEI – Diversity, equity, and inclusion: a conceptual framework that promotes the fair treatment and full participation of all people, especially in the workplace, including populations who have historically been underrepresented or subject to discrimination because of their background, identity, disability, etc.

Disparate Impact – Refers to practices in academics, employment, housing, and other areas that adversely affect one group of people of a protected characteristic more than another. When these "practices" do not exist—it is absurd to attribute the absence of proportional representation in the STEM fields, say, to bias.

Equality of Outcomes – It means that given the same opportunity and privileges two people should end up in the same position or at least equal position. But "equality of opportunity" does not promise "equality in the outcome." People have different levels of skill and put different amounts of effort into work they do.

Illiberalism – The 21st century term is used to describe an attitude that is close-minded, intolerant, and bigoted.

Implicit Bias Training – Are programs purport to expose people to their implicit biases, provide tools to adjust automatic patterns of thinking, and ultimately eliminate discriminatory behaviors.

Intersectionality – A theoretical framework for understanding how aspects of one's social and political identities might combine to create unique modes of discrimination.

Marxism – The political, economic, and social principles and policies advocated by Karl Marx and a theory and practice of socialism including the labor theory of value, dialectical materialism, the class struggle, and dictatorship of the proletariat until the establishment of a classless society.

Meritocracy – Is the only way a free people can create an efficient, prosperous, opportunity society. Without it, nobody has any incentive to innovate or work hard. The capable and hard-working become cynical and resentful, while the incompetent and the indolent know they don't have to step up, because they can live for free. This is the inherent flaw of Marxism, communism, and socialism.

Microaggression – It has entered the national conversation to mean brief, subtle verbal or nonverbal exchanges—often unintended—that send denigrating messages because of the recipient's group membership.

Multiculturalism – The view that cultures, races, and ethnicities, particularly those of minority groups, deserve special acknowledgement of their differences within a dominant political culture.

Political Correctness – A term used to describe language, policies, or measures that are intended to avoid offense or disadvantage to members of particular groups in society.

Progressivism – A political philosophy in support of social reform based on the idea of progress in which advancements in science, technology, economic development, and social organization are vital to improve the human condition.

Restorative Justice – Is an approach to justice where one of the responses to a crime is to organize a meeting between the victim and the offender, sometimes with representatives of the wider community.

Social Justice – A political and philosophical theory which asserts that there are dimensions to the concept of justice beyond those embodied in the principles of civil or criminal law, economic supply and demand, or traditional moral frameworks.

Viewpoint Diversity – Viewpoint diversity occurs when members of a group or community approach problems or questions from a range of perspectives.

White Privilege – The set of social and economic advantages that white people have by virtue of their race in a culture characterized by racial inequality.

White Supremacy – The term "white supremacy" can be confusing because it can mean an actual belief in the superiority of white people, in which case it is despicable. However, it is nearly always employed to mean something much larger—anything from classical philosophers to Enlightenment thinkers to the Industrial Revolution.

Woke – The Oxford dictionary describes it as an alertness "to racial or social discrimination and injustice," and it's a term progressives and liberals aspire to be—while conservatives view it as akin to a joke, and sometimes, a social evil, like cancel culture. "At its heart, wokeness is divisive, exclusionary, and hateful. It basically gives mean people a shield to be mean and cruel, armored in false virtue," as stated by Twitter CEO, Elon Musk.

Words Are Violence – An illiberal notion meant to stifle free speech and viewpoint diversity and sis popularized by Millennial and Zillennials aged college students affected by the tyranny of feelings.

References

About the Free Speech Alliance Alumni. Free Speech Alliance. June 3, 2022. https://alumnifreespeechalliance.com/.

Akan, Emel. "Lockdowns Reduce COVID-19 Mortality?" *Epoch Times*. January 26, 2022. https://www.theepochtimes.com/do-lockdowns-reduce-covid-19-mortality_4232386.html.

Andrzejewski, Adam. "Chicago's Big Education, Inc." *City Journal*. February 17, 2021. https://www.city-journal.org/reining-in-the-chicago-teachers-union.

Blankley, Bethany. "DeSantis introduces 'Stop WOKE Act' to ban critical race theory in schools." Just the News. December 16, 2021. https://justthenews.com/nation/states/desantis-introduces-stop-woke-act-ban-critical-race-theory-schools?utm_source=ground.news&utm_medium=referral.

Blanks Jr., Walter. "Teachers' Unions Deserve Much of the Blame for Pandemic-Era Learning Loss." *National Review*. September 6, 2022. https://www.nationalreview.com/2022/09/teachers-unions-deserve-much-of-the-blame-for-pandemic-era-learning-loss/.

Boehm, Eric. "The Pandemic Set Off a Homeschooling Boom. Don't Be So Sure That a Bust Is Coming." Reason. January 28, 2022. https://reason.com/2022/01/28/the-pandemic-set-off-a-homeshooling-boom-dont-be-so-sure-that-a-bust-is-coming/.

Buck, Daniel and Garion Frankel. "How Public Schools Went Woke—and What to Do about It." *National Review*. March 5, 2022. https://www.nationalreview.com/2022/03/how-public-schools-went-woke-and-what-to-do-about-it/.

Calvert, Scott. "Schools Are Back and Confronting Severe Learning Losses." *Wall Street Journal*. September 6, 2022. https://readingresultspdx.org/learninglosseswsj/.

Cass, Oren. "How the Other Half Learns." *City Journal*. Winter 2019. https://www.city-journal.org/html/how-other-half-learns-16403.html.

Cass, Oren. "What Are Public Schools For?" *City Journal*. December 14, 2021. https://www.city-journal.org/parents-and-educators-disagree-on-purpose-of-public-schools.

Chin, Wai Wah. "Charters for All." *City Journal*. February 18, 2022. https://www.city-journal.org/new-york-needs-more-charter-schools.

Cohen, Steve. "How to Fix the Student Debt Crisis: Stop Loaning Money to Students; Loan it to Colleges Instead." *City Journal*. November 30, 2015. https://www.city-journal.org/html/how-fix-student-debt-crisis-14065.html.

Copland, James R., John Ketcham and Christopher F. Rufo. "Next Step for the Parents' Movement: Curriculum Transparency." *City Journal*. December 1, 2021. https://www.city-journal.org/how-to-achieve-transparency-in-schools.

Dallmeyer, Mckenna. "Diversity Statements Can Determine Who Gets Hired at Universities." Campus Reform. April 25, 2022. https://www.campusreform.org/article?id=19424.

DeSanctis, Alexandra. "Nearly Three-Quarters of Americans Support School Choice." *National Review.* March 1, 2022. https://www.nationalreview.com/corner/nearly-three-quarters-of-americans-support-school-choice/.

Domanico, Ray. "Richard Carranza's Deflections." *City Journal.* July 2, 2019. https://www.city-journal.org/richard-carranza-racial-bias.

Dorman, Sam. "Legal Coalition Forming to Stop Critical Race Theory Training Around the Country." Fox News. January 2021. https://www.foxnews.com/politics/legal-coalition-critical-race-theory.

Dougherty, Michael Brendan. "Why the Fight Over Critical Race Theory Matters." *National Review.* June 24, 2021. https://www.nationalreview.com/magazine/2021/07/12/dewey-defeats-critical-race-theory/.

Eden, Max. "Taking Off the Mask." *City Journal.* April 20, 2021. https://www.city-journal.org/critical-race-theory-in-civics-education.

Education Freedom Report Card: State Rankings for Parents. The Heritage Foundation. September 9, 2022. https://www.heritage.org/educationreportcard/.

Edwards, Ph.D., Lee. "Confucius Institutes: China's Trojan Horse." The Heritage Foundation. May 27, 2021. https://www.heritage.org/homeland-security/commentary/confucius-institutes-chinas-trojan-horse.

Egalite, Anna J. "How Family Background Influences Student Achievement." Education Next. Vol. 16, No. 2. https://www.educationnext.org/how-family-background-influences-student-achievement/.

Elder, Larry. "Top High Schools Scrap Merit-Based Admission." Front Page Magazine. March 26, 2021. https://www.frontpagemag.com/top-high-schools-scrap-merit-based-admissionwill-larry-elder/.

Ellwanger, Adam. "The Art of Teaching and the End of Wokeness." National Association of Scholars. Winter 2021. https://www.nas.org/academic-questions/34/4/the-art-of-teaching-and-the-end-of-wokeness.

Fillat, Andrew I. and Henry I. Miller. "Diversity Smokescreen." *City Journal.* March 21, 2022. https://www.city-journal.org/diversity-is-a-smokescreen-in-college-admissions.

Finn Jr., Chester E. "A Nation Still at Risk." Hoover Digest. Winter 2022 No. 1. https://www.hoover.org/research/nation-still-risk-1.

Fitzhenry, Jack. "Parents' Guide to Children's Rights Aims to Save America's Public Schools From CRT." The Heritage Foundation. June 14, 2022. https://www.heritage.org/education/commentary/parents-guide-childrens-rights-aims-save-americas-public-schools-crt.

Goldberg, Zach and Eric Kaufmann. "Yes, Critical Race Theory Is Being Taught in Schools." *City Journal.* October 20, 2022. https://www.city-journal.org/yes-critical-race-theory-is-being-taught-in-schools.

Gorka, Katharine Cornell. "The Great Parent Revolt." The Heritage Foundation. Aug. 12, 2021. https://www.heritage.org/education/commentary/the-great-parent-revolt.

Greene, Ph.D., Jay and Frederick M. Hess. "It's Time to Roll Back Campus DEI Bureaucracies." *National Review.* September 18, 2022. https://www.nationalreview.com/2022/09/its-time-to-roll-back-campus-dei-bureaucracies/.

Greene, Ph.D., Jay and Ian Kingsbury "Empowering Parents with School Choice Reduces Wokeism in Education" The Heritage Foundation. November 15, 2022 https://www.heritage.org/education/report/empowering-parents-school-choice-reduces-wokeism-education

Greene, Ph.D., Jay and James Paul. "Time for the School Choice Movement to Embrace the Culture War." The Heritage Foundation. February 9, 2022. https://www.heritage.org/education/report/time-the-school-choice-movement-embrace-the-culture-war.

Greenhut, Steven. "Teachers Unions Continue to Exploit COVID to Serve Themselves." American Spectator. September 7, 2022. https://spectator.org/teachers-unions-continue-to-exploit-covid-to-serve-themselves/.

Gutmann, Andrew and Paul Rossi. "Inside the Woke Indoctrination Machine." *The Wall Street Journal*. February 11, 2022. https://www.wsj.com/articles/inside-the-woke-indoctrination-machine-diversity-equity-inclusion-bipoc-schools-conference-11644613908.

Hanson, Victor Davis. "Universities Breed Anger, Ignorance, and Ingratitude." *National Review* October 22, 2019. https://www.nationalreview.com/2019/10/universities-breed-anger-ignorance-ingratitude/.

Hilditch, Cameron. "Bonfire of the Sanities: California's Deranged Revival of the Aztec Gods." *National Review*. March 28, 2021. https://www.nationalreview.com/2021/03/bonfire-of-the-sanities-californias-deranged-revival-of-the-aztec-gods/.

Hill, Bailee. "Teachers union infuriates parents with 'astonishing' tweet: 'Trying to gaslight Americans.'" Fox News. November 15, 2022. https://www.foxnews.com/media/teachers-union-infuriates-parents-astonishing-tweet-trying-gaslight-americans.

Hughes, Coleman. "What the New Integrationists Fail to See." *City Journal*. July 2, 2018. https://www.city-journal.org/html/black-only-schools-16000.html.

Institutional Neutrality: Blueprint for Reform. The James G. Martin Center for Academic Renewal. https://www.jamesgmartin.center/wp-content/uploads/2020/08/Blueprint-for-Reform-Institutional-Neutrality.pdf.

Jilani, Zaid. "Progressives Against Transparency." *City Journal*. January 26, 2022. https://www.city-journal.org/progressives-against-school-transparency.

Kaufmann, Eric. "A Necessary Intervention." *City Journal*. March 4, 2021. https://www.city-journal.org/govt-must-regulate-universities-to-protect-free-speech.

Kersten, Katherine. "No Thug Left Behind." *City Journal*. Winter 2017. https://www.city-journal.org/html/no-thug-left-behind-14951.html.

Kilgannon, Meg. "The SPLC's Radical 'Learning For Justice' Program: What Parents, Teachers, and Administrators Need to Know." Family Research Council. 2021. https://www.frc.org/booklet/the-splcs-radical-learning-for-justice-program.

Kurtz, Stanley. "The Greatest Education Battle of Our Lifetimes." *National Review*. March 15, 2021. https://www.nationalreview.com/corner/the-greatest-education-battle-of-our-lifetimes/?utm_source=recirc-desktop&utm_medium=homepage&utm_campaign=right-rail&utm_content=corner&utm_term=second.

Leroux, Robert. "Woke Madness and the University." National Association of Scholars. Winter 2021. https://www.NAS.org/academic-questions/34/4/woke-madness-and-the-university.

Lopez, Clare M. "Marxism in the Classroom, Riots in the Streets." Front Page Magazine. July 25, 2020. https://www.frontpagemag.com/marxism-classroom-riots-streets-clare-m-lopez/.

Mac Donald, Heather. "Back to Discipline." *City Journal*. December 19, 2018. https://www.city-journal.org/disparate-impact-analysis.

Mac Donald, Heather. "Conformity to a Lie." *City Journal*. Summer 2020. https://www.city-journal.org/academia-systemic-racism.

Mac Donald, Heather. "Grievance Proxies." *City Journal*. May 16, 2019. https://www.city-journal.org/college-boards-sat-adversity-score.

Malanga, Steven. "School Choice Rising." *City Journal*. Summer 2022. https://www.city-journal.org/school-choice-rising.

Malanga, Steven. "The Union Map of School Closings" *City Journal* February 17, 2022 https://www.city-journal.org/strong-teachers-unions-mean-more-covid-restrictions.

Manning, Teresa R. "Speaking Up." *City Journal*. September 22, 2021. https://www.city-journal.org/can-legislation-protect-free-speech-on-campus.

McDonald, Kerry. "How Hybrid Schools Are Reshaping Education." Foundation for Economic Education. April 1, 2022 https://fee.org/articles/how-hybrid-schools-are-reshaping-education/.

McDonald, Kerry. "Teachers Unions Are More Powerful Than You Realize—but That May Be Changing." Cato Institute. August 31, 2020. https://www.cato.org/commentary/teachers-unions-are-more-powerful-you-realize-may-be-changing

McManus, Bob. "Classrooms of the Absurd." *City Journal*. July 22, 2019. https://www.city-journal.org/new-york-charter-schools-success.

McManus, Bob. "New York's Toxic Schools Chancellor." *City Journal*. June 3, 2019. https://www.city-journal.org/richard-carranza-implicit-bias.

McManus, Bob. "Re-Sinking CUNY." *City Journal*. August 5, 2019. https://www.city-journal.org/cuny-objective-testing.

McManus, Bob. "Richard Carranza's Deflections." City Journal. July 2, 2019. https://www.city-journal.org/richard-carranza-racial-bias.

Newman, Alex. "How Socialists Used Teachers Unions Such as the NEA to Destroy Education." *Epoch Times. May 20, 2020.* https://www.theepochtimes.com/how-socialists-used-teachers-unions-such-as-the-nea-to-destroy-education_3149507.html.

Newman, Alex. "Schools Using Fake 'History' to Kill America." *Epoch Times. September 29,* 2020. https://www.theepochtimes.com/schools-using-fake-history-to-kill-america_3514284.html

Owens, Candace. "A Short History of Slavery." Prager U. August 23, 2021. https://www.prageru.com/video/whats-wrong-with-the-1619-project.

Piereson, James and Naomi Schaefer Riley. "Less Than Meets the Eye." *City Journal*. May 4, 2021. https://www.city-journal.org/scoreless-admissions-set-minority-students-up-for-failure.

Pioneering ACTA Analysis Confirms That Higher Education Tuition Is Linked To Spending, With Minimal Effect On Graduation Rates. ACTA. August 17, 2021. https://www.goacta.org/2021/08/pioneering-acta-analysis-confirms-that-higher-education-tuition-is-linked-to-spending-with-minimal-effect-on-graduation-rates/.

Pondiscio, Robert. "Educating Patriots." *City Journal*. October 25, 2020. https://www.city-journal.org/restoring-the-public-purpose-of-american-education.

Pulliam, Mark. "The Campus Diversity Swarm." *City Journal*. October 10, 2018. https://www.city-journal.org/campus-diversity-bureaucracies-16223.html.

Randall, David. "Charting Academic Freedom." National Association of Scholars. January 15, 2018. https://www.nas.org/reports/charting-academic-freedom-103-years-of-debate/full-report.

Randall, David. "Gov. Youngkin Bans Critical Race Theory, but More Reform is Necessary." National Association of Scholars. January 18, 2022. https://www.nas.org/blogs/article/gov-youngkin-bans-critical-race-theory-but-more-reform-is-necessary.

Randall, David. "Kick the '1619 Project' Out of Schools." National Association of Scholars. August 10, 2020. https://www.nas.org/blogs/article/kick-the-1619-project-out-of-schools.

Randall, David. "Learning for Self-Government." National Association of Scholars. February 15, 2022. https://www.nas.org/reports/learning-for-self-government/full-report.

Randall, David. "Social Justice Education in America." National Association of Scholars. November 29, 2019. https://www.nas.org/reports/social-justice-education-in-america/full-report.

Reilly, Wilfred. "What Is Critical Race Theory, Really?" *City Journal*. October 13, 2021. https://www.city-journal.org/what-is-critical-race-theory-really.

Reilly, Wilfred. "What's Wrong With the 1619 Project?" Prager U. https://assets.ctfassets.net/qnesrjodfi80/6pHowieMH6mlh35Bs5SqVX/f65d59b627651783162f5edcfe42ce0b/Reilly-Whats_Wrong_With_the_1619_Project-Transcript.pdf.

Report Finds that America's Leading Science Curriculum Fails Students. National Association of Scholars. April 08, 2021. https://www.nas.org/blogs/article/report-finds-the-americas-leading-science-curriculum-fails-students.

Report Finds Title IX Offices are Sex Monitors, not Education Monitors. National Association of Scholars. October 29, 2020. https://www.nas.org/blogs/press_release/report-finds-title-ix-offices-are-sex-monitors-not-education-monitors.

Rufo, Christopher F. "Banging Beyond Binaries." *City Journal*. May 17, 2022. https://www.city-journal.org/philadelphia-schools-tout-radical-transgender-conference.

Rufo, Christopher F. "Biden Criminalizes CRT Dissent." *City Journal*. October 6, 2021. https://www.city-journal.org/biden-criminalizes-critical-race-theory-dissent.

Rufo, Christopher F. "Disingenuous Defenses of Critical Race Theory." *New York Post*. July 9, 2021. https://nypost.com/2021/07/09/disingenuous-defenses-of-critical-race-theory/.

Rufo, Christopher F. "Going All In." *City Journal*. July 15, 2021. https://www.city-journal.org/nea-to-promote-critical-race-theory-in-schools.

Rufo, Christopher F. "Radical Gender Lessons for Young Children." *City Journal*. April 21, 2022. https://www.city-journal.org/radical-gender-lessons-for-young-children.

Rufo, Christopher F. "Sexual Liberation in Public Schools." *City Journal*. July 20, 2022. https://www.city-journal.org/sexual-liberation-in-public-schools.

Rufo, Christopher F. "Subversive Education." *City Journal*. March 17, 2021. https://www.city-journal.org/critical-race-theory-in-wake-county-nc-schools.

Rufo, Christopher F. "Teaching Hate." *City Journal*. December 18, 2020. https://www.city-journal.org/racial-equity-programs-seattle-schools.

Sabo, Mike. "The 1776 Commission Report Reinvigorates the American Mind." National Association of Scholars. January 22, 2021. https://www.nas.org/blogs/article/the-1776-commission-report-reinvigorates-the-american-mind.

Sailer, John D. and Ray M. Sanchez. "An Overt Political Litmus Test." *City Journal*. May 16, 2022. https://www.city-journal.org/california-community-colleges-impose-political-litmus-test.

Salzman, Philip Carl. "National Suicide by Education." Minding the Campus. September 23, 2022. https://www.mindingthecampus.org/2022/09/23/national-suicide-by-education/.

Sand, Larry. "Hypocrisy, Inc." *City Journal*. February 20, 2018. https://www.city-journal.org/html/hypocrisy-inc-15728.html.

Sand, Larry. "What School Shutdowns Have Wrought." *City Journal*. March 16, 2021. https://www.city-journal.org/what-school-shutdowns-have-wrought.

Sanzi, Erika. "The Monster Is in the Classroom." *City Journal*. April 30, 2021. https://www.city-journal.org/elementary-schools-go-woke.

Schalin, Jay. "Bolstering the Board: Trustees Are Academia's Best Hope for Reform." The James G. Martin Center for Academic Renewal. July 14, 2020. https://www.jamesgmartin.center/2020/07/bolstering-the-board-trustees-are-academias-best-hope-for-reform/.

Schalin, Jay. "The Pushback Against Classroom Indoctrination Begins." The James G. Martin Center for Academic Renewal. July 20, 2022. https://www.jamesgmartin.center/2022/07/the-pushback-against-classroom-indoctrination-begins/.

Schrager, Allison. "Don't Cancel School." *City Journal*. August 5, 2020. https://www.city-journal.org/negative-effects-of-closed-schools-covid.

Seminara, Dave. "The Very Intersectional Caterpillar" *City Journal* October 15, 2021 https://www.city-journal.org/the-politicization-of-childrens-books

Sidamon-Eristoff, Andrew. "Online Learning Finds Its Moment." *City Journal*. April 3, 2020. https://www.city-journal.org/covid-19-online%20education-revolution.

Smith, Ember and Richard V. Reeves. "SAT Math Scores Mirror and Maintain Racial Inequity." Brookings Institute. December 1, 2020. https://www.brookings.edu/blog/up-front/2020/12/01/sat-math-scores-mirror-and-maintain-racial-inequity/.

Smith, Wesley J. "Johns Hopkins Analysis: 'Lockdowns Should be Rejected Out of Hand'." *National Review*. February 1, 2022. https://www.nationalreview.com/corner/johns-hopkins-analysis-lockdowns-should-be-rejected-out-of-hand/?utm_source=onesignal&utm_medium=push&utm_campaign=article.

Spivak, Kennin M. "Patriotism Starts in the Classroom." *National Review*. July 3, 2022. https://www.nationalreview.com/2022/07/patriotism-starts-in-the-classroom/.

Statement by the American Council of Trustees and Alumni (ACTA) on President Biden's Loan Forgiveness Plan. ACTA. August 24, 2022. https://www.goacta.org/resource/statement-by-the-american-council-of-trustees-and-alumni-on-president-bidens-loan-forgiveness-plan/.

Stern, Sol. "Curriculum Is the Cure." *City Journal*. December 12, 2016. https://www.city-journal.org/html/curriculum-cure-14897.html.

Stern, Sol. "E. D. Hirsch's Curriculum for Democracy." *City Journal*. Autumn 2009. https://www.city-journal.org/html/e-d-hirsch%E2%80%99s-curriculum-democracy-13234.html.

The Challenge from Action Civics. National Association of Scholars. https://www.nas.org/civics-alliance/our-mission-and-vision/challenge-action-civics.

The Civics Alliance: A Toolkit. National Association of Scholars. March 22, 2021. https://www.nas.org/blogs/article/the-civics-alliance-a-toolkit.

Tierney, John. "Lockdown Addicts." *City Journal*. November 20, 2020. https://www.city-journal.org/bidens-covid-advisors-ignore-high-costs-of-lockdowns.

Todd-Smith, Ph.D., Laurie. "School Choice Advances in States." America First Policy Institute. November 12, 2021. https://americafirstpolicy.com/latest/school-choice-advances-in-states.

Tolson, Patricia. "Statistics Show America's Education System is Failing: CRT and Lower Expectation Equals Fewer Literate Graduates, Expert Says." *Epoch Times. January 2, 2022.* https://www.theepochtimes.com/statistics-show-americas-education-system-is-failing-crt-and-lower-expectation-equals-fewer-literate-graduates-expert-says_4179014.html.

Tuccille, J.D. "Microschools Have a Big Future." Reason. January 28, 2022. https://reason.com/2022/01/28/microschools-have-a-big-future/.

Valdary, Chloé. "Reconciliation, or Grievance?" *City Journal*. June 6, 2019. https://www.city-journal.org/diversity-training.

Weissmueller, Zach. "Florida Parents Take Back the Classroom." Reason. January 28,.2022. https://reason.com/video/2022/01/28/florida-parents-take-back-the-classroom/.

Wiborg, Susanne. "The Politics of Closing Schools." Education Next. August 25, 2021. https://www.educationnext.org/politics-of-closing-schools-teachers-unions-covid-19-pandemic-europe/.

Wilson, Corey Lee. *California Madness: A SAPIENT Being's Guide to the State's Recall, Leftist Policies & Progressive Downward Spiral.* Fratire Publishing, LLC. Corona, California. 2022.

Wilson, Corey Lee. *Free Speech Madness: A SAPIENT Being's Guide to the War Against Truth, Conservative Ideals & Freedom of Speech.* Fratire Publishing, LLC. Corona, California. 2022.

Wilson, Corey Lee. *The S.A.P.I.E.N.T. Being: Enhancing Viewpoint Diversity and Intellectual Humility to Make Free Speech Again on Campus.* Fratire Publishing, LLC. Corona, California. 2019.

Woke Schooling: A Toolkit for Concerned Parents. Manhattan Institute. June 17, 2021. https://www.manhattan-institute.org/woke-schooling-toolkit-for-concerned-parents.

Wong, Alia. "Did Republicans take over school boards? Key education takeaways from the 2022 midterms." *USA Today*. November 20, 2022. https://www.usatoday.com/story/news/education/2022/11/20/midterms-take-classroom-how-education-fared-2022-elections/10713535002/

Wood, Peter W. "Skewed History: Textbook Coverage of Early America and the New Deal." National Association of Scholars. April 2021. https://www.nas.org/reports/skewed-history/full-report.

Xu, Kenny. "Diversity—Unless You're Asian." *City Journal*. June 3, 2021. https://www.city-journal.org/harvard-race-conscious-admissions-policy.

Zinberg, Joel. "An Affirmative Action Endgame?" *City Journal*. January 25, 2022. https://www.city-journal.org/supreme-court-to-hear-affirmative-action-cases.

Index

X

Y

Z

Author Bio

Author: Corey Lee Wilson.

Corey Lee Wilson was raised an atheist by his liberal *Playboy* Bunny mother, has three Anglo-Hispanic siblings, a bi-racial daughter, a brother who died of AIDS, baptized a Protestant by his conservative grandparents, attended temple with his Jewish foster parents, baptized again as a Catholic for his first Filipina wife, attends Buddhist ceremonies with his second Thai wife, became an agnostic on his own free will for most of his life, and is a lifetime independent voter.

Corey felt the sting of intellectual humility by repeating the 4th grade and attended eighteen different schools before putting himself through college (without parents) at Mt. San Antonio College and Cal Poly Pomona University (while on triple secret probation). Named Who's Who of American College Students in 1984, he received a BS in Economics and won his fraternity's most prestigious undergraduate honor, the Phi Kappa Tau Fraternity's Shideler Award, both in 1985. In 2020, he became a member of the Heterodox Academy and in 2021 a member of the National Association of Scholars and 1776 Unites.

As a satirist and fraternity man, Corey started Fratire Publishing in 2012 and transformed the fiction "fratire" genre to a respectable and viewpoint diverse non-fiction genre promoting practical knowledge and wisdom to help everyday people navigate safely through the many hazards of life. In 2018, he founded the SAPIENT Being to help promote freedom of speech, viewpoint diversity, intellectual humility and most importantly advance sapience in America's students and campuses.

The SAPIENT Being has three programs: Make Free Speech Again On Campus (MFSAOC) Program, Free Speech Alumni Ambassador (FSAA) Program, and the Sapient Conservative Textbooks (SCT) Program—all working together to promote its mission and vision of sapience.

If you're interested in the MFSAOC Program and starting a S.A.P.I.E.N.T. Being club, chapter, or alliance on or off campus, please go to https://www.SapientBeing.org/start-a-chapter, e-mail SapientBeing@att.net, or call (951) 638-5562 for more information.

If you're interested in becoming a conservative campus advisor for right-leaning campus organizations as part of the CCA Program from the S.A.P.I.E.N.T. Being, please e-mail at SapientBeing@att.net, or call (951) 638-5562 for more information.

If you're interested as an educator, administrator, or student in the SCT Program and their 40 MADNESS series of textbooks from the S.A.P.I.E.N.T. Being, please check them out at the Fratire Publishing website at https://www.FratirePublishing.com/madnessbooks, for more information.

Hopefully, this book was enlightening and your journey through it—along with mine—made you aware of the issues and challenges ahead of us. If it has, your quest and mine towards becoming a sapient being has begun. If it hasn't, there's no better time to start than now. Come join us in creating a society advancing personal intelligence and enlightenment now together (S.A.P.I.E.N.T.) and become a sapient being.

www.ingramcontent.com/pod-product-compliance
Lightning Source LLC
Chambersburg PA
CBHW042358030426
42337CB00032B/5140